Power Maths

Year 2A

A Guide to Teaching for Mastery

Series Editor: Tony Staneff

Contents

Introduction

Foreword by the series editor and author, Tony Staneff

 For far too long in the UK, maths has been feared by learners – and by many teachers, too. As a result, most learners consistently underachieve. More crucially, negative beliefs about ability, aptitude and the nature of maths are entrenched in children's thinking from an early age.

Yet, as someone who has loved maths all my life, I've always believed that every child has the capacity to succeed in maths. I've also had the great pleasure of leading teams and departments who share that belief and passion. Teaching for mastery, as practised in China and other South-East Asian jurisdictions since the 1980s, has confirmed my conviction that maths really is for everyone and not just those who have a special talent. In recent years my team and I at Trinity Academy, Halifax, have had the privilege of researching with and working with some of the finest mastery practitioners from the UK and beyond, whose impact on learners' confidence, achievement and attitude is an inspiration.

The mastery approach recognises the value of developing the power to think rather than just do. It also recognises the value of making a coherent journey in which whole-class groups tackle concepts in very small steps, one by one. You cannot build securely on loose foundations – and it is just the same with maths: by creating a solid foundation of deep understanding, our children's skills and confidence will be strong and secure. What's more, the mindset of learner and teacher alike is fundamental: everyone can do maths… EVERYONE CAN!

I am proud to have been part of the extensive team responsible for turning the best of the world's practice, research, insights, and shared experiences into *Power Maths*, a unique teaching and learning resource developed especially for UK classrooms. *Power Maths* embodies our vision to help and support primary maths teachers to transform every child's mathematical and personal development. 'Everyone can!' has become our mantra and our passion, and we hope it will be yours, too.

Now, explore and enjoy all the resources you need to teach for mastery, and please get back to us with your *Power Maths* experiences and stories!

What is *Power Maths*?

Created especially for UK primary schools, and aligned with the new National Curriculum, *Power Maths* is a whole-class, textbook-based mastery resource that empowers every child to understand and succeed. *Power Maths* rejects the notion that some people simply 'can't do' maths. Instead, it develops growth mindsets and encourages hard work, practice and a willingness to see mistakes as learning tools.

Best practice consistently shows that mastery of small, cumulative steps builds a solid foundation of deep mathematical understanding. *Power Maths* combines interactive teaching tools, high-quality textbooks and continuing professional development (CPD) to help you equip children with a deep and long lasting understanding. Based on extensive evidence, and developed in partnership with practising teachers, *Power Maths* ensures that it meets the needs of children in the UK.

Power Maths and Mastery

Power Maths makes mastery practical and achievable by providing the structures, pathways, content, tools and support you need to make it happen in your classroom.

To develop mastery in maths children must be enabled to acquire a deep understanding of maths concepts, structures and procedures, step by step. Complex mathematical concepts are built on simpler conceptual components and when children understand every step in the learning sequence, maths becomes transparent and makes logical sense. Interactive lessons establish deep understanding in small steps, as well as effortless fluency in key facts such as tables and number bonds. The whole class works on the same content and no child is left behind.

Power Maths

- Builds every concept in small, progressive steps
- Is built with interactive, whole-class teaching in mind
- Provides the tools you need to develop growth mindsets
- Helps you check understanding and ensure that every child is keeping up
- Establishes core elements such as intelligent practice and reflection

The *Power Maths* approach

Everyone can!

Founded on the conviction that every child can achieve, *Power Maths* enables children to build number fluency, confidence and understanding, step by step.

Child-centred learning

Children master concepts one step at a time in lessons that embrace a concrete-pictorial-abstract (C-P-A) approach, avoid overload, build on prior learning and help them see patterns and connections. Same-day intervention ensures sustained progress.

Continuing professional development

Embedded teacher support and development offer every teacher the opportunity to continually improve their subject knowledge and manage whole-class teaching for mastery.

Whole-class teaching

An interactive, whole-class teaching model encourages thinking and precise mathematical language and allows children to deepen their understanding as far as they can.

Introduction to the author team

Power Maths arises from the work of maths mastery experts who are committed to proving that, given the right mastery mindset and approach, **everyone can do maths**. Based on robust research and best practice from around the world, *Power Maths* was developed in partnership with a group of UK teachers to make sure that it not only meets our children's wide-ranging needs but also aligns with the National Curriculum in England.

Tony Staneff, Series Editor and Author

Vice Principal at Trinity Academy, Halifax, Tony also leads a team of mastery experts who help schools across the UK to develop teaching for mastery via nationally recognised CPD courses, problem-solving and reasoning resources, schemes of work, assessment materials and other tools.

A team of experienced authors, including:

- **Josh Lury** – a specialist maths teacher, author and maths consultant with a passion for innovative and effective maths education
- **Jenny Lewis, Stephen Monaghan, Beth Smith and Kelsey Brown** – skilled maths teachers and mastery experts
- **Cherri Moseley** – a maths author, former teacher and professional development provider
- **Paul Wrangles** – a maths author and former teacher, Paul's goal is to "ignite creative thought in teachers and pupils by providing creative teaching resources".

Professor Jian Liu, Series Consultant and author, and his team of mastery expert authors:

- **Hou Huiying, Huang Lihua, Wang Mingming, Yin Lili, Zhang Dan, Zhang Hong and Zhou Da**

Used by over 20 million children, Professor Liu's textbook programme is one of the most popular in China. He and his author team are highly experienced in intelligent practice and in embedding key maths concepts using a C-P-A approach.

A group of 15 teachers and maths co-ordinators

We have consulted our teacher group throughout the development of *Power Maths* to ensure we are meeting their real needs in the classroom.

Your *Power Maths* resources

To help you teach for mastery, *Power Maths* comprises a variety of high-quality resources.

Pupil Textbooks

'Discover', 'Share' and 'Think together' sections promote discussion and introduce mathematical ideas logically, so that children understand more easily.

Using a Concrete-Pictorial-Abstract approach, clear mathematical models help children to make connections and grasp concepts.

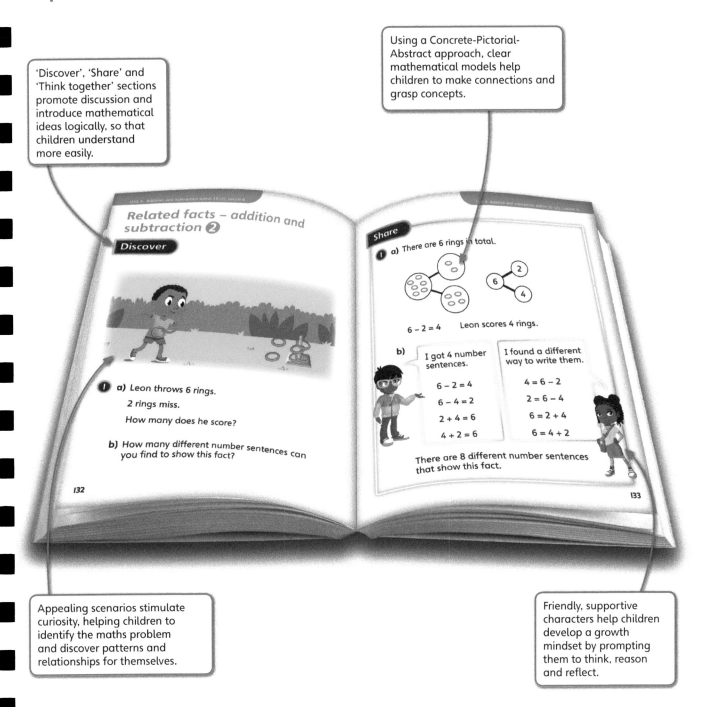

Appealing scenarios stimulate curiosity, helping children to identify the maths problem and discover patterns and relationships for themselves.

Friendly, supportive characters help children develop a growth mindset by prompting them to think, reason and reflect.

The coherent *Power Maths* lesson structure carries through into the vibrant, high-quality textbooks. Setting out the core learning objectives for each class, the lesson structure follows a carefully mapped journey through the curriculum and supports children on their journey to deeper understanding.

Pupil Practice Books

The Practice Books offer just the right amount of intelligent practice for children to complete independently in the final section of each lesson.

The practice questions are for everyone – each question varies one small element to move children on in their thinking. Look at the different parts in question 1!

Calculations are connected so that children think about the underlying concept. In question 3, children have to write out the calculation to find the answer. Concepts are presented differently again in question 4 to challenge children.

Practice questions are finely tuned to move children forward in their thinking and to reveal misconceptions.

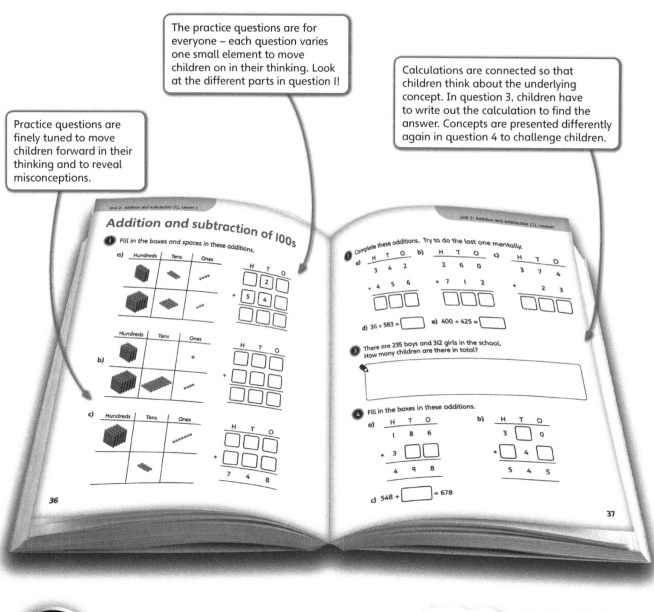

Challenge questions allow children to delve deeper into a concept.

Reflect questions reveal the depth of each child's understanding before they move on.

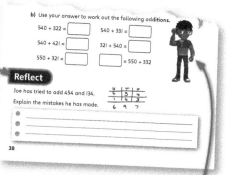

The *Power Maths* characters support and encourage children to think and work in different ways.

Online subscriptions

The online subscription will give you access to additional resources.

eTextbooks

Digital versions of *Power Maths* Textbooks allow class groups to share and discuss questions, solutions and strategies. They allow you to project key structures and representations at the front of the class, to ensure all children are focusing on the same concept.

Teaching tools

Here you will find interactive versions of key *Power Maths* structures and representations.

Power Ups

Use this series of daily activities to promote and check number fluency.

Online versions of Teacher Guide pages

PDF pages give support at both unit and lesson levels. You will also find help with key strategies and templates for tracking progress.

Unit videos

Watch the professional development videos at the start of each unit to help you teach with confidence. The videos explore common misconceptions in the unit, and include intervention suggestions as well as suggestions on what to look out for when assessing mastery in your students.

End of unit Strengthen and Deepen materials

Each Strengthen activity at the end of every unit addresses a key misconception and can be used to support children who need it. The Deepen activities are designed to be low ceiling / high threshold and will challenge those children who can understand more deeply. These resources will help you ensure that every child understands and will help you keep the class moving forward together. These printable activities provide an optional resource bank for use after the assessment stage.

Underpinning all of these resources, *Power Maths* is infused throughout with continual professional development, supporting you at every step.

The *Power Maths* teaching model

At the heart of *Power Maths* is a clearly structured teaching and learning process that helps you make certain that every child masters each maths concept securely and deeply. For each year group, the curriculum is broken down into core concepts, taught in units. A unit divides into smaller learning steps – lessons. Step by step, strong foundations of cumulative knowledge and understanding are built.

Quick check on prerequisite skills and a warm-up for children.

Rich assessments show mastery of key skills combined with a pupil self-assessment and reflection opportunity.

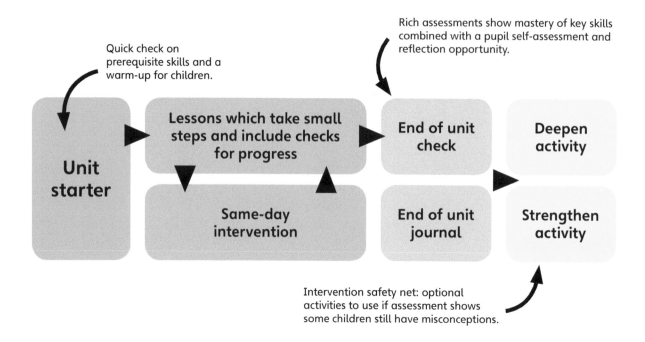

Intervention safety net: optional activities to use if assessment shows some children still have misconceptions.

Unit starter

Each unit begins with a unit starter, which introduces the learning context along with key mathematical vocabulary and structures and representations.

- The Pupil Textbooks include a check on readiness and a warm-up task for children to complete.

- Your Teacher Guide gives support right from the start on important structures and representations, mathematical language, common misconceptions and intervention strategies.

- Unit-specific videos develop your subject knowledge and insights so you feel confident and fully equipped to teach each new unit. These are available via the online subscription.

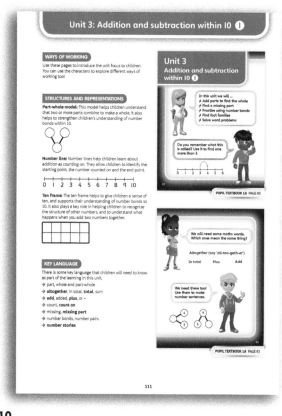

Lesson

Once a unit has been introduced, it is time to start teaching the series of lessons.

- Each lesson is scaffolded with Pupil Textbook and Practice Book activities and always begins with a Power Up activity (available via online subscription).

- *Power Maths* identifies lesson by lesson what concepts are to be taught.

- Your Teacher Guide offers lots of support for you to get the most from every child in every lesson. As well as highlighting key points, tricky areas and how to handle them, you will also find question prompts to check on understanding and clarification on why particular activities and questions are used.

Same-day intervention

Same-day interventions are vital in order to keep the class progressing together. Therefore, *Power Maths* provides plenty of support throughout the journey.

- Intervention is focused on keeping up now, not catching up later, so interventions should happen as soon as they are needed.

- Practice section questions are designed to bring misconceptions to the surface, allowing you to identify these easily as you circulate during independent practice time.

- Child-friendly assessment questions in the Teacher Guide help you identify easily which children need to strengthen their understanding.

End of unit check and journal

At the end of a unit, summative assessment tasks reveal essential information on each child's understanding. An End of unit check in the Pupil Textbook lets you see which children have mastered the key concepts, which children have not and where their misconceptions lie. The Practice Book also includes an End of unit journal in which children can reflect on what they have learned. Each unit also offers Strengthen and Deepen activities, available via the online subscription.

> The Teacher Guide offers different ways of managing the End of unit assessments as well as giving support with handling misconceptions.

> The End of unit check presents four multiple-choice questions. Children think about their answer, decide on a solution and explain their choice.

> The End of unit journal is an opportunity for children to test out their learning and reflect on how they feel about it. Tackling the 'journal' problem reveals whether a child understands the concept deeply enough to move on to the next unit.

Unit 1: Numbers to 10 → Textbook 1A p56

End of unit check

My journal

Bea has 5 red ◯ and 1 yellow ◯. Colour them in.

◯◯◯◯◯

Seth has 3 red ◯ and 3 yellow ◯. Colour them in.

◯◯◯◯◯◯

What is the same? _____

_____

What is different? _____

_____

These words might help you.

balloon   I   one
less   3   three
more   5   five

42

Unit 1: Numbers to 10

End of unit check

Your teacher will ask you these questions.

1. What is the missing number?

_____ I   2   3

A 4   B I   C 0   D 5

2. What is the number?

A 3   B 4   C 5   D 7

3. Demi is counting from I to I0. She says, 'four'. What numbers come next?

A 3, 2, I   C 5, 6, 7
B 5, 7, 6   D 4, 5, 6

56

The *Power Maths* lesson sequence

At the heart of *Power Maths* is a unique lesson sequence designed to empower children to understand core concepts and grow in confidence. Embracing the National Centre for Excellence in the Teaching of Mathematics' (NCETM's) definition of mastery, the sequence guides and shapes every *Power Maths* lesson you teach.

Flexibility is built into the *Power Maths* programme so there is no one-to-one mapping of lessons and concepts and you can pace your teaching according to your class. While some children will need to spend longer on a particular concept (through interventions or additional lessons), others will reach deeper levels of understanding. However, it is important that the class moves forward together through the termly schedules.

Power Up ⏱ 5 minutes

Each lesson begins with a Power Up activity (available via the online subscription) which supports fluency in key number facts.

The whole-class approach depends on fluency, so the Power Up is a powerful and essential activity.

TOP TIP
If the class is struggling with the task, revisit it later and check understanding.

Power Ups reinforce the two key things that are essential for success: times-tables and number bonds.

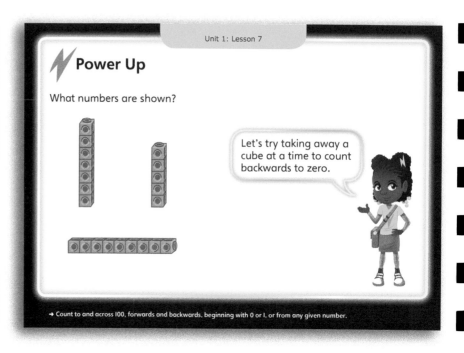

Discover ⏱ 10 minutes

A practical, real-life problem arouses curiosity. Children find the maths through story telling.

TOP TIP
Discover works best when run at tables, in pairs with concrete objects.

Question ① a) tackles the key concept and question ① b) digs a little deeper. Children have time to explore, play and discuss possible strategies.

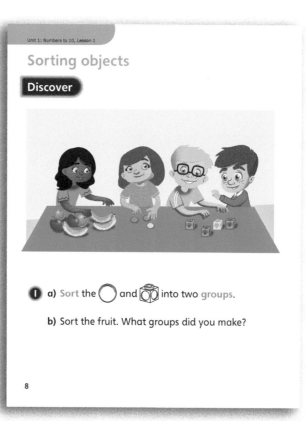

Share ⏱ 10 minutes

Teacher-led, this interactive section follows the Discover activity and highlights the variety of methods that can be used to solve a single problem.

TOP TIP

Bring children to the front or onto the carpet to discuss their methods. Pairs sharing a textbook is a great format for this!

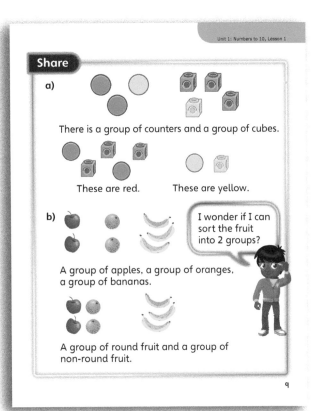

Share

a)

There is a group of counters and a group of cubes.

These are red.   These are yellow.

b)

I wonder if I can sort the fruit into 2 groups?

A group of apples, a group of oranges, a group of bananas.

A group of round fruit and a group of non-round fruit.

Your Teacher Guide gives target questions for children. The online toolkit provides interactive structures and representations to link concrete and pictorial to abstract concepts.

Bring children to the front to share and celebrate their solutions and strategies.

Think together

⏱ 10 minutes

Children work in groups on the carpet or at tables, using their textbooks or eBooks.

TOP TIP

Make sure children have mini whiteboards or pads to write on if they are not at their tables.

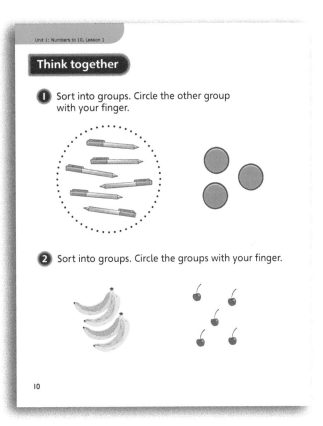

Think together

1 Sort into groups. Circle the other group with your finger.

2 Sort into groups. Circle the groups with your finger.

Using the Teacher Guide, model question 1 for your class.

Question 2 is less structured. Children will need to think together in their groups, then discuss their methods and solutions as a class.

Question 3 – the openness of the Challenge question helps to check depth of understanding.

Practice 🕐 15 minutes

Using their Practice Books, children work independently while you circulate and check on progress.

Questions follow small steps of progression to deepen learning.

TOP TIP
Some children could work separately with a teacher or assistant.

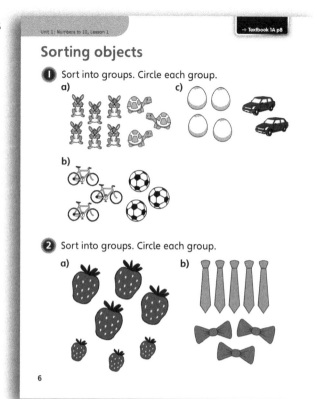

Are some children struggling? If so, work with them as a group, using mathematical structures and representations to support understanding as necessary.

There are no set routines: for real understanding, children need to think about the problem in different ways.

Reflect 🕐 5 minutes

'Spot the mistake' questions are great for checking misconceptions.

The Reflect section is your opportunity to check how deeply children understand the target concept.

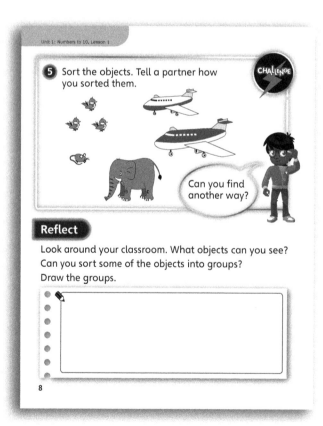

The Practice Books use various approaches to check that children have fully understood each concept.

Looking like they understand is not enough! It is essential that children can show they have grasped the concept.

Using the *Power Maths* Teacher Guide

Think of your Teacher Guides as *Power Maths* handbooks that will guide, support and inspire your day-to-day teaching. Clear and concise, and illustrated with helpful examples, your Teacher Guides will help you make the best possible use of every individual lesson. They also provide wrap-around professional development, enhancing your own subject knowledge and helping you to grow in confidence about moving your children forward together.

There is a Teacher Guide per year group for every term with unit and lesson level guidance and support.

Tips and advice on key elements such as C-P-A approaches, misconceptions, language, modelling growth mindsets and same-day intervention.

Annotations for every Pupil Textbook and Practice Book page, providing prompts for key questions to ask to expose understanding and explanations as to why key questions have been chosen.

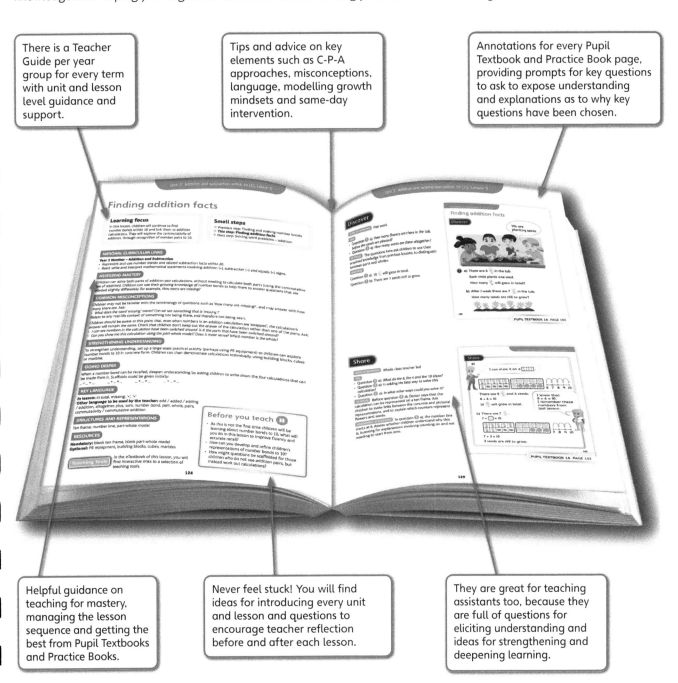

Helpful guidance on teaching for mastery, managing the lesson sequence and getting the best from Pupil Textbooks and Practice Books.

Never feel stuck! You will find ideas for introducing every unit and lesson and questions to encourage teacher reflection before and after each lesson.

They are great for teaching assistants too, because they are full of questions for eliciting understanding and ideas for strengthening and deepening learning.

At the end of each unit, your Teacher Guide helps you identify who has fully grasped the concept, who has not and how to move every child forward. This is covered later in the Assessment strategies section.

Power Maths Year 2, yearly overview

Textbook	Strand	Unit	Number of Lessons	
Textbook A / Practice Workbook A (Term 1)	Number – number and place value	1	Numbers to 100	10
	Number – addition and subtraction	2	Addition and subtraction (1)	12
	Number – addition and subtraction	3	Addition and subtraction (2)	9
	Measurement	4	Money	9
	Number – multiplication and division	5	Multiplication and division (1)	9
Textbook B / Practice Workbook B (Term 2)	Number – multiplication and division	6	Multiplication and division (2)	9
	Statistics	7	Statistics	7
	Measurement	8	Length and height	5
	Geometry – properties of shape	9	Properties of shapes	12
	Number – fractions	10	Fractions	14
Textbook C / Practice Workbook C (Term 3)	Geometry – position and direction	11	Position and direction	4
	Number – addition and subtraction	12	Problem solving and efficient methods	12
	Measurement	13	Time	9
	Measurement	14	Weight, volume and temperature	10

Power Maths Year 2, Textbook 2A (Term I) overview

Strand 1	Unit		Lesson number	Lesson title	NC Objective 1	NC Objective 2	NC Objective 3
Number – number and place value	Unit 1	Numbers to 100	1	Counting objects to 100	Count, read and write numbers to 100 in numerals; count in multiples of 2s, 5s and 10s (year 1)		
Number – number and place value	Unit 1	Numbers to 100	2	Representing numbers to 100	Identify, represent and estimate numbers using different representations, including the number line		
Number – number and place value	Unit 1	Numbers to 100	3	Tens and ones (1)	Recognise the place value of each digit in a 2-digit number (10s, 1s)	Identify, represent and estimate numbers using different representations, including the number line	
Number – number and place value	Unit 1	Numbers to 100	4	Tens and ones (2)	Recognise the place value of each digit in a 2-digit number (10s, 1s)	Identify, represent and estimate numbers using different representations, including the number line	
Number – number and place value	Unit 1	Numbers to 100	5	Representing numbers on a place value grid	Recognise the place value of each digit in a 2-digit number (10s, 1s)	Identify, represent and estimate numbers using different representations, including the number line	
Number – number and place value	Unit 1	Numbers to 100	6	Comparing numbers (1)	Compare and order numbers from 0 up to 100; use <, > and = signs	Identify, represent and estimate numbers using different representations, including the number line	
Number – number and place value	Unit 1	Numbers to 100	7	Comparing numbers (2)	Compare and order numbers from 0 up to 100; use <, > and = signs		
Number – number and place value	Unit 1	Numbers to 100	8	Ordering numbers	Compare and order numbers from 0 up to 100; use <, > and = signs		
Number – number and place value	Unit 1	Numbers to 100	9	Counting in 2s, 5s and 10s	Count in steps of 2, 3, and 5 from 0, and in 10s from any number, forward and backward		
Number – number and place value	Unit 1	Numbers to 100	10	Counting in 3s	Count in steps of 2, 3, and 5 from 0, and in 10s from any number, forward and backward	Identify, represent and estimate numbers using different representations, including the number line	
Number – addition and subtraction	Unit 2	Addition and subtraction (1)	1	Related facts – addition and subtraction	Recall and use addition and subtraction facts to 20 fluently, and derive and use related facts up to 100		
Number – addition and subtraction	Unit 2	Addition and subtraction (1)	2	Using number facts to check calculations	Recall and use addition and subtraction facts to 20 fluently, and derive and use related facts up to 100	Recognise and use the inverse relationship between addition and subtraction and use this to check calculations and solve missing number problems	Show that addition of two numbers can be done in any order (commutative) and subtraction of one number from another cannot
Number – addition and subtraction	Unit 2	Addition and subtraction (1)	3	Comparing number sentences	Solve problems with addition and subtraction: using concrete objects and pictorial representations, including those involving numbers, quantities and measures	Recall and use addition and subtraction facts to 20 fluently, and derive and use related facts up to 100	
Number – addition and subtraction	Unit 2	Addition and subtraction (1)	4	Finding related facts	Recall and use addition and subtraction facts to 20 fluently, and derive and use related facts up to 100		
Number – addition and subtraction	Unit 2	Addition and subtraction (1)	5	Making number bonds to 100	Solve problems with addition and subtraction: using concrete objects and pictorial representations, including those involving numbers, quantities and measures	Recall and use addition and subtraction facts to 20 fluently, and derive and use related facts up to 100	
Number – addition and subtraction	Unit 2	Addition and subtraction (1)	6	Adding and subtracting 1s	Add and subtract numbers using concrete objects, pictorial representations, and mentally, including: a 2-digit number and 1s	Solve problems with addition and subtraction: using concrete objects and pictorial representations, including those involving numbers, quantities and measures	
Number – addition and subtraction	Unit 2	Addition and subtraction (1)	7	Finding 10 more and 10 less	Count in steps of 2, 3, and 5 from 0, and in 10s from any number, forward and backward	Solve problems with addition and subtraction: using concrete objects and pictorial representations, including those involving numbers, quantities and measures	
Number – addition and subtraction	Unit 2	Addition and subtraction (1)	8	Adding and subtracting 10s	Add and subtract numbers using concrete objects, pictorial representations, and mentally, including: a 2-digit number and 10s	Solve problems with addition and subtraction: using concrete objects and pictorial representations, including those involving numbers, quantities and measures	

Strand 1	Unit		Lesson number	Lesson title	NC Objective 1	NC Objective 2	NC Objective 3
Number – addition and subtraction	Unit 2	Addition and subtraction (1)	9	Adding a 2-digit and 1-digit number (1)	Add and subtract numbers using concrete objects, pictorial representations, and mentally, including: a 2-digit number and 1s	Solve problems with addition and subtraction: using concrete objects and pictorial representations, including those involving numbers, quantities and measures	
Number – addition and subtraction	Unit 2	Addition and subtraction (1)	10	Adding a 2-digit and 1-digit number (2)	Add and subtract numbers using concrete objects, pictorial representations, and mentally, including: a 2-digit number and 1s	Solve problems with addition and subtraction: using concrete objects and pictorial representations, including those involving numbers, quantities and measures	
Number – addition and subtraction	Unit 2	Addition and subtraction (1)	11	Subtracting a 1-digit number from a 2-digit number (1)	Add and subtract numbers using concrete objects, pictorial representations, and mentally, including: a 2-digit number and 1s	Solve problems with addition and subtraction: using concrete objects and pictorial representations, including those involving numbers, quantities and measures	
Number – addition and subtraction	Unit 2	Addition and subtraction (1)	12	Subtracting a 1-digit number from a 2-digit number (2)	Add and subtract numbers using concrete objects, pictorial representations, and mentally, including: a 2-digit number and 1s	Solve problems with addition and subtraction: applying their increasing knowledge of mental and written methods	
Number – addition and subtraction	Unit 3	Addition and subtraction (2)	1	Adding two 2-digit numbers (1)	Add and subtract numbers using concrete objects, pictorial representations, and mentally, including: two 2-digit numbers	Solve problems with addition and subtraction: applying their increasing knowledge of mental and written methods	
Number – addition and subtraction	Unit 3	Addition and subtraction (2)	2	Adding two 2-digit numbers (2)	Add and subtract numbers using concrete objects, pictorial representations, and mentally, including: two 2-digit numbers	Solve problems with addition and subtraction: applying their increasing knowledge of mental and written methods	
Number – addition and subtraction	Unit 3	Addition and subtraction (2)	3	Subtracting a 2-digit number from another 2-digit number (1)	Add and subtract numbers using concrete objects, pictorial representations, and mentally, including: two 2-digit numbers	Solve problems with addition and subtraction: applying their increasing knowledge of mental and written methods	
Number – addition and subtraction	Unit 3	Addition and subtraction (2)	4	Subtracting a 2-digit number from another 2-digit number (2)	Add and subtract numbers using concrete objects, pictorial representations, and mentally, including: two 2-digit numbers	Solve problems with addition and subtraction: applying their increasing knowledge of mental and written methods	
Number – addition and subtraction	Unit 3	Addition and subtraction (2)	5	Subtracting a 2-digit number from another 2-digit number (3)	Add and subtract numbers using concrete objects, pictorial representations, and mentally, including: two 2-digit numbers	Solve problems with addition and subtraction: applying their increasing knowledge of mental and written methods	
Number - addition and subtraction	Unit 3	Addition and subtraction (2)	6	Subtracting a 2-digit number from another 2-digit number (4)	Add and subtract numbers using concrete objects, pictorial representations, and mentally, including: two 2-digit numbers	Solve problems with addition and subtraction: applying their increasing knowledge of mental and written methods	
Number – addition and subtraction	Unit 3	Addition and subtraction (2)	7	Adding three 1-digit numbers	Add and subtract numbers using concrete objects, pictorial representations and mentally, including: adding three 1-digit numbers	Solve problems with addition and subtraction: applying their increasing knowledge of mental and written methods	
Number – addition and subtraction	Unit 3	Addition and subtraction (2)	8	Solving word problems – the bar model (1)	Solve problems with addition and subtraction: using concrete objects and pictorial representations, including those involving numbers, quantities and measures		
Number – addition and subtraction	Unit 3	Addition and subtraction (2)	9	Solving word problems – the bar model (2)	Solve problems with addition and subtraction: using concrete objects and pictorial representations, including those involving numbers, quantities and measures		
Measurement	Unit 4	Money	1	Counting money – coins	Recognise and use signs for pounds (£) and pence (p); combine amounts to make a particular value	Recognise and know the value of different denominations of coins and notes (year 1)	
Measurement	Unit 4	Money	2	Counting money – notes	Recognise and use signs for pounds (£) and pence (p); combine amounts to make a particular value	Recognise and know the value of different denominations of coins and notes (year 1)	
Measurement	Unit 4	Money	3	Counting money – coins and notes	Recognise and use signs for pounds (£) and pence (p); combine amounts to make a particular value		

18

Strand 1	Unit		Lesson number	Lesson title	NC Objective 1	NC Objective 2	NC Objective 3
Measurement	Unit 4	Money	4	Showing equal amounts of money (1)	Find different combinations of coins that equal the same amounts of money	Recognise and know the value of different denominations of coins and notes (year 1)	
Measurement	Unit 4	Money	5	Showing equal amounts of money (2)	Find different combinations of coins that equal the same amounts of money	Recognise and know the value of different denominations of coins and notes (year 1)	
Measurement	Unit 4	Money	6	Comparing amounts of money	Solve simple problems in a practical context involving addition and subtraction of money of the same unit, including giving change	Recognise and know the value of different denominations of coins and notes (year 1)	
Measurement	Unit 4	Money	7	Calculating the total amount	Solve simple problems in a practical context involving addition and subtraction of money of the same unit, including giving change		
Measurement	Unit 4	Money	8	Finding change	Solve simple problems in a practical context involving addition and subtraction of money of the same unit, including giving change		
Measurement	Unit 4	Money	9	Solving two-step word problems	Solve simple problems in a practical context involving addition and subtraction of money of the same unit, including giving change		
Number – multiplication and division	Unit 5	Multiplication and division (1)	1	Making equal groups	Solve one-step problems involving multiplication and division by calculating the answer using concrete objects, pictorial representations and arrays with the support of the teacher (year 1)		
Number – multiplication and division	Unit 5	Multiplication and division (1)	2	Multiplication as equal groups	Calculate mathematical statements for multiplication and division within the multiplication tables and write them using the multiplication (×), division (÷) and equals (=) signs	Solve problems involving multiplication and division, using materials, arrays, repeated addition, mental methods, and multiplication and division facts, including problems in contexts	
Number – multiplication and division	Unit 5	Multiplication and division (1)	3	Adding equal groups	Solve problems involving multiplication and division, using materials, arrays, repeated addition, mental methods, and multiplication and division facts, including problems in contexts	Solve one-step problems involving multiplication and division, by calculating the answer using concrete objects, pictorial representations and arrays with the support of the teacher (year 1)	
Number – multiplication and division	Unit 5	Multiplication and division (1)	4	Multiplication sentences	Solve problems involving multiplication and division, using materials, arrays, repeated addition, mental methods, and multiplication and division facts, including problems in contexts		
Number – multiplication and division	Unit 5	Multiplication and division (1)	5	Using arrays	Calculate mathematical statements for multiplication and division within the multiplication tables and write them using the multiplication (×), division (÷) and equals (=) signs	Solve problems involving multiplication and division, using materials, arrays, repeated addition, mental methods, and multiplication and division facts, including problems in contexts	
Number – multiplication and division	Unit 5	Multiplication and division (1)	6	2 times-table	Recall and use multiplication and division facts for the 2, 5 and 10 multiplication tables, including recognising odd and even numbers		
Number – multiplication and division	Unit 5	Multiplication and division (1)	7	5 times-table	Recall and use multiplication and division facts for the 2, 5 and 10 multiplication tables, including recognising odd and even numbers		
Number – multiplication and division	Unit 5	Multiplication and division (1)	8	10 times-table	Recall and use multiplication and division facts for the 2, 5 and 10 multiplication tables, including recognising odd and even numbers		
Number – multiplication and division	Unit 5	Multiplication and division (1)	9	Solving word problems – multiplication	Solve problems involving multiplication and division, using materials, arrays, repeated addition, mental methods, and multiplication and division facts, including problems in contexts		

Mindset: an introduction

Global research and best practice deliver the same message: learning is greatly affected by what learners perceive they can or cannot do. What is more, it is also shaped by what their parents, carers and teachers perceive they can do. Mindset – the thinking that determines our beliefs and behaviours – therefore has a fundamental impact on teaching and learning.

Everyone can!

Power Maths and mastery methods focus on the distinction between 'fixed' and 'growth' mindsets (Dweck, 2007).[1] Those with a fixed mindset believe that their basic qualities (for example, intelligence, talent and ability to learn) are pre-wired or fixed: 'If you have a talent for maths, you will succeed at it. If not, too bad!' By contrast, those with a growth mindset believe that hard work, effort and commitment drive success and that 'smart' is not something you are or are not, but something you become. In short, everyone can do maths!

Key mindset strategies

A growth mindset needs to be actively nurtured and developed. *Power Maths* offers some key strategies for fostering healthy growth mindsets in your classroom.

It is okay to get it wrong

Mistakes are valuable opportunities to re-think and understand more deeply. Learning is richer when children and teachers alike focus on spotting and sharing mistakes as well as solutions.

Praise hard work

Praise is a great motivator, and by focusing on praising effort and learning rather than success, children will be more willing to try harder, take risks and persist for longer.

Mind your language!

The language we use around learners has a profound effect on their mindsets. Make a habit of using growth phrases, such as, 'Everyone can!', 'Mistakes can help you learn' and 'Just try for a little longer'. The king of them all is one little word, 'yet... I can't solve this...yet!' Encourage parents and carers to use the right language too.

Build in opportunities for success

The step-by-small-step approach enables children to enjoy the experience of success. In addition, avoid ability grouping and encourage every child to answer questions and explain or demonstrate their methods to others.

[1] Dweck, C (2007) The New Psychology of Success, Ballantine Books: New York

The *Power Maths* characters

The *Power Maths* characters model the traits of growth mindset learners and encourage resilience by prompting and questioning children as they work. Appearing frequently in the Textbooks and Practice Books, they are your allies in teaching and discussion, helping to model methods, alternatives and misconceptions, and to pose questions. They encourage and support your children, too: they are all hardworking, enthusiastic and unafraid of making and talking about mistakes.

Meet the team!

Creative Flo is open-minded and sometimes indecisive. She likes to think differently and come up with a variety of methods or ideas.

Determined Dexter is resolute, resilient and systematic. He concentrates hard, always tries his best and he'll never give up – even though he doesn't always choose the most efficient methods!

"Let's try again."

"Mistakes are cool!"

"Have I found all of the solutions?"

"Let's try it this way…"

"Can we do it differently?"

"I've got another way of doing this!"

"I'm going to try this!"

"I know how to do that!"

"Want to share my ideas?"

Curious Ash is eager, interested and inquisitive, and he loves solving puzzles and problems. Ash asks lots of questions but sometimes gets distracted.

"What if we tried this…?"

"I wonder…"

"Is there a pattern here?"

Sparks the Cat

Miaow!

Brave Astrid is confident, willing to take risks and unafraid of failure. She's never scared to jump straight into a problem or question, and although she often makes simple mistakes she's happy to talk them through with others.

Mathematical language

Traditionally, we in the UK have tended to try simplifying mathematical language to make it easier for young children to understand. By contrast, evidence and experience show that by diluting the correct language, we actually mask concepts and meanings for children. We then wonder why they are confused by new and different terminology later down the line! *Power Maths* is not afraid of 'hard' words and avoids placing any barriers between children and their understanding of mathematical concepts. As a result, we need to be planned, precise and thorough in building every child's understanding of the language of maths. Throughout the Teacher Guides you will find support and guidance on how to deliver this, as well as individual explanations throughout the Pupil Textbooks.

Use the following key strategies to build children's mathematical vocabulary, understanding and confidence.

Precise and consistent

Everyone in the classroom should use the correct mathematical terms in full, every time. For example, refer to 'equal parts', not 'parts'. Used consistently, precise maths language will be a familiar and non-threatening part of children's everyday experience.

Full sentences

Teachers and children alike need to use full sentences to explain or respond. When children use complete sentences, it both reveals their understanding and embeds their knowledge.

Stem sentences

These important sentences help children express mathematical concepts accurately, and are used throughout the *Power Maths* books. Encourage children to repeat them frequently, whether working independently or with others. Examples of stem sentences are:

"4 is a part, 5 is a part, 9 is the whole."

"There are .... groups. There are .... in each group."

Key vocabulary

The unit starters highlight essential vocabulary for every lesson. In the Pupil Textbooks, characters flag new terminology and the Teacher Guide lists important mathematical language for every unit and lesson. New terms are never introduced without a clear explanation.

Symbolic language

Symbols are used early on so that children quickly become familiar with them and their meaning. Often, the *Power Maths* characters will highlight the connection between language and particular symbols.

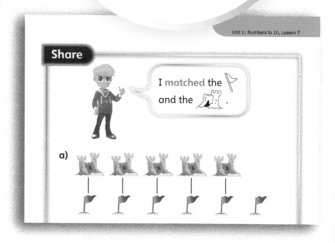

The role of talk and discussion

When children learn to talk purposefully together about maths, barriers of fear and anxiety are broken down and they grow in confidence, skills and understanding. Building a healthy culture of 'maths talk' empowers their learning from day one.

Explanation and discussion are integral to the *Power Maths* structure, so by simply following the books your lessons will stimulate structured talk. The following key 'maths talk' strategies will help you strengthen that culture and ensure that every child is included.

Sentences, not words

Encourage children to use full sentences when reasoning, explaining or discussing maths. This helps both speaker and listeners to clarify their own understanding. It also reveals whether or not the speaker truly understands, enabling you to address misconceptions as they arise.

Working together

Working with others in pairs, groups or as a whole class is a great way to support maths talk and discussion. Use different group structures to add variety and challenge. For example, children could take timed turns for talking, work independently alongside a 'discussion buddy', or perhaps play different *Power Maths* character roles within their group.

Think first – then talk

Provide clear opportunities within each lesson for children to think and reflect, so that their talk is purposeful, relevant and focused.

Give every child a voice

Where the 'hands up' model allows only the more confident child to shine, *Power Maths* involves everyone. Make sure that no child dominates and that even the shyest child is encouraged to contribute – and praised when they do.

Assessment strategies

Teaching for mastery demands that you are confident about what each child knows and where their misconceptions lie: therefore, practical and effective assessment is vitally important.

Formative assessment within lessons

The **Think together** section will often reveal any confusions or insecurities: try ironing these out by doing the first Think together question as a class. For children who continue to struggle, you or your teaching assistant should provide support and enable them to move on.

Performance in **Practice** can be very revealing: check Practice Books and listen out both during and after practice to identify misconceptions.

The **Reflect** section is designed to check on the all-important depth of understanding. Be sure to review how the children performed in this final stage before you teach the next lesson.

End of unit check – Textbook

Each unit concludes with a summative check to help you assess quickly and clearly each child's understanding, fluency, reasoning and problem-solving skills. Your Teacher Guide will suggest ideal ways of organising a given activity and offer advice and commentary on what children's responses mean. For example, 'What misconception does this reveal?'; 'How can you reinforce this particular concept?'

For Year 1 and Year 2 children, assess in small, teacher-led groups, giving each child time to think and respond while also consolidating correct mathematical language. Assessment with young children should always be an enjoyable activity, so avoid one-to-one individual assessments, which they may find threatening or scary. If you prefer, the End of unit check can be carried out as a whole-class group using whiteboards and Practice Books.

End of unit check – Practice Book

The Practice Book contains further opportunities for assessment, and can be completed by children independently whilst you are carrying out diagnostic assessment with small groups. Your Teacher Guide will advise you on what to do if children struggle to articulate an explanation – or perhaps encourage you to write down something they have explained well. It will also offer insights into children's answers and their implications for next learning steps. It is split into three main sections, outlined below.

My journal and Think

My journal is designed to allow children to show their depth of understanding of the unit. It can also serve as a way of checking that children have grasped key mathematical vocabulary. The question children should answer is first presented in the Pupil Textbook in the Think section. This provides an opportunity for you to discuss the question first as a class to ensure children have understood their task. Children should have some time to think about how they want to answer the question, and you could ask them to talk to a partner about their ideas. Then children should write their answer in their Practice Book, using the word bank provided to help them with vocabulary.

Power check

The Power check allows pupils to self-assess their level of confidence on the topic by colouring in different smiley faces. You may want to introduce the faces as follows:

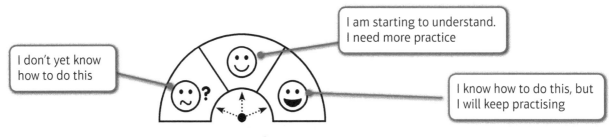

I don't yet know how to do this

I am starting to understand. I need more practice

I know how to do this, but I will keep practising

Power play or Power puzzle

Each unit ends with either a Power play or a Power puzzle. This is an activity, puzzle or game that allows children to use their new knowledge in a fun, informal way.

How to ask diagnostic questions

The diagnostic questions provided in children's Practice Books are carefully structured to identify both understanding and misconceptions (if children answer in a particular way, you will know why). The simple procedure below may be helpful:

Ask the question, offering the selection of answers provided.

▼

Children take time to think about their response.

▼

Each child selects an answer and shares their reasoning with the group.

▼

Give minimal and neutral feedback (for example, 'That's interesting', or 'Okay').

▼

Ask, 'Why did you choose that answer?', then offer an opportunity to change their mind by providing one correct and one incorrect answer.

▼

Note which children responded and reasoned correctly first time and everyone's final choices.

▼

Reflect that together, we can get the right answer.

▼

Record outcomes on the assessment grid (on the next page).

Power Maths Unit Assessment Grid

Year ___   **Unit** ___ _____

Record only as much information as you judge appropriate for your assessment of each child's mastery of the unit and any steps needed for intervention.

Name	Q1	Q2	Q3	Q4	Q5	My journal	Power check	Power play/puzzle	Mastery	Intervention/ Strengthen

Keeping the class together

Traditionally, children who learn quickly have been accelerated through the curriculum. As a consequence, their learning may be superficial and will lack the many benefits of enabling children to learn with and from each other.

By contrast, *Power Maths'* mastery approach values real understanding and richer, deeper learning above speed. It sees all children learning the same concept in small, cumulative steps, each finding and mastering challenge at their own level. Remember that when you teach for mastery, EVERYONE can do maths! Those who grasp a concept easily have time to explore and understand that concept at a deeper level. The whole class therefore moves through the curriculum at broadly the same pace via individual learning journeys.

For some teachers, the idea that a whole class can move forward together is revolutionary and challenging. However, the evidence of global good practice clearly shows that this approach drives engagement, confidence, motivation and success for all learners, and not just the high flyers. The strategies below will help you keep your class together on their maths journey.

Mix it up

Do not stick to set groups at each table. Every child should be working on the same concept, and mixing up the groupings widens children's opportunities for exploring, discussing and sharing their understanding with others.

Recycling questions

Reuse the Pupil Textbook and Practice Book questions with concrete materials to allow children to explore concepts and relationships and deepen their understanding. This strategy is especially useful for reinforcing learning in same-day interventions.

Strengthen at every opportunity

The next lesson in a *Power Maths* sequence always revises and builds on the previous step to help embed learning. These activities provide golden opportunities for individual children to strengthen their learning with the support of teaching assistants.

Prepare to be surprised!

Children may grasp a concept quickly or more slowly. The 'fast graspers' won't always be the same individuals, nor does the speed at which a child understands a concept predict their success in maths. Are they struggling or just working more slowly?

Depth and breadth

Just as prescribed in the National Curriculum, the goal of *Power Maths* is never to accelerate through a topic but rather to gain a clear, deep and broad understanding.

"Pupils who grasp concepts rapidly should be challenged through being offered rich and sophisticated problems before any acceleration through new content. Those who are not sufficiently fluent with earlier material should consolidate their understanding, including through additional practice, before moving on."

National Curriculum: Mathematics programmes of study: KS1 & 2, 2013

The lesson sequence offers many opportunities for you to deepen and broaden children's learning, some of which are suggested below.

Discover

As well as using the questions in the Teacher Guide, check that children are really delving into why something is true. It is not enough to simply recite facts, such as '6 + 3 = 9'. They need to be able to see why, explain it, and to demonstrate the solution in several ways.

Share

Make sure that every child is given chances to offer answers and expand their knowledge and not just those with the greatest confidence.

Think together

Encourage children to think about how they solved the problem and explain it to their partner. Be sure to make concrete materials available on group tables throughout the lesson to support and reinforce learning.

Practice

Avoid any temptation to select questions according to your assessment of ability: practice questions are presented in a logical sequence and it is important that each child works through every question.

Reflect

Open-ended questions allow children to deepen their understanding as far as they can by finding new ways of finding answers. For example, *Give me another way of working out how high the wall is... And another way?*

Online materials

For each unit you will find additional strengthening activities to support those children who need it and to deepen the understanding of those who need the additional challenge.

Same-day intervention

Since maths competence depends on mastering concepts one by one in a logical progression, it is important that no gaps in understanding are ever left unfilled. Same-day interventions – either within or after a lesson – are a crucial safety net for any child who has not fully made the small step covered that day. In other words, intervention is always about keeping up, not catching up, so that every child has the skills and understanding they need to tackle the next lesson. That means presenting the same problems used in the lesson, with a variety of concrete materials to help children model their solutions.

We offer two intervention strategies below, but you should feel free to choose others if they work better for your class.

Within-lesson intervention

The Think together activity will reveal those who are struggling, so when it is time for Practice, bring these children together to work with you on the first practice questions. Observe these children carefully, ask questions, encourage them to use concrete models and check that they reach and can demonstrate their understanding.

After-lesson intervention

You might like to use Think together before an assembly, giving you or teaching assistants time to recap and expand with slow graspers during assembly time. Teaching assistants could also work with strugglers at other convenient points in the school day.

The role of practice

Practice plays a pivotal role in the *Power Maths* approach. It takes place in class groups, smaller groups, pairs, and independently, so that children always have the opportunities for thinking as well as the models and support they need to practice meaningfully and with understanding.

Intelligent practice

In *Power Maths*, practice never equates to the simple repetition of a process. Instead we embrace the concept of intelligent practice, in which all children become fluent in maths through varied, frequent and thoughtful practice that deepens and embeds conceptual understanding in a logical, planned sequence. To see the difference, take a look at the following examples.

Traditional practice

- Repetition can be rote – no need for a child to think hard about what they are doing

- Praise may be misplaced

- Does this prove understanding?

Intelligent practice

- Varied methods – concrete, pictorial and abstract

- Calculations expressed in different ways, requiring thought and understanding

- Constructive feedback

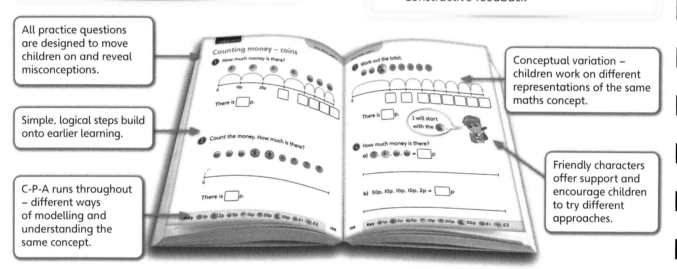

All practice questions are designed to move children on and reveal misconceptions.

Simple, logical steps build onto earlier learning.

C-P-A runs throughout – different ways of modelling and understanding the same concept.

Conceptual variation – children work on different representations of the same maths concept.

Friendly characters offer support and encourage children to try different approaches.

A carefully designed progression

The Pupil Practice Books provide just the right amount of intelligent practice for children to complete independently in the final sections of each lesson. It is really important that all children are exposed to the practice questions, and that children are not directed to complete different sections. That is because each question is different and has been designed to challenge children to think about the maths they are doing. The questions become more challenging so children grasping concepts more quickly will start to slow down as they progress. Meanwhile, you have the chance to circulate and spot any misconceptions before they become barriers to further learning.

Homework and the role of carers

While *Power Maths* does not prescribe any particular homework structure, we acknowledge the potential value of practice at home. For example, practising fluency in key facts, such as number bonds and times tables, is an ideal homework task for Key Stage 1 children, and carers could work through uncompleted Practice Book questions with children at either primary stage.

However, it is important to recognise that many parents and carers may themselves lack confidence in maths, and few, if any, will be familiar with mastery methods. A Parents' and Carers' Evening that helps them understand the basics of mindsets, mastery and mathematical language is a great way to ensure that children benefit from their homework. It could be a fun opportunity for children to teach their families that everyone can do maths!

Structures and representations

Unlike most other subjects, maths comprises a wide array of abstract concepts – and that is why children and adults so often find it difficult. By taking a concrete-pictorial-abstract (C-P-A) approach, *Power Maths* allows children to tackle concepts in a tangible and more comfortable way.

Non-linear stages

Concrete

Replacing the traditional approach of a teacher working through a problem in front of the class, the concrete stage introduces real objects that children can use to 'do' the maths – any familiar object that a child can manipulate and move to help bring the maths to life. It is important to appreciate, however, that children must always understand the link between models and the objects they represent. For example, children need to first understand that three cakes could be represented by three pretend cakes, and then by three counters or bricks. Frequent practice helps consolidate this essential insight. Although they can be used at any time, good concrete models are an essential first step in understanding.

Pictorial

This stage uses pictorial representations of objects to let children 'see' what particular maths problems look like. It helps them make connections between the concrete and pictorial representations and the abstract maths concept. Children can also create or view a pictorial representation together, enabling discussion and comparisons. The *Power Maths* teaching tools are fantastic for this learning stage, and bar modelling is invaluable for problem-solving throughout the primary curriculum.

Abstract

Our ultimate goal is for children to understand abstract mathematical concepts, symbols and notation and, of course, some children will reach this stage far more quickly than others. To work with abstract concepts, a child must be comfortable with the meaning of, and relationships between, concrete, pictorial and abstract models and representations. The C-P-A approach is not linear, and children may need different types of models at different times. However, when a child demonstrates with concrete models and pictorial representations that they have grasped a concept, we can be confident that they are ready to explore or model it with abstract symbols such as numbers and notation.

Use at any time and with any age to support understanding

Variation helps visualisation

Children find it much easier to visualise and grasp concepts if they see them presented in a number of ways, so be prepared to offer and encourage many different representations.

For example, the number six could be represented in various ways:

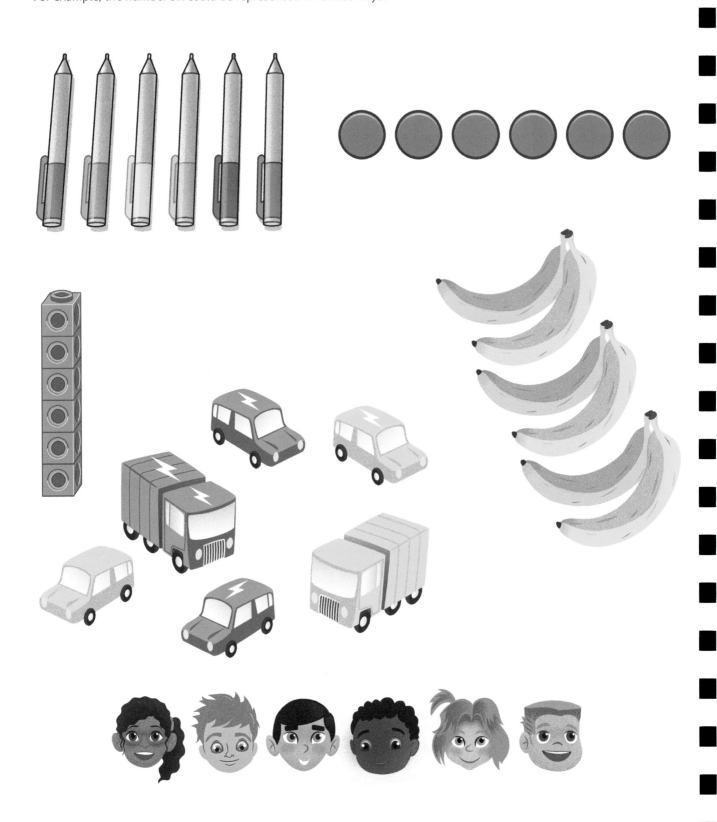

Getting started with *Power Maths*

As you prepare to put *Power Maths* into action, you might find the tips and advice below helpful.

STEP 1: Train up!

A practical, up-front full-day professional development course will give you and your team a brilliant head-start as you begin your *Power Maths* journey. You will learn more about the ethos, how it works and why.

STEP 2: Check out the progression

Take a look at the yearly and termly overviews. Next take a look at the unit overview for the unit you are about to teach in your Teacher Guide, remembering that you can match your lessons and pacing to your class.

STEP 3: Explore the context

Take a little time to look at the context for this unit: what are the implications for the unit ahead? (Think about key language, common misunderstandings and intervention strategies, for example.) If you have the online subscription, don't forget to watch the corresponding unit video.

STEP 4: Prepare for your first lesson

Familiarise yourself with the objectives, essential questions to ask and the resources you will need. The Teacher Guide offers tips, ideas and guidance on individual lessons to help you anticipate children's misconceptions and challenge those who are ready to think more deeply.

STEP 5: Teach and reflect

Deliver your lesson — and enjoy!

Afterwards, reflect on how it went... Did you cover all five stages? Does the lesson need more time? How could you improve it?

Unit I
Numbers to 100

Mastery Expert tip! "The reflect sections of this unit are excellent for developing children's reasoning skills. I often asked children to develop their ideas independently and then justify them to their partner. It allowed them to develop their vocabulary use and support each other in their learning."

Don't forget to watch the Unit 1 video!

WHY THIS UNIT IS IMPORTANT

This unit focuses on children's ability to read and understand numbers to 100. They will use their growing understanding of place value to help them sort, compare and order numbers.

Within this unit, children will revise their understanding of different representations of numbers and also meet other representations for the first time. They will use these representations to show a number's 'tens' and 'ones' and use this to help them compare and order. Children will use part-whole models and place value grids to show their partitioning of numbers and use these to support their reasoning when comparing and ordering.

Moving on from partitioning and ordering numbers, the children will begin to develop their ability to count forwards and backwards efficiently in steps of 2, 3, 5, and 10.

WHERE THIS UNIT FITS

→ **Unit 1: Numbers to 100**

→ Unit 2: Addition and Subtraction (1)

Before they start this unit, it is expected that children:
- know how to group objects into groups of ten
- count up and back in ones.

ASSESSING MASTERY

Children who have mastered this unit will be able to confidently partition any 2-digit number in different ways and be able to recognise how many tens and ones make up any given 2-digit number. They will be able to use multiple concrete, pictorial and abstract representations of numbers, such as place value grids and part-whole models, to support their reasoning and justification of their ideas.

COMMON MISCONCEPTIONS	STRENGTHENING UNDERSTANDING	GOING DEEPER
Children may have more trouble counting backwards than forwards.	Give children games to play such as hide and seek where they will get to practise counting down (10, 9…3, 2, 1, coming!). Sing songs such as 'Ten Green Bottles'. Practise counting over the 10s bridges (for example 42, 41, 40, 39…).	Give children images of castles built with cubes (as in Lesson 10 – **Think together**). If you add three blocks each time, can they predict what the 4th castle in the pattern will be? What about the 7th? Can children explain how they know?
Children may place the tens number in a place value grid, as opposed to just the digit representing how many tens (50 instead of 5 for example).	Use digit cards to generate two numbers, say 5 and 2. Arrange the cards to make 52 and 25, discussing the value of each digit in both numbers. Reinforce the description: 5 tens and 2 ones is the same as 52; 2 tens and 5 ones is the same as 25.	

WAYS OF WORKING

Use these pages to introduce the focus to children. You can use the characters to explore different ways of working too.

STRUCTURES AND REPRESENTATIONS

Part-whole model: This model helps children understand that two or more parts combine to make a whole. It also helps to strengthen children's understanding of number bonds within 100.

Number line: Number lines help children to represent the order of numbers. They will help children count on and back from a given starting point and help them identify patterns within the count.

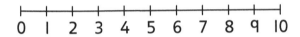

Place value grid: Place value grids help children to record and describe how a number is 'made'. This representation can empower children to more efficiently describe and order numbers.

Tens	Ones

KEY LANGUAGE

There is some key language that children will need to know as part of the learning in this unit:

→ less than, fewer, smaller, less, (<)

→ greater than, larger, bigger, more, (>)

→ equal to, (=)

→ greatest, biggest

→ fewest, smallest

→ tens, ones

→ how many?, count, partition

→ place value grid, part-whole model

PUPIL TEXTBOOK 2A PAGE 6

PUPIL TEXTBOOK 2A PAGE 7

Counting objects to 100

Learning focus

In this lesson, children will learn to count objects to 100 efficiently, using their understanding of counting in tens and ones.

Small steps

→ **This step: Counting objects to 100**
→ Next step: Representing numbers to 100

NATIONAL CURRICULUM LINKS

Year 2 Number – Number and Place Value

Count, read and write numbers to 100 in numerals; count in multiples of 2s, 5s and 10s (year 1 revision).

ASSESSING MASTERY

Children can confidently count from 0 to any number up to 100. They can use their understanding of counting in tens and ones to help them count efficiently and can use multiple representations to support their counting and reasoning.

COMMON MISCONCEPTIONS

When counting groups of 10, children may continue counting in tens after all the 10 groups have been counted. For example, if counting up to 52, children may count: 0, 10, 20, 30, 40, 50, 60, 70, instead of 0, 10, 20, 30, 40, 50, 51, 52. Ask:
• *Are there 10 blocks under that jump along the number line? How many blocks are there?*

STRENGTHENING UNDERSTANDING

Introduce this lesson through play acting the scenario shown in the **Discover** section. Drop a large collection of objects and discuss how best to count them. Ask:
• *Counting in ones is taking a long time. How could we make this quicker?*

GOING DEEPER

To explore the concept more deeply, encourage children to count in multiples of 10 more efficiently. You could ask children how they could make counting the tens quicker. For example, instead of counting to 30 by counting three sets of 10 (0, 10, 20, 30), children could be encouraged to recognise three tens as 30 and so count from 0 to 30 in one jump.

KEY LANGUAGE

In lesson: count, tens, ones, group, all number names and numerals from 0 to 100

Other language to be used by the teacher: number line, check

STRUCTURES AND REPRESENTATIONS

Number line

RESOURCES

Mandatory: blank number lines

Optional: collections of countable objects, bead strings

 In the eTextbook of this lesson, you will find interactive links to a selection of teaching tools.

Before you teach ⏸

• What resources will you use to support children's counting?
• Are children able to find groups of 10 objects?

Discover

WAYS OF WORKING Pair work

ASK

- *What is the same and what is different about the objects the girl has dropped?*
- *How could we group and sort the cubes?*
- *How could the boy help her count them?*
- *What will make counting the cubes more difficult?*
- *Would sorting them by colour help?*
- *How many would be left if the boy hid 3 of them?*

IN FOCUS Question ❶ a) offers the opportunity to begin discussing with children how they would go about sorting the cubes to make them easier to count. This activity would be most effective if same coloured cubes as in the picture were available for children to manipulate, group and sort.

ANSWERS

Question ❶ a): There are 28 ▱.

Question ❶ b): There are 30 ▱ now.

Share

WAYS OF WORKING Whole class teacher led

ASK

- *Who do you think will finish counting the blocks first, Dexter or Astrid?*
- *Did you group the blocks differently to Astrid?*
- *Why do you think she chose to group them in tens?*
- *How did you find out what 2 more was?*
- *How did you represent 2 more? Did anyone represent it differently?*
- *How does the number line make the counting clear?*

IN FOCUS Discuss question ❶ a) and how it is similar or different to the children's chosen method of counting. Children should recognise that counting in tens and then counting on from a multiple of 10 is an efficient method. Ask children to group their blocks like this to give them the opportunity to practise the skill in a concrete manner.

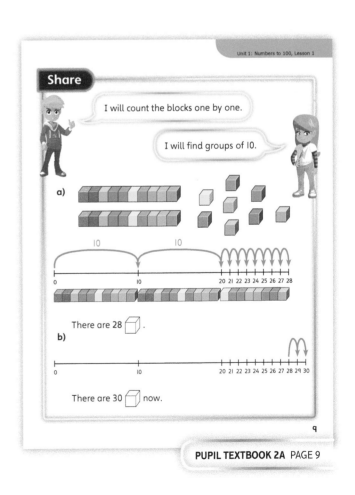

Think together

WAYS OF WORKING Whole class teacher led (I do, We do, You do)

ASK

- Question ❶ : *How have the stars been organised in the picture?*
- Question ❶ : *How have the stars been organised along the number line?*
- Question ❶ : *How will you count along the number line?*
- Question ❷ : *Are you sure the cubes are grouped correctly? How could you check?*

IN FOCUS Question ❶ supports children in making the link between counting and grouping the objects into groups of 10, to presenting this along a number line. For this question, children are scaffolded in where the missing numbers are needed along the number line. Question ❷ removes the scaffold of the missing number boxes, offering children the opportunity to demonstrate their understanding of how the number line can be used to represent the method of counting.

STRENGTHEN To strengthen understanding of question ❶ and question ❷ , ask children how the objects have been grouped and how the groups relate to the jumps on the number line. Use cubes in two groups of 10 to check how many there are.

DEEPEN Question ❸ offers the opportunity to ensure that children understand the need to group in tens. Ask children how they would represent their thinking and prove their ideas.

ASSESSMENT CHECKPOINT Question ❷ assesses whether children can count by finding groups of 10 and then counting the remaining few. They can link this to jumps along a blank number line.

ANSWERS

Question ❶ : There are 32 stars.

Question ❷ : There are 45 cubes.

Question ❸ : Emma has mistakenly made groups of 11 and 10, then added 5.

Jim has mistakenly made groups of 10 and 9, then added 7.

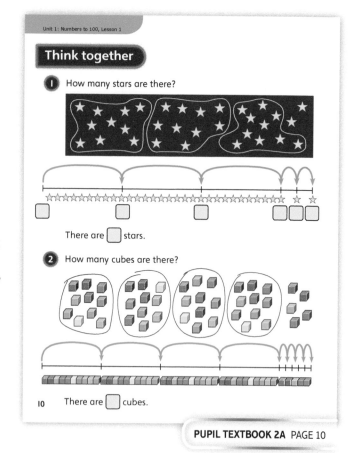

PUPIL TEXTBOOK 2A PAGE 10

PUPIL TEXTBOOK 2A PAGE 11

Practice

IN FOCUS Questions in this section offer the opportunity for children to experience groups of 10 in different representations. Questions ❶ and ❷ a) show the groups of 10 within each amount in a concrete way, allowing children the opportunity to develop independence with the concept. Question ❷ b) shows the groups of 10 in a more abstract way. Question ❸ gives children the chance to complete a blank number line to represent their counting.

STRENGTHEN In question ❷ b), support children by giving them straws tied in bundles of 10. If they untie these bundles they will be able to see the 10 in a more concrete way.

DEEPEN Question ❸ could be extended by asking children what the number line would look like if you added another 2 dots to the overall amount. Question ❹ uses less regular arrangements of the cubes in tens comprised of 6 and 4 and emphasises the need to count the number of tens accurately. To deepen children's thinking around this question, ask why Emma thinks she needs 70 cubes and how they could arrange the cubes differently to make them easier to count. Question ❺ uses a number line and number tracks to develop children's abilities to count up and down in tens.

ASSESSMENT CHECKPOINT Question ❷ b) should help you decide whether pupils are able to count in tens and then ones to find the total. Question ❺ provides the opportunity to test their fluency in counting up and down in tens.

ANSWERS Answers for the **Practice** part of the lesson appear in the separate **Practice and Reflect answer guide**.

Reflect

IN FOCUS The **Reflect** part of the lesson requires children to practise the skill of counting in tens and ones again. More important than why option 2 is correct is why options 1 and 3 are incorrect. Children should be given the opportunity to discuss their ideas with their partner and justify their conclusions.

ASSESSMENT CHECKPOINT Assess whether children have understood the correct method of counting tens and ones to find a total. Can children convince you that option 2 is correct and options 1 and 3 are incorrect? Can they identify where the mistakes have been made and can they use the picture and number sequences to support their reasoning?

ANSWERS Answers for the **Reflect** part of the lesson appear in the separate **Practice and Reflect answer guide**.

After the lesson ⏸

- How confident were children with using a blank number line?
- Do children recognise why 10 is an important number in our number system?

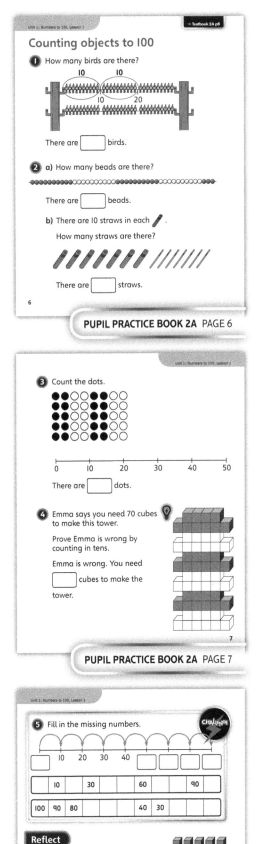

PUPIL PRACTICE BOOK 2A PAGE 6

PUPIL PRACTICE BOOK 2A PAGE 7

PUPIL PRACTICE BOOK 2A PAGE 8

Representing numbers to 100

Learning focus

In this lesson, children will learn to recognise and represent numbers to 100 in different ways. They will investigate concrete and pictorial representations of numbers.

Small steps

→ Previous step: Counting objects to 100
→ **This step: Representing numbers to 100**
→ Next step: Tens and ones (1)

NATIONAL CURRICULUM LINKS

Year 2 Number – Number and Place Value

Identify, represent and estimate numbers using different representations, including the number line.

ASSESSING MASTERY

Children can confidently use different resources, pictures and numerals to represent numbers in different ways. They can use these representations to represent the tens and ones within a number.

COMMON MISCONCEPTIONS

Some of the representations shown, such as a bundle of 10 straws, do not represent the cardinality of the number. Children may struggle to identify the tens of some items. Ask:

• *How could you check how many are in each bundle? How could we organise these to make them easier to count?*

STRENGTHENING UNDERSTANDING

To strengthen initial understanding of the concept, ask children to count and group objects around the classroom. This will also help to support their recognition of groups of 10 where cardinality is unclear. For example, ask how they could find out how many blue pencils there are, encouraging them to put them into bundles of 10.

GOING DEEPER

For children who can confidently partition numbers into tens and ones, discuss how they could more efficiently count the remaining ones, for example grouping them into twos or fives. Ask how they could make the ones quicker to count.

KEY LANGUAGE

In lesson: tens, count, represent, all number names and numerals from 0 to 100

Other language to be used by the teacher: ones, check

STRUCTURES AND REPRESENTATIONS

Number line, Base 10 equipment, bead string, ten frame

RESOURCES

Mandatory: blank number lines

Optional: cubes, ten frames, selections of countable objects including straws, number cards

 In the eTextbook of this lesson, you will find interactive links to a selection of teaching tools.

Before you teach

• How confident are children at grouping in tens?
• How could you link this concept to a real-life context?
• What other resources and representations could you provide for children to count?

Discover

WAYS OF WORKING Pair work

ASK

- *What has happened in the picture?*
- *What might the girl be thinking?*
- *What has she already done with the cones?*
- *What objects will be easiest to count?*
- *How many red cones are there?*

IN FOCUS The picture offers a good chance to discuss why grouping in tens enables efficient counting. Discussing the similarities and differences in how the objects have been arranged should lead to the conclusion that the cones are much easier to count as they have been put into tens.

ANSWERS

Question ① a): There are 43 🛆 in total.

Question ① b): There are now 47 🛆 .

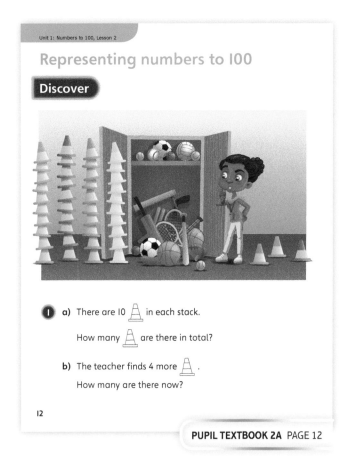

PUPIL TEXTBOOK 2A PAGE 12

Share

WAYS OF WORKING Whole class teacher led

ASK

- *Did anyone count the cones in a different way to Astrid?*
- *Was your way more or less efficient than Astrid's?*
- *What is the same and different about the pile of cones and the cubes or number line?*
- *Can you think of any other ways to represent the tens and ones? Is your way clearer?*

IN FOCUS Both questions provide the opportunity to make the link with the previous lesson's learning. Before moving on to the next part of the lesson, discuss with children other ways they could represent the numbers, before they are given the lesson's suggestions in **Think together**.

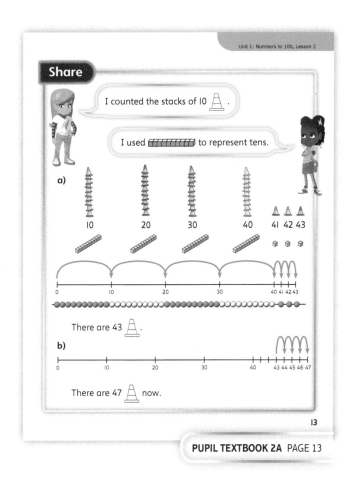

PUPIL TEXTBOOK 2A PAGE 13

Think together

Whole class teacher led (I do, We do, You do)

ASK

- Question ❶ : *How can you count the stickers quickly?*
- Question ❶ : *What do the cubes show?*
- Question ❶ : *What will you put in the empty boxes below the number line?*
- Question ❷ : *What should you count first: the tens or the ones?*
- Question ❷ : *Which do you predict is the biggest number? Which do you predict is the smallest number?*

IN FOCUS Question ❷ offers the opportunity to use the representations that have been taught so far to support the counting needed to match the numbers to the straws. Provide children with physical straws, bundled as in the picture, to support their counting.

STRENGTHEN When counting any of the numbers or arrangements of pictures and resources in any of the three questions, it could help children to have the cube representations of 10 and 1 printed on cards to be easily manipulated, as this will be a representation they should be comfortable with; alternatively, use pre-constructed columns of Base 10 equipment. Either the cards or the cubes could be used to create the number more physically.

DEEPEN For question ❸ b), ensure that children have access to many different resources to allow for their creativity when constructing representations. Ask: *Which is the clearest? Which makes it easiest to count? Which makes it more difficult to count?*

ASSESSMENT CHECKPOINT Question ❸ a) assesses whether children are able to identify different representations of ten and one. Question ❸ b) provides the opportunity to identify whether they are able to create their own representation of a number between 0 and 100.

ANSWERS

Question ❶ : There are 56 red stickers.

Question ❷ a): 33

Question ❷ b): 73

Question ❷ c): 53

Question ❸ a): They represent the number 42.

Question ❸ b): Children justify their representation, which should show the number 32 in tens and ones.

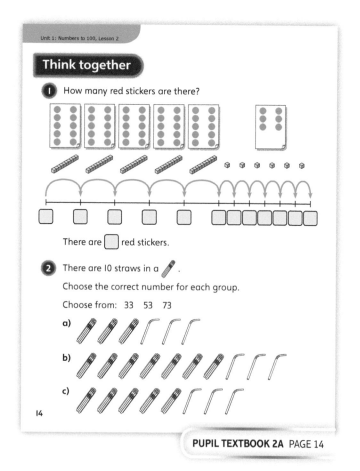

PUPIL TEXTBOOK 2A PAGE 14

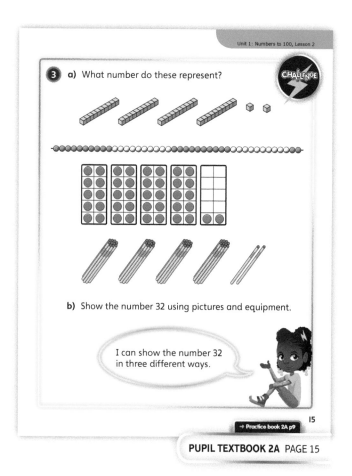

PUPIL TEXTBOOK 2A PAGE 15

Practice

WAYS OF WORKING Independent thinking

IN FOCUS Questions ① and ② provide children with more opportunities to work with different representations of numbers.

STRENGTHEN For questions ① and ② it may be helpful to have the real objects (or replicas) pictured in the question. Ask children to make the picture out of the objects. In question ① b), for example, ask how many cups are in the first pyramid, the second pyramid, and so on.

DEEPEN Question ④ challenges the assumptions children may be making at this point. For example, questions ④ a) and ④ b) both show tens as lines of cubes and ones as single cubes. Question ④ c) presents the tens and ones out of the normal order children will have grown accustomed to. Encourage children to consider whether 10 ones are the same as or different from the single ten. Ask them how they would write a number with 5 tens and 10 ones.

ASSESSMENT CHECKPOINT Questions ① and ② should help you decide whether children can confidently identify different representations of ten and one, are confident when seeing these representations used in different ways and can link these representations to numbers between 0 and 100. Question ③ assesses whether children are able to draw their own representations of numbers between 0 and 100.

ANSWERS Answers for the **Practice** part of the lesson appear in the separate **Practice and Reflect answer guide**.

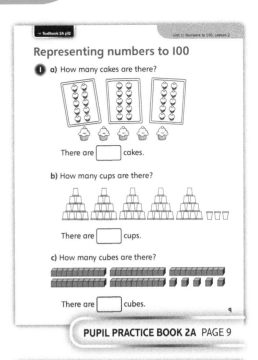

PUPIL PRACTICE BOOK 2A PAGE 9

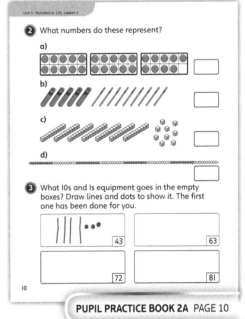

PUPIL PRACTICE BOOK 2A PAGE 10

Reflect

WAYS OF WORKING Pair work

IN FOCUS The **Reflect** part of the lesson requires children to work on their own representation. Use this opportunity to have children share their representations and discuss them with their partner. Ask whose is the clearer representation, and why.

ASSESSMENT CHECKPOINT Assess whether children are confident creating, and justifying the use of, different representations for any number between 0 and 100.

ANSWERS Answers for the **Reflect** part of the lesson appear in the separate **Practice and Reflect answer guide**.

After the lesson ⏸

- Did having the representations presented in different ways demonstrate any misconceptions or assumptions?
- Were there any representations children came up with that would be useful in future lessons? How will you record or display these?

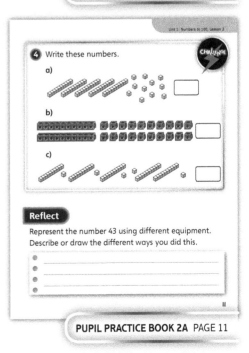

PUPIL PRACTICE BOOK 2A PAGE 11

Tens and ones

Learning focus

In this lesson, children will partition numbers into tens and ones. They will also name a number when given the tens and ones.

Small steps

→ Previous step: Representing numbers to 100
→ **This step: Tens and ones (1)**
→ Next step: Tens and ones (2)

NATIONAL CURRICULUM LINKS

Year 2 Number – Number and Place Value

- Recognise the place value of each digit in a 2-digit number (tens, ones).
- Identify, represent and estimate numbers using different representations, including the number line.

ASSESSING MASTERY

Children can partition any number between 0 and 100 into its tens and ones. They can confidently name any number between 0 and 100, when given the tens and ones separately.

COMMON MISCONCEPTIONS

Children may find it difficult to associate '5 tens' with 50, instead saying '50 tens'. Make sure that the representations from the previous lessons (cube towers, ten frames and so on) are available to scaffold their understanding. Ask:
- *What does each tower represent? How many towers are there?*

STRENGTHENING UNDERSTANDING

Prepare boxes or sets of 10 and individual objects. Introduce the concept by copying the scenario shown in the **Discover** picture. Give children their own shopping list and ask them to collect the correct number of groups of ten and ones.

GOING DEEPER

Encourage children to think of other ways of partitioning a given number into two amounts.

KEY LANGUAGE

In lesson: tens, ones, count, all number names and numerals from 0 to 100

Other language to be used by the teacher: represent, partition, digit, check

STRUCTURES AND REPRESENTATIONS

Base 10 equipment, place value cards, ten frame

RESOURCES

Mandatory: place value cards

Optional: Base 10 equipment, counters, collections of countable objects sorted into tens and ones

 In the eTextbook of this lesson, you will find interactive links to a selection of teaching tools.

Before you teach

- What other representations worked well in the last lesson?
- How can you integrate those representations into this lesson?

Discover

WAYS OF WORKING Pair work

ASK

- *What does Simon need?*
- *How has Simon represented the numbers on his list?*
- *How will Simon know how many pens to take?*
- *How many full boxes of pens should he pick up?*
- *How can you work out how many boxes of pencils Simon needs?*
- *Are there enough rubbers for him to collect for his class?*

IN FOCUS Use this picture to begin discussing how numbers can be partitioned into tens and ones. Ensure children make the link between 3 tens and 30, 4 tens and 40, and so on.

ANSWERS

Question ❶ a): Simon needs 4 [10 pencils] . He needs 6 ✏.

Question ❶ b): Molly needs 3 [10 pens] . She needs 1 ✏.

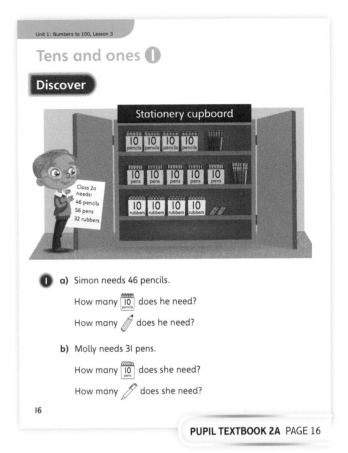

Share

WAYS OF WORKING Whole class teacher led

ASK

- *How did you know how many boxes of 10 would be needed?*
- *How did you know how many ones would be needed?*
- *What would the number have looked like if Simon needed 1 fewer pencils? 10 fewer?*
- *How else could you represent the number?*

IN FOCUS Question ❶ a) reinforces the idea of '4 tens' being equal to 40 and not '40 tens'. Using place value cards will support this understanding.

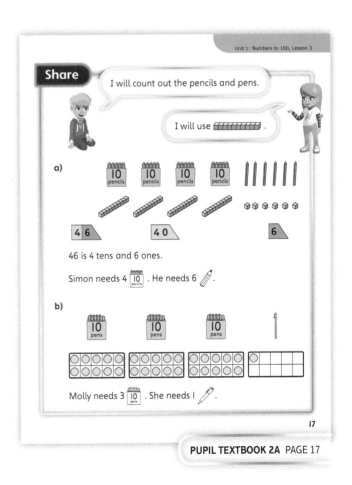

Think together

Think together

Unit 1: Numbers to 100, Lesson 3

WAYS OF WORKING Whole class teacher led (I do, We do, You do)

ASK
- *Which digit tells you how many tens you need?*
- *Which digit shows how many ones you need?*
- *How else could you represent the number?*

IN FOCUS Question **1** a) scaffolds children's understanding of partitioning a number into tens and ones. Use this opportunity to reinforce that 5 tens is the same as 50, and so on. Question **2** links this lesson's learning with the representations covered in the previous lesson. Have these resources available to help support the link in children's learning.

STRENGTHEN For question **1** b), it may be useful to have either real boxes of 10 rubbers, or pictures of them, each on an individual card. Children could use these to create the number in the same way as in question **1** a). Ask:
- *Can you show me what that number would look like?*
- *How many boxes of 10 rubbers do you have?*
- *How many single rubbers do you have?*
- *How many tens are there? How many ones?*

DEEPEN In question **3** , it is important that children recognise that 50 can be represented as 5 tens and 0 ones or 0 tens and 50 ones. Establish that more than one of the statements may be correct. Ask how this could be and whether one way is better than the other.

ASSESSMENT CHECKPOINT Question **2** should determine whether children can partition a number into tens and ones, and name a number when given the tens and ones separately. They should be able to link this understanding to the representations they have looked at in previous lessons.

ANSWERS

Question **1** a): 56 is 5 tens and 6 ones.

Simon needs 5 [10 pens] .

He needs 6 ✏ .

Question **1** b): 32 is 3 tens and 2 ones.

Simon needs 3 [10 rubbers] .

He needs 2 ▱ .

Question **2** a): 33 is 3 tens and 3 ones.

Question **2** b): 53 is 5 tens and 3 ones.

Question **2** c): 36 is 3 tens and 6 ones.

Question **3** : Both Bella and Dev are correct.

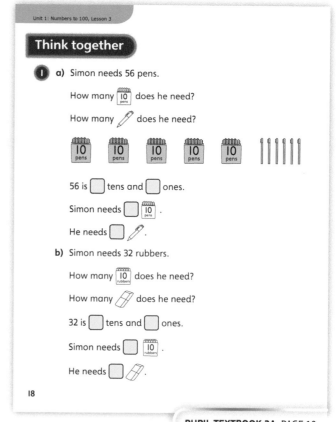

1 a) Simon needs 56 pens.

How many [10 pens] does he need?

How many ✏ does he need?

56 is ☐ tens and ☐ ones.

Simon needs ☐ [10 pens] .

He needs ☐ ✏ .

b) Simon needs 32 rubbers.

How many [10 rubbers] does he need?

How many ▱ does he need?

32 is ☐ tens and ☐ ones.

Simon needs ☐ [10 rubbers] .

He needs ☐ ▱ .

18

PUPIL TEXTBOOK 2A PAGE 18

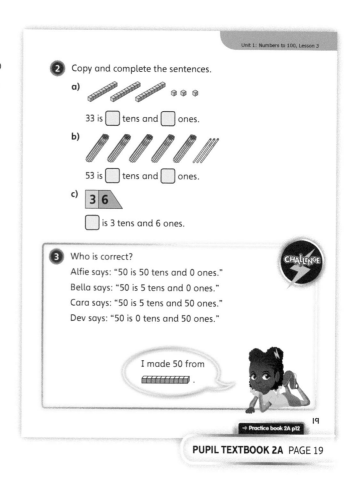

2 Copy and complete the sentences.

a)

33 is ☐ tens and ☐ ones.

b)

53 is ☐ tens and ☐ ones.

c) **3 6**

☐ is 3 tens and 6 ones.

3 Who is correct?

Alfie says: "50 is 50 tens and 0 ones."

Bella says: "50 is 5 tens and 0 ones."

Cara says: "50 is 5 tens and 50 ones."

Dev says: "50 is 0 tens and 50 ones."

I made 50 from [▭▭▭▭▭] .

→ Practice book 2A p12

19

PUPIL TEXTBOOK 2A PAGE 19

Practice

WAYS OF WORKING Independent thinking

IN FOCUS Questions ❶ and ❷ give children the chance to independently make the link between their learning from the previous two lessons and this one. Encourage children to use the concrete and pictorial resources to support their ideas and thinking.

STRENGTHEN In question ❸, it could help to have the representations from the previous lesson and a set of place value cards to assist children in partitioning. Ask how the resources can help them find out how many tens and ones they need.

DEEPEN In question ❹, encourage children to use the representations they have been working with as proof to develop their reasoning. In question ❺, ask children to explain how they know what numbers appear where. Encourage them to use the numbers that are already on the number line to help them.

ASSESSMENT CHECKPOINT Use question ❸ to assess whether children can partition a 2-digit number into its tens and ones.

ANSWERS Answers for the **Practice** part of the lesson appear in the separate **Practice and Reflect answer guide**.

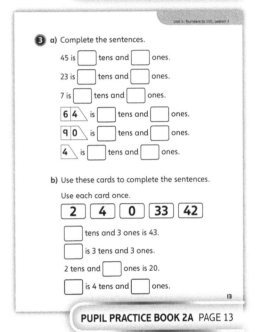

PUPIL PRACTICE BOOK 2A PAGE 12

PUPIL PRACTICE BOOK 2A PAGE 13

Reflect

WAYS OF WORKING Pair work

IN FOCUS The **Reflect** part of the lesson requires children to find a solution to the question, which they can then share with their partner. Encourage children to find more than one possible number, challenging them to find as many as they can.

ASSESSMENT CHECKPOINT Assess if children are able to create a 2-digit number with 9 ones and if they understand which digit is determined by the number of ones.

ANSWERS Answers for the **Reflect** part of the lesson appear in the separate **Practice and Reflect answer guide**.

After the lesson

- Are children able to partition confidently?
- Can children describe how many tens are in a number fluently and accurately?

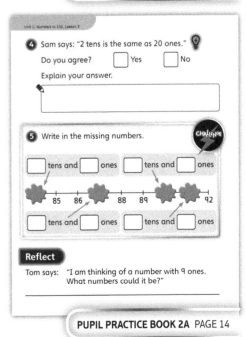

PUPIL PRACTICE BOOK 2A PAGE 14

Tens and ones ❷

Learning focus

In this lesson, children will continue to develop their understanding of partitioning 2-digit numbers, recording this as an addition calculation.

Small steps

→ Previous step: Tens and ones (1)
→ **This step: Tens and ones (2)**
→ Next step: Representing numbers on a place value grid

NATIONAL CURRICULUM LINKS

Year 2 Number – Number and Place Value

- Recognise the place value of each digit in a 2-digit number (tens, ones).
- Identify, represent and estimate numbers using different representations, including the number line.

ASSESSING MASTERY

Children can confidently partition 2-digit numbers using the part-whole model. They can record their partitioning using addition calculations.

COMMON MISCONCEPTIONS

Children may not recognise that a number can be partitioned in any other way than just tens and ones. Representing the number as counters in ten frames will help. Ask:
- *Can you think of another way to split this number? Can you show me how you would partition it?*

STRENGTHENING UNDERSTANDING

Give children Base 10 equipment or counters with ten frames to create the numbers. Encourage children to put the tens and ones into two different groups. When they are confident in this, ask whether they can move some tens to make different groups.

GOING DEEPER

When children are confident at writing an addition calculation using the two numbers they have created from partitioning, encourage them to think of other ways of writing the calculation. This will help develop their understanding of addition's commutativity and reinforce = sign as 'equal to' and not 'here comes the answer'. Ask whether they could write the addition by swapping the numbers around, and which numbers they can swap.

KEY LANGUAGE

In lesson: tens, ones, partition, part-whole, all number names and numerals from 0 to 100

Other language to be used by the teacher: represent, count, digit

STRUCTURES AND REPRESENTATIONS

Part-whole model, Base 10 equipment, place value cards, ten frame

RESOURCES

Mandatory: Base 10 equipment, place value cards, ten frames

Optional: counters, collections of countable objects

 In the eTextbook of this lesson, you will find interactive links to a selection of teaching tools.

Before you teach

- Are children ready to partition 2-digit numbers in different ways beyond a number's tens and ones?

Discover

WAYS OF WORKING Pair work

ASK

- *What are the children looking at?*
- *What do you think they have been doing?*
- *What number is in the circle?*
- *What do you think might go in the two circles below?*
- *Have the children used any equipment you recognise? What might they have used it for?*

IN FOCUS The picture should remind children of their previous learning as it references resources and equipment they met in the previous lesson. Question ① a) develops the idea that an addition calculation can be written using the two numbers created from partitioning.

ANSWERS

Question ① a): 56 = 50 + 6

Question ① b): Children's explanation of how they would change their representation to create 46 should include changing the tens.

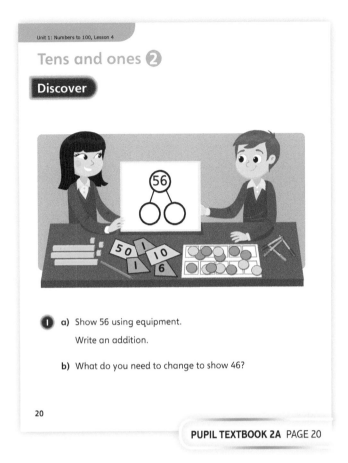

Tens and ones ②

Discover

① a) Show 56 using equipment.

Write an addition.

b) What do you need to change to show 46?

20

PUPIL TEXTBOOK 2A PAGE 20

Share

WAYS OF WORKING Whole class teacher led

ASK

- *How did you show 56? What equipment did you use?*
- *Can you make it another way? Which way is clearer?*
- *How will you change it to show 46?*
- *How are the different representations similar? How are they different?*
- *How can you write this as an addition?*

IN FOCUS Both questions reinforce the representation of 2-digit numbers with the resources children have been using in the unit so far and develop the use of the part-whole model.

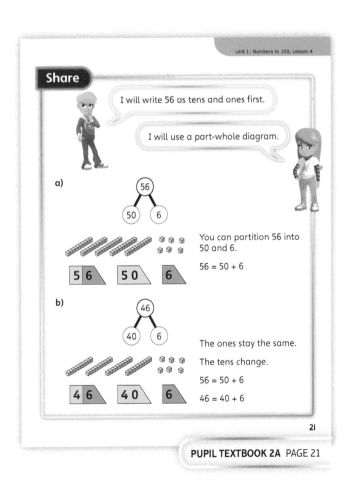

Share

I will write 56 as tens and ones first.

I will use a part-whole diagram.

a)

You can partition 56 into 50 and 6.

56 = 50 + 6

b)

The ones stay the same.

The tens change.

56 = 50 + 6

46 = 40 + 6

21

PUPIL TEXTBOOK 2A PAGE 21

Think together

WAYS OF WORKING Whole class teacher led (I do, We do, You do)

ASK

- *What equipment will you use to represent the number?*
- *How will you find how many tens and ones are in the number?*
- *Can you complete the part-whole diagram?*
- *How can you turn this into an addition?*

IN FOCUS Questions ❶ and ❷ build children's confidence when moving from the concrete representation of a number, using resources, to the abstract numerals and then finally to the linked addition calculation. Question ❷ approaches the concept that a number may not have any ones but that this can still be shown as an addition.

STRENGTHEN To support children's ability to use the partitioned number to create an addition calculation, it may be useful to have a large printed blank addition frame ready, such as: ? + ? = 35. Can children place the place value cards that made 35 into the addition frame? Having done this, they could then record the addition.

DEEPEN Question ❸ approaches the idea that a number can be partitioned in ways beyond just finding its tens and ones. Particularly important are the questions at the bottom of the page, regarding what is the same and what is different. Children should recognise that while they are partitioned differently, they are the same number.

ASSESSMENT CHECKPOINT Questions ❶ and ❷ will help you decide whether children can partition numbers into tens and ones, and use these numbers to write an addition. Assess whether they are becoming more confident at partitioning numbers in other ways, including using the part-whole model.

ANSWERS

Question ❶: 30 + 5 = 35

Question ❷ a): 23 = 20 + 3

Question ❷ b): 40 = 40 + 0

Question ❷ c): 24 = 20 + 4

Question ❷ d): 39 = 30 + 9

Question ❸:

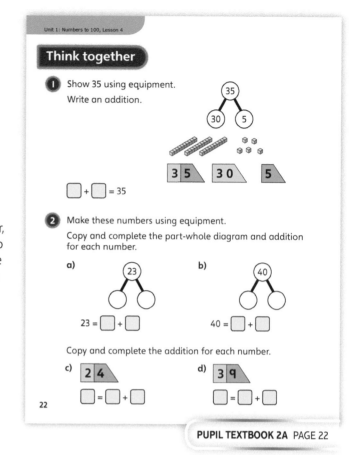

PUPIL TEXTBOOK 2A PAGE 22

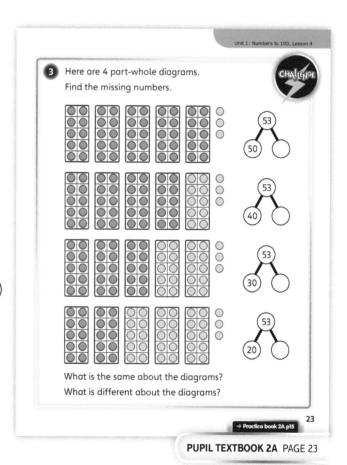

PUPIL TEXTBOOK 2A PAGE 23

Practice

Independent thinking

IN FOCUS In questions **1** and **2**, children independently practise the skills they have been learning so far. Both questions show numbers in different ways, including all the representations children have been using. Question **2** develops children's fluency with the part-whole model by showing it in a different orientation. Question **3** extends the concept of partitioning, by partitioning the same number in different ways.

STRENGTHEN In question **3**, ask children to discuss the similarities and differences. Ask what the pictures show and why some of the counters are different colours. Then focus on the part-whole diagrams and ask how they change and how they stay the same.

DEEPEN When children are explaining their ideas in question **4**, encourage them to prove their ideas using different representations. Challenge them to prove their answer to you and to explain the mistakes in the incorrect part-whole diagrams.

ASSESSMENT CHECKPOINT Questions **1** and **2** assess whether children can partition numbers into tens and ones, including using the part-whole model, and use these numbers to write an addition. Question **3** helps you determine whether they are able to partition numbers in other ways. Look for children supporting their ideas through the use of resources and accurately recorded addition calculations.

ANSWERS Answers for the **Practice** part of the lesson appear in the separate **Practice and Reflect answer guide**.

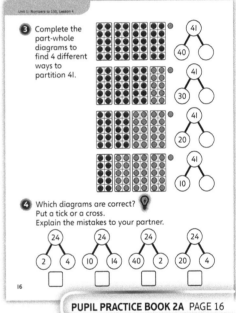

PUPIL PRACTICE BOOK 2A PAGE 15

PUPIL PRACTICE BOOK 2A PAGE 16

Reflect

Pair work

IN FOCUS The **Reflect** part of the lesson requires children to practise different ways of partitioning the same number. Once children have worked on their own ideas, ask them to discuss their ideas with their partner. Challenge them to find as many ways to partition the number as they can, and to explain whether they think they have found all the possible ways.

ASSESSMENT CHECKPOINT Assess whether children recognise that a number can be partitioned in more ways than just finding its tens and ones, and whether they can represent and explain this fluently.

ANSWERS Answers for the **Reflect** part of the lesson appear in the separate **Practice and Reflect answer guide**.

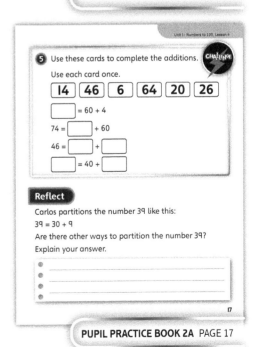

PUPIL PRACTICE BOOK 2A PAGE 17

After the lesson ⏸

- How confident were children in recording addition calculations?
- How confident were children in partitioning in different ways?
- Did any children begin to recognise addition's commutativity?

Representing numbers on a place value grid

Learning focus

In this lesson, children will learn to use a place value grid to show the value of digits within a 1- or 2-digit number.

Small steps

→ Previous step: Tens and ones (2)
→ **This step: Representing numbers on a place value grid**
→ Next step: Comparing numbers (1)

NATIONAL CURRICULUM LINKS

Year 2 Number – Number and Place Value

- Recognise the place value of each digit in a 2-digit number (tens, ones).
- Identify, represent and estimate numbers using different representations, including the number line.

ASSESSING MASTERY

Children can show the value of the digits in a 1- or 2-digit number using a place value grid. They can convert different concrete and pictorial representations of numbers into tens and ones and place these correctly into the place value grid.

COMMON MISCONCEPTIONS

When filling in the place value grid, children may fill the tens column with, for example, 60, instead of 6, when recording a number such as 63. Ask:

- *Can you show that number using cubes? How many tens can you count? Are there 60 tens or 6?*

STRENGTHENING UNDERSTANDING

To strengthen understanding of the place value grid, provide children with pre-made representations of tens and ones. Using a large version of the place value grid, encourage children to make the number first, before putting the tens and ones in the correct columns. Once this is done children can count how many tens and how many ones there are and complete the columns with digit cards.

GOING DEEPER

Encourage children to find patterns. Ask them to find all the numbers that have a 3 in the ones column, then all the numbers that have a 3 in the tens column. Ask what is the same and what is different about the numbers.

KEY LANGUAGE

In lesson: number, tens, ones, place value

Other language to be used by the teacher: digit, value

STRUCTURES AND REPRESENTATIONS

Place value grid, Base 10 equipment, number line

RESOURCES

Mandatory: place value grid, Base 10 equipment

Optional: large place value grid

 In the eTextbook of this lesson, you will find interactive links to a selection of teaching tools.

Before you teach

- Which resources will best support recognising the tens and ones in a number?
- How will you link this lesson to the previous lesson on partitioning?

Discover

WAYS OF WORKING Pair work

ASK

- *How do you know how many tens a number has?*
- *How many numbers in the picture have 3 tens?*
- *Whose number is easier to find?*
- *Can you show the numbers in a different way?*

IN FOCUS Use this part of the lesson to play a similar game in the classroom. Either you or the children could give the rest of the class clues about a number in the grid. Encourage children to give their reasoning when offering their suggestions.

ANSWERS

Question ❶ a): Mr Taylor's number is 32.

Question ❶ b): Mia's number is 62.

Representing numbers on a place value grid

Discover

a) What is Mr Taylor's number?

b) What is Mia's number?

24

PUPIL TEXTBOOK 2A PAGE 24

Share

WAYS OF WORKING Whole class teacher led

ASK

- *Is Flo's idea a good one?*
- *How does the place value grid organise the numbers more clearly?*
- *Why is there a '3' underneath 30 cubes in the tens column?*
- *What is the same about '3 tens' and 30? What is different?*
- *Can Mia's number be 60?*

IN FOCUS Questions ❶ a) and ❶ b) show how the place value grid works. Ensure children are aware of how to complete the grid accurately, recording tens as a single digit, rather than the full tens number.

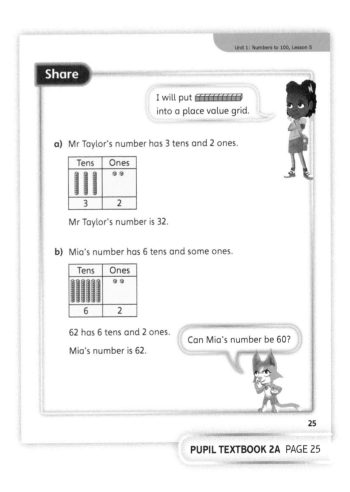

Share

I will put ▱▱▱▱ into a place value grid.

a) Mr Taylor's number has 3 tens and 2 ones.

Tens	Ones
3	2

Mr Taylor's number is 32.

b) Mia's number has 6 tens and some ones.

Tens	Ones
6	2

62 has 6 tens and 2 ones.

Mia's number is 62.

Can Mia's number be 60?

25

PUPIL TEXTBOOK 2A PAGE 25

Think together

WAYS OF WORKING Whole class teacher led (I do, We do, You do)

ASK

- Question ❶: *What clues do you have about Rav's number?*
- Question ❶: *What numbers will it not be? How do you know?*
- Question ❶: *How could you show Rav's number?*
- Question ❷: *How do you know how many tens and ones there are in the number?*
- Question ❷: *How will you record the tens? How will you record the ones?*

IN FOCUS Question ❶ gives children the opportunity to justify their ideas. Encourage them to show proof of their ideas through the use of resources and pictures, supporting the place value grid.

STRENGTHEN Use question ❷ to ensure that children understand how to accurately fill in the tens column on the place value grid. If children record the tens as a tens number, rather than a single digit, ask them how many tens there are and how they recorded this in the previous lesson.

DEEPEN Use Dexter and Flo's conversation in question ❸ to discuss what 0 in the tens column would represent. For example, ask how much 0 tens is and whether it is possible to put 0 in the tens column. Discuss whether Flo is correct. Encourage children to share their ideas. Have they found any different solutions? Ask them to check each other's solutions to make sure they are correct.

ASSESSMENT CHECKPOINT Use questions ❶ and ❷ to assess whether children can read and complete a place value grid. Check that they are aware that each place value is recorded with a single digit number.

ANSWERS

Question ❶: Rav's number is 35 or 65.

Question ❷ a): 6 tens / 2 ones

Question ❷ b): 4 tens / 0 ones

Question ❷ c): 4 tens / 7 ones

Question ❷ d): 5 tens / 1 one

Question ❸: The possible numbers are 2, 5, 25, 50, 52

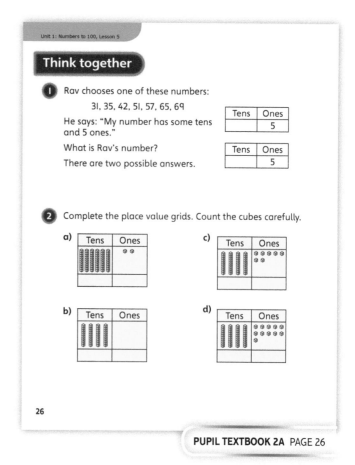

PUPIL TEXTBOOK 2A PAGE 26

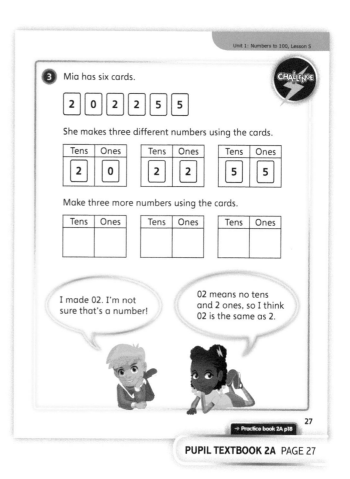

PUPIL TEXTBOOK 2A PAGE 27

Practice

WAYS OF WORKING Independent thinking

IN FOCUS Questions ❶ and ❷ scaffold children's understanding by providing representations of numbers already partitioned into their tens and ones. Question ❸ provides the opportunity to identify patterns along the number line. Ask children what changes and what stays the same in the place value grid as they count up and down along the number line.

STRENGTHEN For question ❷, provide children with Base 10 equipment and a large version of the place value grid. Suggest that they first build the number with cubes and place them into the grid as demonstrated. Ask how many tens they put into the tens column, and how they should record this.

DEEPEN In Question ❹ b), discuss what the tens digit could be. Ask whether a number can have a tens digit which is greater than 9. Encourage children to represent and prove their ideas. Ask whether they can predict what might happen after 9 tens.

ASSESSMENT CHECKPOINT Questions ❷ and ❸ will help you to decide whether children can show a number's place value confidently, using a place value grid. Children can link the place value grid to what they already know about partitioning and representing numbers.

ANSWERS Answers for the **Practice** part of the lesson appear in the separate **Practice and Reflect answer guide**.

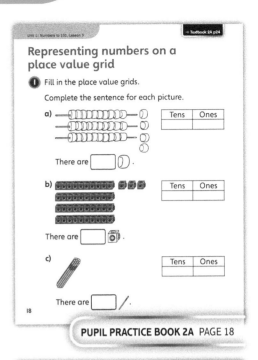

PUPIL PRACTICE BOOK 2A PAGE 18

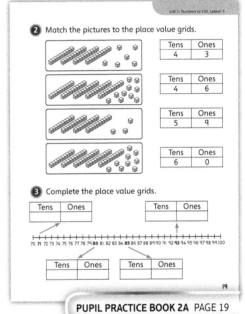

PUPIL PRACTICE BOOK 2A PAGE 19

Reflect

WAYS OF WORKING Pair work

IN FOCUS The **Reflect** part of the lesson requires children to demonstrate the value of each '8' digit. Encourage children to use a place value grid to help them. Once children have worked independently on the problem, give them the opportunity to share their ideas with their partner.

ASSESSMENT CHECKPOINT Assess whether children can confidently explain the place value of each number, using a place value grid to support their thinking and justifications.

ANSWERS Answers for the **Reflect** part of the lesson appear in the separate **Practice and Reflect answer guide**.

After the lesson ⏸

- Are children able to use the place value grid correctly, recording the tens and units accurately?
- Were children able to identify the differences between the partitioning they have done previously and how they use the place value grid?

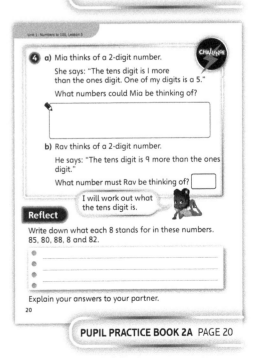

PUPIL PRACTICE BOOK 2A PAGE 20

Comparing numbers ①

Learning focus

In this lesson, children will develop their understanding of comparing numbers. Children will start to use their understanding of place value to aid them in their comparisons.

Small steps

→ Previous step: Representing numbers on a place value grid
→ **This step: Comparing numbers (1)**
→ Next step: Comparing numbers (2)

NATIONAL CURRICULUM LINKS

Year 2 Number – Number and Place Value

- Compare and order numbers from 0 up to 100; use <, > and = signs.
- Identify, represent and estimate numbers using different representations, including the number line.

ASSESSING MASTERY

Children can prove that one group is greater than another, by matching up and comparing concrete and pictorial representations of numbers.

COMMON MISCONCEPTIONS

Children may not compare the numbers in an efficient way. Ask:
- *Is there a quicker way to make the comparison? Could you show the comparison in another way?*

STRENGTHENING UNDERSTANDING

Introduce the lesson through role playing a scene of two dolls sharing sweets. Share the sweets in different ways, both equally and unequally. Ask who has more and who has fewer. If the sweets are shared unequally, ask children how they could change the amounts so it is fair.

GOING DEEPER

Deepen understanding of different contexts by offering short word problems. For example: *Tim has 63p and Milly has 74p. Who has the most money to spend at the shops?* and *Taylor needs 59 cm of ribbon to wrap a present. He found 45 cm of ribbon. Does he have enough?* Encourage children to represent these problems with the resources they have used previously.

KEY LANGUAGE

In lesson: more, less, greater, tens, ones, compare, <, >, =

Other language to be used by the teacher: larger, bigger, smaller, fewer, equal

STRUCTURES AND REPRESENTATIONS

Multilink cubes, Base 10 equipment

RESOURCES

Optional: multilink cubes, Base 10 equipment, counters

 In the eTextbook of this lesson, you will find interactive links to a selection of teaching tools.

Before you teach

- Are children confident with the <, > and = signs?
- Will children be confident at comparing numbers clearly in different representations?

Discover

WAYS OF WORKING Pair work

ASK

- *Who do you predict has more? How did you make your prediction?*
- *Is it fair at the moment?*
- *Can you write Matt's number of cubes as a written number?*
- *How many will Anna have after she has given 10 cubes away?*
- *How have the children organised their cubes? Why do you think they did that?*

IN FOCUS The picture reinforces the previous lessons by grouping the cubes in tens.

ANSWERS

Question ❶ a): Anna has more .

Question ❶ b): Matt has more now.

PUPIL TEXTBOOK 2A PAGE 28

Share

WAYS OF WORKING Whole class teacher led

ASK

- *Who do you think will be able to compare the numbers more quickly, Dexter or Astrid?*
- *Should we compare the tens or ones first?*
- *Why is it important to compare the last row?*
- *Did anyone start by comparing the last row? Would this work all the time?*
- *Can you think of any other ways to show the numbers?*
- *Why has the sign > been used?*

IN FOCUS Questions ❶ a) and ❶ b) remind children of the importance of arranging cubes systematically in tens and ones. Question ❶ a) involves comparing 3 ones and a ten (or 10 ones) in the last row, whereas in question ❶ b) children need to compare the tens.

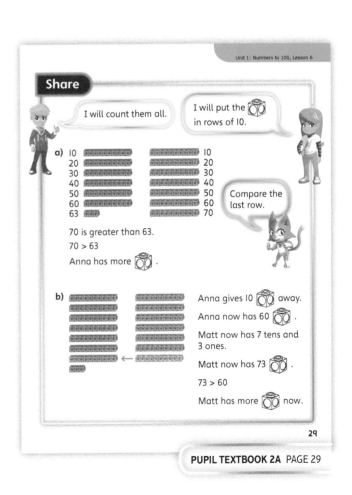

PUPIL TEXTBOOK 2A PAGE 29

Think together

WAYS OF WORKING Whole class teacher led (I do, We do, You do)

ASK

- *What should you do first?*
- *Are the cubes organised in a way that makes it easy to compare?*
- *Which number is bigger?*
- *Which number will go before > and <? Which number will go after it?*

IN FOCUS Questions ❶ and ❷ scaffold children in their ability to compare numbers, gradually reducing the amount of pre-completed elements. The tens and ones are arranged differently in questions ❶ and ❷, giving children the opportunity to work out which they think is clearer.

STRENGTHEN Encourage children to make concrete representations of the numbers using cubes or other countable objects. Remind them to arrange the objects so that they can easily see which is the bigger number.

DEEPEN Question ❸ presents numbers arranged in unfamiliar ways. Ask children whether the objects are arranged so they can count them quickly, and whether they could change the arrangements to make their counting more efficient. Discuss whether Flo is correct.

ASSESSMENT CHECKPOINT Questions ❶ and ❷ assess whether children can compare representations of two numbers. Children can recognise, and demonstrate through their comparisons, that they need to compare the tens first, then the ones.

ANSWERS

Question ❶ : 30 is greater than 24.

         30 > 24

         Ros has more cubes.

Question ❷ a): 30 is less than 43.

         30 < 43

Question ❷ b): 43 is equal to 43.

         43 = 43

Question ❸ a): 51 = 51

Question ❸ b): 48 > 46 or 46 < 48

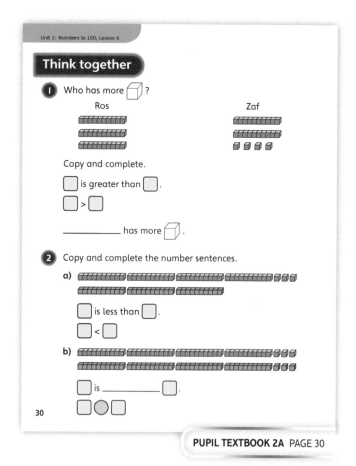

PUPIL TEXTBOOK 2A PAGE 30

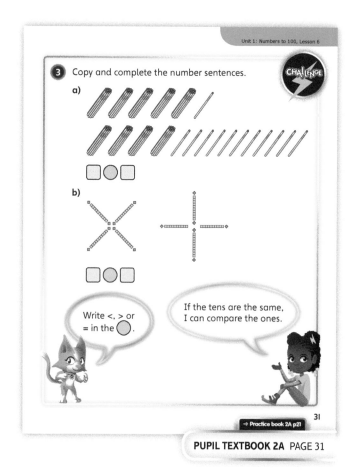

PUPIL TEXTBOOK 2A PAGE 31

Practice

WAYS OF WORKING Independent thinking

IN FOCUS Questions **1** and **2** give the children opportunity to practise with different representations of numbers. Question **1** scaffolds their solutions while question **2** requires more independence. Question **3** reminds children of the multiple different representations of numbers they have studied.

STRENGTHEN In question **3**, which uses some more abstract representations, encourage children to represent 40 in one of the more concrete ways shown in the question. Ask how they could make the numbers easier to compare. Suggest that they represent all the numbers in the same way.

DEEPEN In question **4**, use Flo's comment to deepen children's problem-solving ability. Ask why she is going to leave the second box blank. Discuss with children what would happen if she guessed a number for the second box, and whether she could be sure that she was correct. Encourage children to prove their ideas.

ASSESSMENT CHECKPOINT Questions **1**, **2** and **3** should help you to determine whether children can compare numbers using multiple representations, and recognise that it is important and more efficient to compare the tens first, then the ones.

ANSWERS Answers for the **Practice** part of the lesson appear in the separate **Practice and Reflect answer guide**.

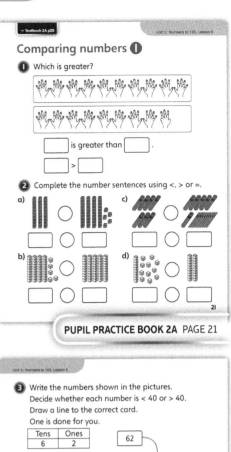

PUPIL PRACTICE BOOK 2A PAGE 21

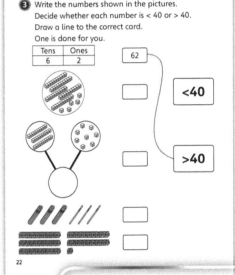

PUPIL PRACTICE BOOK 2A PAGE 22

Reflect

WAYS OF WORKING Pair work

IN FOCUS The **Reflect** part of the lesson requires children to justify their answer. They could share their ideas and proof with their partner.

ASSESSMENT CHECKPOINT Assess whether children can explain how their choice of evidence shows that 47 is less than 54.

ANSWERS Answers for the **Reflect** part of the lesson appear in the separate **Practice and Reflect answer guide**.

After the lesson ⏸

- Were children confident using the signs and vocabulary of comparison?
- Ideas of 'more' and 'fewer' occur in many situations – including games, role play (for example, shopping activities) and classroom jobs like organising resources or putting pupils into groups.
- What opportunities can you identify to reinforce and apply this lesson's learning?

PUPIL PRACTICE BOOK 2A PAGE 23

Comparing numbers ②

Learning focus

In this lesson, children will continue developing their ability to compare numbers, using more abstract representations.

Small steps

→ Previous step: Comparing numbers (1)
→ **This step: Comparing numbers (2)**
→ Next step: Ordering numbers

NATIONAL CURRICULUM LINKS

Year 2 Number – Number and Place Value

Compare and order numbers from 0 up to 100; use <, > and = signs.

ASSESSING MASTERY

Children can confidently compare numbers using place value to help and can recognise and explain why it is important to compare the larger part of two numbers first. Children are able to use more abstract representations to represent the numbers they are comparing.

COMMON MISCONCEPTIONS

Children may find comparing numbers with a 0 in the ones column confusing. Reinforce that they need to compare the tens column first. Ask:

• *How can you represent the numbers? What will you do first? The tens numbers are the same. What will you do now?*

STRENGTHENING UNDERSTANDING

Ensure that children who are unsure about comparing concrete and pictorial representations of numbers are given the opportunity to practise and develop this skill. Provide a large printed place value grid in which children can arrange the numbers in a concrete way, such as with cubes, before completing the more abstract grid. Possible approaches include comparing cube towers grouped in tens and ones, and comparing groups of objects through classroom jobs or role play, for example, pencils on tables or sharing sweets between two cuddly toys.

GOING DEEPER

Give children a 2-digit number (for example, 86). Ask how they could make the number smaller or larger by only changing the ones. Then ask how they could make the number smaller or larger by only changing the tens. This problem could give children the opportunity to work with problems that have either more than one solution or no solution at all.

KEY LANGUAGE

In lesson: more, less, greater, fewer, tens, ones, place value, number line, compare, equal, <, >

Other language to be used by the teacher: larger, bigger, smaller

STRUCTURES AND REPRESENTATIONS

Number line, place value grid

RESOURCES

Optional: cubes, large printed place value grid

 In the eTextbook of this lesson, you will find interactive links to a selection of teaching tools.

Before you teach

• Are children ready to move into the more abstract representations?
• How could you use this lesson to further develop children's problem-solving abilities?

Discover

WAYS OF WORKING Pair work

ASK

- *What could you compare in this picture?*
- *Which tree has the fewest leaves? Are there more leaves on the trees or on the ground?*
- *How can you tell who has more leaves?*
- *How many more leaves should Asif pick up so he has the same number as Beth?*
- *How many different ways could you show the numbers?*

IN FOCUS Questions ❶ a) and ❶ b) both require children to consider how to compare numbers without seeing pictorial representation of the numbers.

ANSWERS

Question ❶ a): Beth has more [leaf] .

Question ❶ b): Dana has fewer [leaf] .

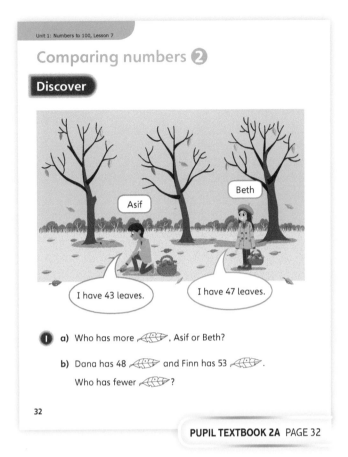

Comparing numbers ❷

Discover

I have 43 leaves.
I have 47 leaves.

❶ a) Who has more [leaf], Asif or Beth?

b) Dana has 48 [leaf] and Finn has 53 [leaf].
Who has fewer [leaf]?

32

PUPIL TEXTBOOK 2A PAGE 32

Share

WAYS OF WORKING Whole class teacher led

ASK

- *How did Dexter and Ash organise the representations to show the comparison?*
- *How does the place value grid help show the value of the number?*
- *What signs could you use to show the comparison?*
- *How do you know which sign to use?*

IN FOCUS Questions ❶ a) and ❶ b) link together the concrete and pictorial representations children used in the previous lesson to compare numbers with the more abstract representations used earlier in the unit, developing the skill of comparing numbers.

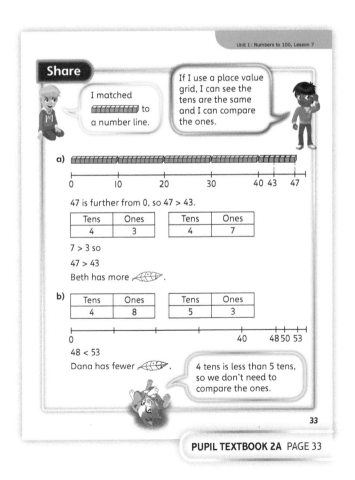

Share

I matched [ten-frame] to a number line.

If I use a place value grid, I can see the tens are the same and I can compare the ones.

a)

47 is further from 0, so 47 > 43.

Tens	Ones
4	3

Tens	Ones
4	7

7 > 3 so

47 > 43

Beth has more [leaf].

b)

Tens	Ones
4	8

Tens	Ones
5	3

48 < 53

Dana has fewer [leaf].

4 tens is less than 5 tens, so we don't need to compare the ones.

33

PUPIL TEXTBOOK 2A PAGE 33

Think together

WAYS OF WORKING Whole class teacher led (I do, We do, You do)

ASK

- Question **1** : *What should you do first?*
- Question **1** : *What sign will you use to show the comparison?*
- Question **1** : *Is there more than one way to write the comparison?*
- Question **1** : *How does the place value grid show the value of the number? How will you use it to compare the numbers?*
- Question **3** : *What column will you look at first when comparing the numbers?*

IN FOCUS Question **1** scaffolds children's move from using concrete resources and pictures to the more abstract representations of a number line and place value grid.

STRENGTHEN Some children may be confused by the partially completed number lines in question **2** , as they will be unable to physically count the ones after the tens. Prepare a number line that shows the ones as well as the tens and ask them to find the numbers on that number line.

DEEPEN Use Astrid and Ash's comments to discuss whether all the comparisons can be solved by looking only at the tens. Ask whether they ever need to look at the ones and challenge them to find an example where they cannot compare by only using the tens.

ASSESSMENT CHECKPOINT Use questions **2** and **3** to assess whether children can compare numbers using their understanding of number lines and place value grids, comparing the tens and then the ones, if necessary.

ANSWERS

Question **1** a): 32 < 42 or 42 > 32

Alexa has more 🐚.

Question **1** b): 65 > 62 or 62 < 65

Oli has more 🐚.

Question **2** a): 49 < 99

Question **2** b): 55 > 50

Question **3** a): 64 > 26

Question **3** b): 57 < 70

Question **3** c): 62 < 66

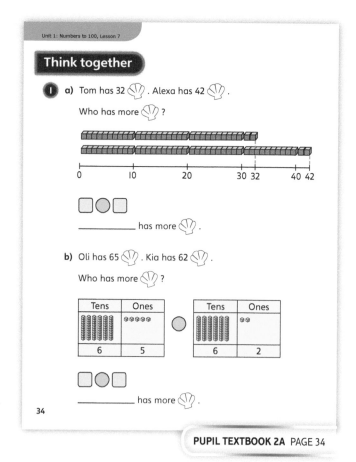

PUPIL TEXTBOOK 2A PAGE 34

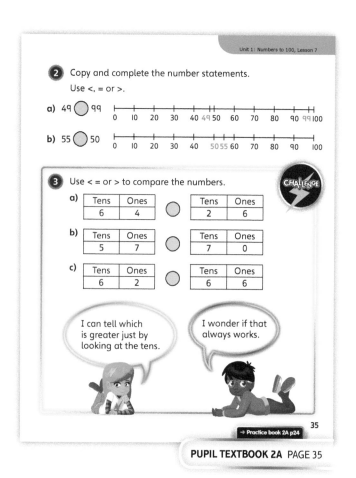

PUPIL TEXTBOOK 2A PAGE 35

Practice

WAYS OF WORKING Independent thinking

IN FOCUS Question ❶ provides different abstract representations for children to compare numbers. From question ❷ onwards, children are given only the numbers. Question ❷ also ensures that children are confident expressing <, > and = in words.

STRENGTHEN In question ❷, when using numbers written in ways that require some problem solving (for example, 'One less than 63', '4 tens and 8 ones'), support children by asking how they would read the number in each picture and encouraging them to use resources to show the number.

DEEPEN Ask children to explain how they solved question ❹. Discuss whether they think Flo's method was the best one. Challenge children to create their own similar number puzzles.

ASSESSMENT CHECKPOINT Use questions ❶ and ❷ to assess whether children can compare 2-digit numbers represented in an abstract form.

ANSWERS Answers for the **Practice** part of the lesson appear in the separate **Practice and Reflect answer guide**.

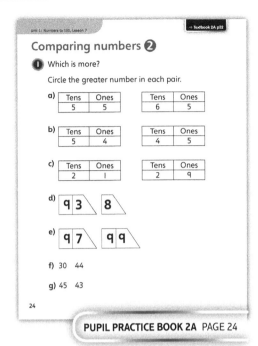

PUPIL PRACTICE BOOK 2A PAGE 24

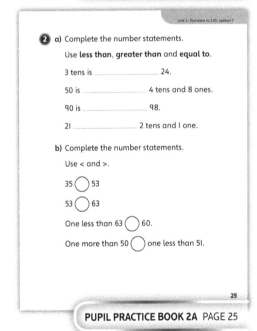

PUPIL PRACTICE BOOK 2A PAGE 25

Reflect

WAYS OF WORKING Pair work

IN FOCUS The **Reflect** part of the lesson requires children to apply and explain their knowledge about comparing 2-digit numbers. Ask children to share their reasoning with their partner, justifying their opinions.

ASSESSMENT CHECKPOINT Assess whether children can fluently explain their reasoning when comparing two numbers, using the appropriate concepts and vocabulary.

ANSWERS Answers for the **Reflect** part of the lesson appear in the separate **Practice and Reflect answer guide**.

After the lesson ⏸

- Were children confident using place value grids to represent numbers?
- Were children able to recognise when there could be more than one correct solution?

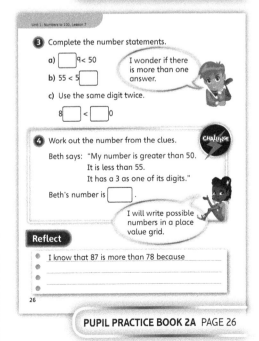

PUPIL PRACTICE BOOK 2A PAGE 26

Ordering numbers

Learning focus

In this lesson, children will use their understanding of place value and comparing numbers to order more than two numbers.

Small steps

→ Previous step: Comparing numbers (2)
→ **This step: Ordering numbers**
→ Next step: Counting in 2s, 5s and 10s

NATIONAL CURRICULUM LINKS

Year 2 Number – Number and Place Value

Compare and order numbers from 0 up to 100; use <, > and = signs.

ASSESSING MASTERY

Children can use their understanding of place value to compare and order numbers. They know to compare the tens in numbers before comparing the ones and can use different representations to support their reasoning.

COMMON MISCONCEPTIONS

Children may demonstrate a lack of organisation in their thinking by trying to compare all three numbers at the same time. Ask:

- *Could you order these numbers in a simpler way? What could you do first?*
- *How will you remember the first comparison? What will you record?*

STRENGTHENING UNDERSTANDING

Approach the concept of this lesson through playing games that score points. Play a short points-based game with three children. Record the scores and at the end of the games ask children how they know who won (has the highest score) and whether they can order the scores from last place to first.

GOING DEEPER

Ask children to sort four numbers and to explain how they sorted them. Repeat with five numbers.

KEY LANGUAGE

In lesson: compare, tens, ones, greatest, fewest, smallest, <, >

Other language to be used by the teacher: larger, greater, bigger, more, smaller, fewer, less, equal

STRUCTURES AND REPRESENTATIONS

Base 10 equipment, multilink cubes, number line

RESOURCES

Optional: Base 10 equipment, multilink cubes, counters, large place value grids

 In the eTextbook of this lesson, you will find interactive links to a selection of teaching tools.

Before you teach

- Can children confidently compare two numbers?
- What real-world contexts could you offer to support the learning?

Discover

WAYS OF WORKING Pair work

ASK

- What have the children measured the sunflowers with?
- Which sunflower is tallest? Whose sunflower is this?
- How could you match the sunflowers with the measurements?

IN FOCUS The picture introduces the concept of ordering more than one number. It may engage children to repeat this activity with plants in the school garden.

ANSWERS

Question ❶ a): Sunflower A is Felix's.

Sunflower B is Dan's.

Sunflower C is Eva's.

Question ❶ b): 33, 38, 45

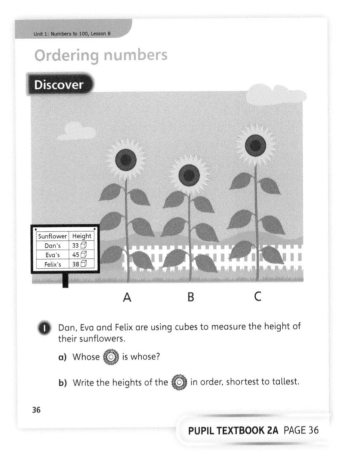

Ordering numbers

Discover

❶ Dan, Eva and Felix are using cubes to measure the height of their sunflowers.

a) Whose 🌻 is whose?

b) Write the heights of the 🌻 in order, shortest to tallest.

36

PUPIL TEXTBOOK 2A PAGE 36

Share

WAYS OF WORKING Whole class teacher led

ASK

- How has Flo chosen to compare the numbers? Did you do the same?
- Is Dexter's idea a good one?
- Could you arrange the cubes in a different way to show the comparison more clearly?
- How did you compare all three numbers?
- Which two did you compare first?

IN FOCUS Question ❶ a) requires the numbers to be compared systematically so that they can be put in order. Use this section to encourage children to look for either the biggest or the smallest number first and then to compare two numbers at a time.

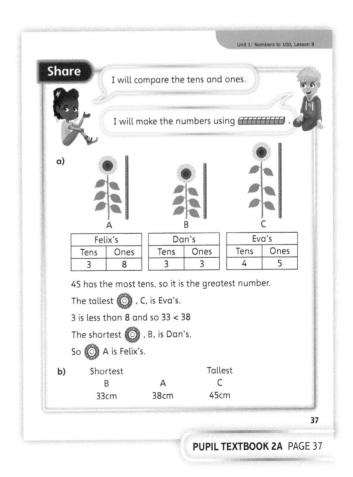

Share

I will compare the tens and ones.

I will make the numbers using ▯▯▯▯▯▯▯▯ .

a)

	Felix's	
Tens		Ones
3		8

	Dan's	
Tens		Ones
3		3

	Eva's	
Tens		Ones
4		5

45 has the most tens, so it is the greatest number.

The tallest 🌻, C, is Eva's.

3 is less than 8 and so 33 < 38

The shortest 🌻, B, is Dan's.

So 🌻 A is Felix's.

b)

Shortest		Tallest
B	A	C
33cm	38cm	45cm

37

PUPIL TEXTBOOK 2A PAGE 37

Think together

Unit 1: Numbers to 100, Lesson 8

Think together

WAYS OF WORKING Whole class teacher led (I do, We do, You do)

ASK
- *What should we do before comparing the numbers?*
- *What representation will you choose to use?*
- *Which representation will be most efficient?*
- *What will tell you which number is the largest?*
- *What number will go in the middle box?*

IN FOCUS Question ❶ helps children to organise their thinking when approaching the ordering of three numbers. The visual representation should make it clear to them which is the greatest, scaffolding a starting point for them to continue ordering.

STRENGTHEN As question ❷ is the first opportunity children have to order three numbers without a pictorial or concrete representation, have pictures or concrete resources available for them to manipulate while ordering. These could include counters or large place value grids with pictures of tens and ones to arrange on them.

DEEPEN Use question ❸ to challenge children to justify their reasoning. Ask how they know what is the smallest or largest possible number and how they can prove it.

ASSESSMENT CHECKPOINT Question ❷ can help you determine whether children can order three numbers. Children are beginning to explain why starting with the biggest or smallest number is an efficient and systematic approach.

ANSWERS

Question ❶ a): The jar with 31 buttons contains the fewest buttons.

Question ❶ b): The greatest number of buttons is 67.

Question ❶ c): 67 > 63 > 31

31 < 63 < 67

Question ❷ a): 28 < 30 < 37

Question ❷ b): 9 < 20 < 70

Question ❸ a): 79, 80, 81

Question ❸ b): 79

Question ❸ c): 81

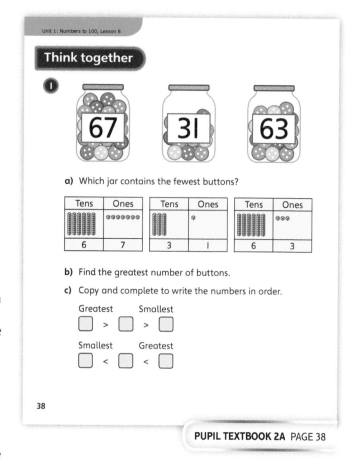

PUPIL TEXTBOOK 2A PAGE 38

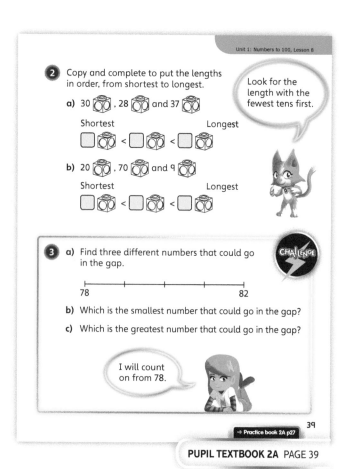

PUPIL TEXTBOOK 2A PAGE 39

Practice

WAYS OF WORKING Independent thinking

IN FOCUS Question ③ offers an opportunity for children to develop their problem-solving skills, with some support from the number line. In question ④, children compare three numbers presented at different levels of abstraction.

STRENGTHEN In question ①, ask children how they could show the numbers and what would make the numbers easier to compare. Guide them towards finding the greatest and the smallest number. If necessary, provide concrete or pictorial resources for them to represent the numbers.

DEEPEN Question ⑥ gives an opportunity for children to independently develop their problem-solving skills. It also reinforces the idea that a problem may have more than one solution. Challenge children to make up their own similar problem for their partner to solve. You could provide pre-written sentence openers.

ASSESSMENT CHECKPOINT Question ⑤ assesses whether children can order three numbers. Assess whether they can recognise efficient and systematic ways to begin comparing and ordering and can use place value to facilitate their comparison.

ANSWERS Answers for the **Practice** part of the lesson appear in the separate **Practice and Reflect answer guide**.

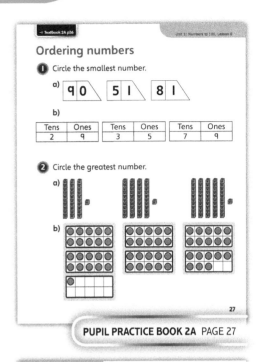

PUPIL PRACTICE BOOK 2A PAGE 27

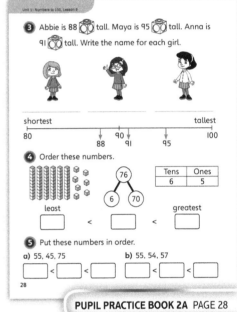

PUPIL PRACTICE BOOK 2A PAGE 28

Reflect

WAYS OF WORKING Independent thinking

IN FOCUS The **Reflect** part of the lesson requires children to order one set of numbers where they need to compare only the tens, and one set where they only need to look at the ones.

ASSESSMENT CHECKPOINT Assess whether children are able to recognise when it is and is not necessary to compare the ones as well as the tens. Children can explain that they only need to compare ones when the tens are the same.

ANSWERS Answers for the **Reflect** part of the lesson appear in the separate **Practice and Reflect answer guide**.

After the lesson ⏸

- How systematic were children in their approach to comparing and sorting numbers?
- Which other curriculum areas require sorting of numbers?

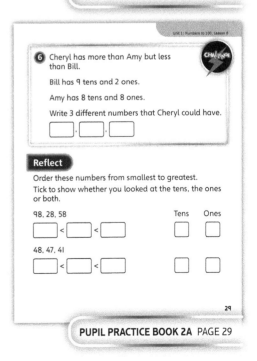

PUPIL PRACTICE BOOK 2A PAGE 29

Counting in 2s, 5s and 10s

Learning focus

In this lesson, children will learn to count forwards and backwards in 2s, 5s and 10s.

Small steps

→ Previous step: Ordering numbers
→ **This step: Counting in 2s, 5s and 10s**
→ Next step: Counting in 3s

NATIONAL CURRICULUM LINKS

Year 2 Number – Number and Place Value

Count in steps of 2, 3, and 5 from 0, and in tens from any number, forwards and backwards.

ASSESSING MASTERY

Children can count reliably forwards and backwards in steps of 2, 5 and 10. They can recognise patterns within their counting, using their knowledge of place value, and can show the patterns using different representations.

COMMON MISCONCEPTIONS

Children may have trouble counting backwards. Using visual representations along a number line, ask:
• *What number am I pointing at? Show me where to point if I counted backwards 2 or 5 or 10. How much do I have now? How was that different to counting forwards?*

STRENGTHENING UNDERSTANDING

This concept could be approached before the lesson through role playing a visit to the shops. For example, if bananas come in bunches of 2, ask children how many bananas in 1 bunch, 2 bunches, 3 bunches, and so on; if oranges are sold in bags of 5, ask how many oranges in 3 bags.

GOING DEEPER

Ask children to investigate which numbers are not counted in the 2s, 5s, and 10s when counting from 0. For example, 3 and 9 will not be counted in any of them. Ask which numbers will never be counted in any of the counts. Ask children to justify their answers.

KEY LANGUAGE

In lesson: altogether, count, pair, twos, fives, tens, less, more

Other language to be used by the teacher: steps, forwards, backwards, increase, decrease, bigger, smaller, pattern

STRUCTURES AND REPRESENTATIONS

Number line, ten frame, number track

RESOURCES

Optional: Base 10 equipment, counters, collections of countable objects

 In the eTextbook of this lesson, you will find interactive links to a selection of teaching tools.

Before you teach

• Are the children confident at spotting patterns around them?
• How could you use this to develop their reasoning skills in this lesson?

Discover

Pair work

ASK

- *How many children are there?*
- *How many children will stand together if they stand in pairs?*
- *What would be different about counting in twos to counting in ones?*
- *Could you organise the children using tens?*
- *Would it help to represent the children with equipment?*

IN FOCUS The teacher in the picture introduces the concept of counting in 2s. This gives children their first opportunity to count in steps greater than one. You could use counters or cubes to represent the children.

ANSWERS

Question ❶ a): There are 32 children altogether.

Question ❶ b): 26 children are still on the 🚌 .

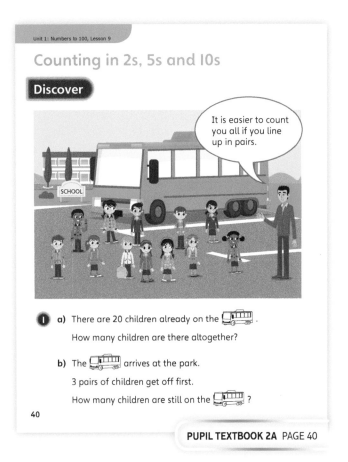

PUPIL TEXTBOOK 2A PAGE 40

Share

Whole class teacher led

ASK

- *How did you represent the children?*
- *Who will count the children more efficiently, Dexter or Flo?*
- *Which representation shows the count most clearly?*
- *Do you notice any patterns? How can these patterns help us count?*
- *Why are some numbers along the number line greyed out?*

IN FOCUS Question ❶ a) gives alternative representations of the number of children and compares the efficiency of counting in ones and 2s. The number line helps children to recognise patterns when counting in 2s.

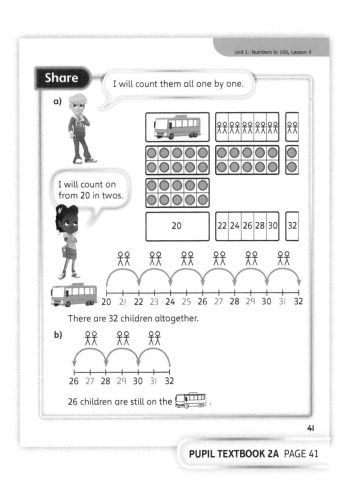

PUPIL TEXTBOOK 2A PAGE 41

Think together

WAYS OF WORKING Whole class teacher led (I do, We do, You do)

ASK

- Question **1** : *Where will you start counting?*
- Question **1** : *What will the pattern look like this time?*
- Question **1** : *Can you explain how the numbers change?*
- Question **2** : *What clues will you look for to know what to count in?*
- Question **2** : *What happens to the pattern if you count back?*
- Question **2** : *How does the pattern change or stay the same?*

IN FOCUS Question **1** demonstrates the counting in a visual way to support children's understanding of the count, including starting from a number other than 0. In question **2** , children count forwards and backwards using numbers without a context.

STRENGTHEN Provide children with a number line. If necessary, provide three different number lines: one that counts in 2s, one in 5s, and one in 10s.

DEEPEN In question **3**, discuss with children why Flo's idea will help. Ask whether they could use anything else to help them check their ideas. Ask whether their answers match the patterns they have seen earlier in the lesson. Be aware that question **3** d) requires children to cross into 3-digit numbers.

ASSESSMENT CHECKPOINT Questions **1** and **2** assess whether children can count forwards and backwards in steps of 2, 5 and 10.

ANSWERS

Question **1** : There are 35 children altogether.

Question **2** a): 36, 38

Question **2** b): 35, 30, 25

Question **2** c): 55, 35, 25

Question **2** d): 86, 84, 80

Question **3** a): 68, 72

Question **3** b): 76, 80

Question **3** c): 65, 75

Question **3** d): 80, 100

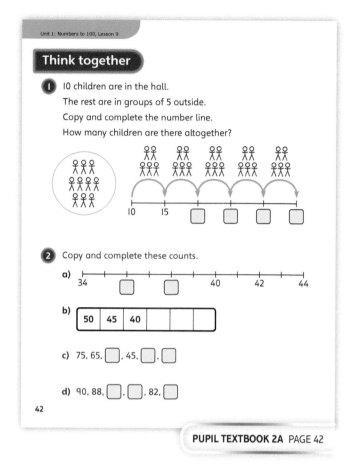

PUPIL TEXTBOOK 2A PAGE 42

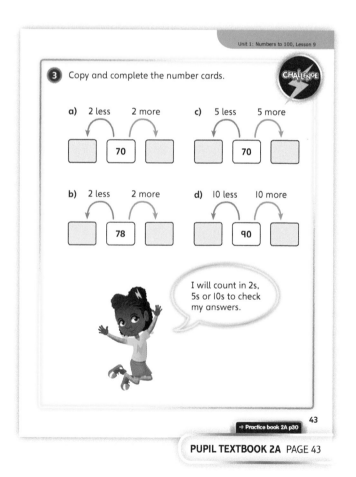

PUPIL TEXTBOOK 2A PAGE 43

Practice

WAYS OF WORKING Independent thinking

IN FOCUS Question ❶ scaffolds children's counting and pattern recognition. The two parts use different representations; note that, while both counts start at 0, the number line shows this while the number track does not. Question ❷ helps to develop children's reasoning ability, by making them decide whether to count in 2s or 5s.

STRENGTHEN For question ❹, offer children a number line to 100. Ask which numbers are greater or less than 20 or 50. Help children to recognise a pattern in the numbers Joe counts.

DEEPEN Question ❺ offers a good opportunity for reasoning and justification. Ask children to justify their answers. Prompt them to prove their answers in more than one way.

ASSESSMENT CHECKPOINT Questions ❶, ❷ and ❸ should help you determine whether children can count forwards and backwards in 2s, 5s and 10s, and can recognise which way to count when given a pattern. Children can explain how counting in this way is more efficient and describe the patterns they find.

ANSWERS Answers for the **Practice** part of the lesson appear in the separate **Practice and Reflect answer guide**.

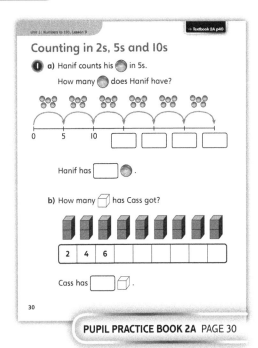

PUPIL PRACTICE BOOK 2A PAGE 30

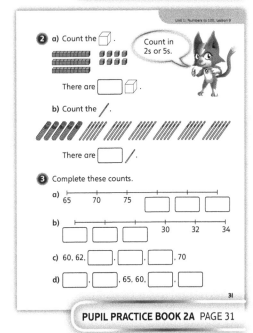

PUPIL PRACTICE BOOK 2A PAGE 31

Reflect

WAYS OF WORKING Pair work

IN FOCUS The **Reflect** part of the lesson requires children to use reasoning to decide whether Leo or Eva will reach the number 10 in their counting. Once children have thought about this question independently, ask them to discuss and develop their ideas with their partner.

ASSESSMENT CHECKPOINT Assess whether children can recognise and show that the count down from 50 will result in saying 10. Children test each count and demonstrate their thinking through clear evidence.

ANSWERS Answers for the **Reflect** part of the lesson appear in the separate **Practice and Reflect answer guide**.

After the lesson ⏸

- Were children more or less confident in a particular count?
- How will you support children to develop their counting skills?

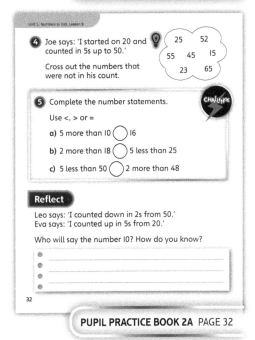

PUPIL PRACTICE BOOK 2A PAGE 32

Counting in 3s

Learning focus

In this lesson, children will learn to count forwards and backwards in 3s.

Small steps

→ Previous step: Counting in 2s, 5s and 10s
→ **This step: Counting in 3s**
→ Next step: Related facts – addition and subtraction

NATIONAL CURRICULUM LINKS

Year 2 Number – Number and Place Value

- Count in steps of 2, 3 and 5 from 0, and in tens from any number, forwards and backwards.
- Identify, represent and estimate numbers using different representations, including the number line.

ASSESSING MASTERY

Children can count reliably forwards and backwards in steps of 3. They can recognise patterns within their counting and can show the patterns using different representations.

COMMON MISCONCEPTIONS

Children may think that every number ending in '3' is a multiple of 3. Using a number line and visual representations of the number, ask:

- *Can you count up one 3 from 0? What number would you be at if you counted on another 3? What do you notice about this number? What about the next one? Does every number have to end in a 3 when counting in 3s?*

STRENGTHENING UNDERSTANDING

To introduce this concept, children could be put into teams of three during a PE lesson. Alternatively, children could be asked to leave and enter a room in groups of three. After each group has entered or left, ask how many children are in the room and how many have left.

GOING DEEPER

Ask children to investigate what happens when they start counting in 3s at a number other than 0. Before they start, ask what they think might change or stay the same when counting from a different number. Ask them to show their reasoning as a picture or with equipment.

KEY LANGUAGE

In lesson: count, threes

Other language to be used by the teacher: steps, forwards, backwards, increase, decrease, bigger, smaller, check

STRUCTURES AND REPRESENTATIONS

Number line, number track, 100 square

RESOURCES

Optional: cubes, counters, collections of countable objects

 In the eTextbook of this lesson, you will find interactive links to a selection of teaching tools.

Before you teach

- Could you provide a counting song to help develop children's confidence and fluency?

Discover

WAYS OF WORKING Pair work

ASK

- *What kind of pattern did Andy make? How would you describe it?*
- *Can you spot any other patterns?*
- *How many sticks did he use for the top triangle?*
- *How many sticks did he use for the second row of triangles? How many sticks did he use for the third row of triangles?*
- *What do you notice?*
- *Can you make the pattern Andy has made? How many sticks did you need in total?*

IN FOCUS Andy's pattern is made from triangles, each using three sticks. This introduces children to the idea of counting in 3s to find the total number of sticks made from 6 triangles.

ANSWERS

Question ❶ a): Andy used 18 ⬭ .

Question ❶ b): Andy needs 12 more ⬭ .

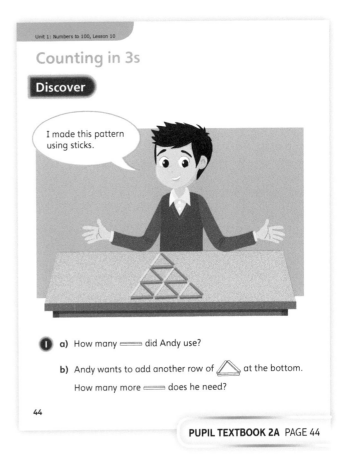

Share

WAYS OF WORKING Whole class teacher led

ASK

- *How have the triangles been organised to make the counting easier?*
- *Does it show 3 more clearly?*
- *How else could you show 3?*

IN FOCUS Both question ❶ a) and ❶ b) make clear how to count in 3s and introduce the patterns that are evident in this method of counting.

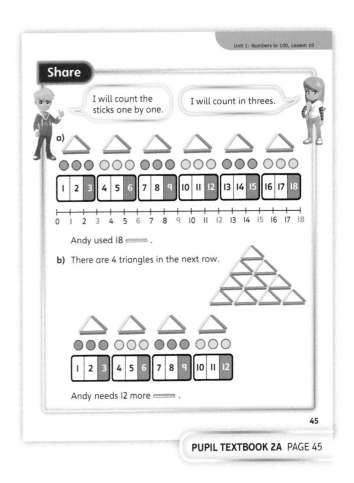

Think together

WAYS OF WORKING Whole class teacher led (I do, We do, You do)

ASK

- Question **1** : *Why are some boxes blank?*
- Question **1** : *How could you use the pictures to help?*
- Question **1** : *What is the same about questions **1** a) and **1** b)? What is different?*
- Question **2** : *What is different about the counting this time?*
- Question **2** : *How will you know where to begin counting?*
- Question **3** : *How can you prove your ideas?*

IN FOCUS Questions in this section offer children different ways of counting in 3s from different starting points.

STRENGTHEN For question **2** , provide children with coloured cubes to build the castles. Each time they add another set of three cubes, ask how many cubes they had to start with and the size of each group. Encourage them to arrange the groups so that they are easier to count.

DEEPEN Use question **1** to begin practising counting back. For example, what if the birds flew away, 3 at a time? For question **3** , ask children whether they can predict what the next common number will be, justifying their answer. Ask what patterns are in the numbers both Jake and Zara write.

ASSESSMENT CHECKPOINT Questions **1** and **2** will help you to decide whether children can count up in 3s and recognise the patterns within their counting.

ANSWERS

Question **1** a): 3, 6, 9, 12

Question **1** b): 3, 6, 9, 12, 15

Question **2** a): 15, 18, 21, 24

Question **2** b): 18, 21, 24, 27

Question **3** : Jake's counting:

2, 4, 6, 8, 10, 12 ,14

Zara's counting:

3, 6, 9, 12, 15, 18, 21

They will both write 6 and 12. Common numbers beyond these will all be multiples of 6.

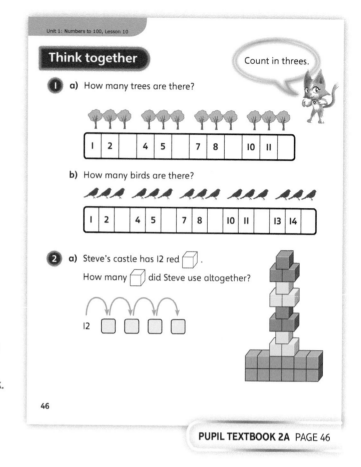

PUPIL TEXTBOOK 2A PAGE 46

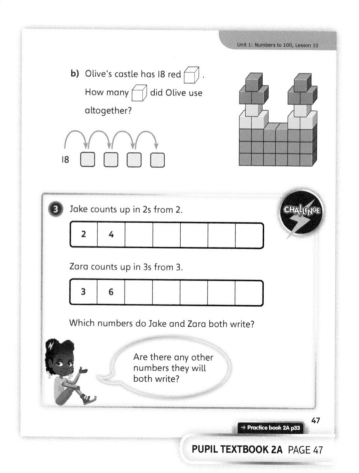

PUPIL TEXTBOOK 2A PAGE 47

Practice

Independent thinking

IN FOCUS Questions ❶, ❷ and ❹ give children opportunity to count in 3s using different representations. Question ❺ provides an interesting opportunity to recognise patterns and to consider how they change in the different number grids.

STRENGTHEN Provide a large number line or number track. For each question, encourage children to represent the count using equipment arranged on one of the number tracks. Ask children to show you how they could use the number track to help them.

DEEPEN Question ❻ offers a good opportunity for problem-solving, reasoning and justification. For parts b) and d), ask children to explain how they find the middle number. Ask how they can check their answer.

ASSESSMENT CHECKPOINT Use question ❸ to assess whether children can count in 3s without concrete or pictorial representation. Question ❺ should help you to decide whether children can recognise the different patterns evident in different ways of counting. Question ❻ assesses whether children can count backwards in 3s as well as forwards.

ANSWERS Answers for the **Practice** part of the lesson appear in the separate **Practice and Reflect answer guide**.

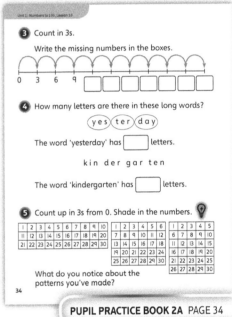

PUPIL PRACTICE BOOK 2A PAGE 33

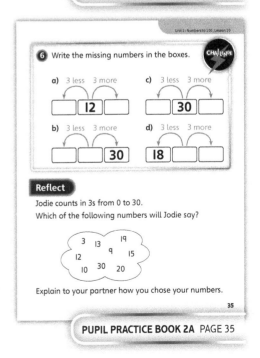

PUPIL PRACTICE BOOK 2A PAGE 34

Reflect

Pair work

IN FOCUS The **Reflect** part of the lesson requires children to identify which numbers in the cloud Jodie would say, by counting from 0 in 3s. When children have had some time to devise their solution and develop their reasoning and justification, ask them to share with their partner.

ASSESSMENT CHECKPOINT Assess whether children can count reliably in 3s and prove their ideas with confident use of the representations used up until this point.

ANSWERS Answers for the **Reflect** part of the lesson appear in the separate **Practice and Reflect answer guide**.

After the lesson

- Were children as confident counting in 3s as in 2s, 5s and 10s?
- Were children able to identify patterns when counting in 3s?

PUPIL PRACTICE BOOK 2A PAGE 35

End of unit check

Don't forget the Power Maths Unit Assessment Grid on p26.

WAYS OF WORKING Group work – adult led

IN FOCUS Questions **1** – **4** all focus on children's understanding of place value and the different representations of numbers they have met across the course of the unit.

Question **5** focuses on children's ability to count in steps of 2, 3 and 5, recognising numbers they will meet in all three patterns.

Think!

WAYS OF WORKING Pair work

IN FOCUS This question has been chosen to assess children's understanding of place value, counting in tens and ones, and use and understanding of the different representations they have worked with.

Focus children on proving their ideas. Ask:
- *How could you show these numbers in a way that makes comparing them clearer?*
- *Could you prove your ideas using resources?*
- *Could you prove it with a picture?*

ANSWERS AND COMMENTARY Children who demonstrate mastery of this concept will be able to recognise the multiple representations of 93 and explain how they are different to the representation of 39. They will recognise and explain the differences between the numbers, potentially using concrete, pictorial and abstract evidence and will be able to explain how their evidence supports their ideas. They will recognise and explain the value of ten and one and relate this to each number, using their ability to compare numbers to support their reasoning. Children may also choose to use a place value grid to support their thinking.

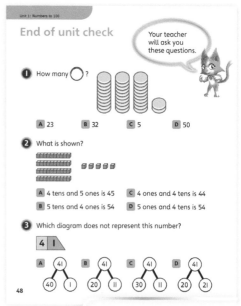

PUPIL TEXTBOOK 2A PAGE 48

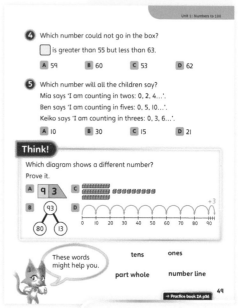

PUPIL TEXTBOOK 2A PAGE 49

Q	A	WRONG ANSWERS AND MISCONCEPTIONS	STRENGTHENING UNDERSTANDING
1	B	A may suggest children have transposed the tens and ones. C may suggest they have counted the columns of ten as one. D may suggest that children have continued counting in tens when counting the ones.	Place value: Give children opportunities to partition 2-digit numbers in different ways. This may be in the context of:
2	A	B and D may suggest children may have transposed the tens and ones. C and D may suggest that children are muddling tens and ones. C and B may suggest children have miscounted.	• dividing items between two people • investigating how many ways a number can be split into two groups.
3	B	C and D may suggest children are unsure about other ways to partition a number beyond its tens and ones.	Children could be encouraged to put the two amounts into a part-whole model. Counting:
4	C	A, B and D may suggest children's understanding of place value and ordering numbers needs reinforcing.	To help children retain the number sequences, it would be beneficial to find, or make up, songs or chants they can sing.
5	B	A, C and D may suggest that children still need more practice counting in these steps.	

My journal

WAYS OF WORKING Independent thinking

ANSWERS AND COMMENTARY Children may record:

I can prove that 39 is a different number because it has 3 tens and 9 ones. All the other numbers have 9 tens and 3 ones.

If children are struggling to compare the numbers, ask:
- *Which representations do you recognise?*
- *What is the same about the representations and what is different?*
- *Can you tell me how they work?*
- *Could you show the number in a different way?*
- *Could you use that method for all the numbers shown?*
- *What do you notice about the representations you have made? What is the same? What is different?*

If children are encouraged to make the number using a representation they are comfortable with, they should find it easier to make the comparisons. When children have explained their observations in words, ask:
- *How could you record that on the page?*
- *What words will you need to use?*
- *Can you use any from the word bank?*
- *Can you say the sentence first?*

Power check

WAYS OF WORKING Independent thinking

ASK
- *What steps could you count in before this unit?*
- *What steps can you count in now?*
- *How confident are you about finding the tens and ones in a number?*
- *How confident do you feel about ordering two 2-digit numbers? How about three?*
- *Do you think you could use a place value grid on your own?*

Power play

WAYS OF WORKING Pair work

IN FOCUS Use this Power play to see if children can work together to follow a route through the maze counting in 2s and 5s. Children should recognise that the 100 they land on when counting in 5s should be closer than the one they land on when counting in 2s.

ANSWERS AND COMMENTARY Look closely at the pattern the children have followed. If they have successfully followed both then this suggests that they are confident in counting in steps of 2 or 5. If they have made a mistake on either of them this could suggest that more practice with that counting pattern is needed.

After the unit ⏸

- Counting in steps of 2, 3, 5 and 10 can be applied to many different real-life contexts (for example, 2p, 5p and 10p when shopping, through games and grouping objects or teams). How could you get the children to apply their learning from this unit in other areas of the curriculum, especially counting in 3s?
- Did the unit assessment show any misconceptions that the class still has? How will you support and develop this area of learning?

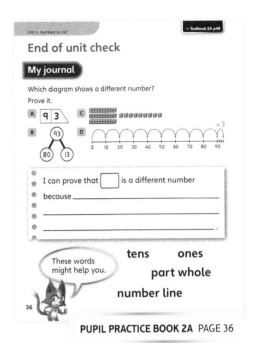

PUPIL PRACTICE BOOK 2A PAGE 36

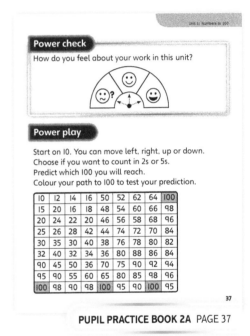

PUPIL PRACTICE BOOK 2A PAGE 37

Strengthen and **Deepen** activities for this unit can be found in the *Power Maths* online subscription.

Unit 2
Addition and subtraction ❶

Mastery Expert tip! "It is important for this unit that children understand the importance of learning key number facts. Children should be encouraged to spot number bonds within 10 and then 20 throughout the unit, all around them in the school environment and in other subject lessons."

Don't forget to watch the Unit 2 video!

WHY THIS UNIT IS IMPORTANT

In this unit, children will build upon the number bonds to 10 that they will have learned in Year 1. Children consolidate this understanding and apply it to number bonds within 20 and to 20 in this unit.

Children are introduced to writing fact families of equations, and to relating addition and subtraction operations. As a result, children learn to use the inverse of one operation to check calculations using the other operation. Children will also be introduced to the concept of 'make 10' to aid mental calculations.

Once this key learning is understood, children are introduced to the column method which they will use throughout their time at school, applying the mental strategies appropriately. This method is introduced alongside a variety of different visual representations to ensure a strong conceptual and procedural understanding.

WHERE THIS UNIT FITS

→ Unit 1: Numbers to 100
→ **Unit 2: Addition and subtraction (1)**
→ Unit 3: Addition and subtraction (2)

This unit builds on the previous unit and applies children's place value understanding to addition and subtraction problems. Unit 2 is the first of two addition and subtraction units. Unit 3 focuses on more complex problems, adding two 2-digit numbers together.

Before they start this unit, it is expected that children:

• know how to partition 2-digit numbers into tens and ones
• understand the value of each digit in a 2-digit number
• know number bonds within 10 and can relate these to bonds within 20.

ASSESSING MASTERY

Children who have mastered this unit will be able to relate each number in a calculation to what it represents within a context. Children will be able to use a variety of manipulatives to represent addition and subtraction and use these alongside the column method. Children will also become fluent at recalling and applying their number bonds within 20 to addition and subtraction equations.

COMMON MISCONCEPTIONS	STRENGTHENING UNDERSTANDING	GOING DEEPER
Children may think the commutative property of addition problems can be applied to subtractions when it cannot.	Allow children to work in pairs to complete problems where one manipulates resources and the other records using the column method.	Use subtraction to check addition calculations and vice versa.
Children may not understand the importance of using known facts within calculations and instead use inefficient strategies such as counting on in ones using their fingers.	Providing children with number facts that are useful to complete calculations will increase the likelihood of children understanding the importance of memorisation.	Children should represent the same calculation in as many different ways as possible using different manipulatives to do so.

WAYS OF WORKING

Use these pages to introduce the unit focus to children as a whole class. You can use the characters to explore different ways of working.

STRUCTURES AND REPRESENTATIONS

Part-whole model: This model helps children understand that two or more parts combine to make a whole. It will also help children understand how addition and subtraction are linked and can be used to calculate an unknown part or whole.

Number line: This model helps children visualise the order of numbers. It helps children to count on and back from a number. Number lines are used to show jumps of different amounts to help children understand the 'make 10' strategy and the steps completed in the column method.

Column method: This representation is introduced to children during this unit and will be built upon for all operations in future units and in later year groups. The column method shows a number broken down into parts based on the place value of its digits and how these digits change as a result of another number being added or subtracted to or from it.

T	O
3	4
+	5
3	9

100 square: This model shows how numbers link to each other and how numbers change when 10 is added or subtracted to or from a number. This model is especially useful to help children make links to the column method.

1	2	3	4	5	6	7	8	9	10
11	12	13	14	15	16	17	18	19	20
21	22	23	24	25	26	27	28	29	30
31	32	33	34	35	36	37	38	39	40
41	42	43	44	45	46	47	48	49	50
51	52	53	54	55	56	57	58	59	60
61	62	63	64	65	66	67	68	69	70
71	72	73	74	75	76	77	78	79	80
81	82	83	84	85	86	87	88	89	90
91	92	93	94	95	96	97	98	99	100

KEY LANGUAGE

There is some key language that children will need to know as a part of the learning in this unit:

→ part, whole and part-whole

→ add, added, plus, total, altogether, sum, calculation, (+)

→ count, count on, count back, left

→ subtract, take away, minus, (–)

→ exchange, compare, greater than, less than, more, less, (>), (<)

→ ones, tens, 10 more, 10 less, place value, column, 1-digit number, 2-digit number

→ number sentence, number bonds, known fact, fact family

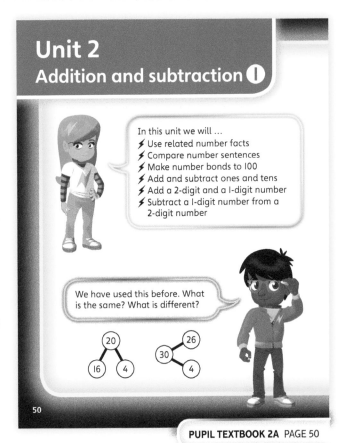

PUPIL TEXTBOOK 2A PAGE 50

PUPIL TEXTBOOK 2A PAGE 51

Related facts – addition and subtraction

Learning focus

In this lesson, children will focus on bonds within 20, using the part-whole diagram to help them see these visually. The focus is not on addition and subtraction, but on recording known facts in different ways within addition and subtraction calculations.

Small steps

→ Previous step: Counting in 3s

→ **This step: Related facts – addition and subtraction**

→ Next step: Using number facts to check calculations

NATIONAL CURRICULUM LINKS

Year 2 Number – Addition and Subtraction

Recall and use addition and subtraction facts to 20 fluently, and derive and use related facts up to 100.

ASSESSING MASTERY

Children can write down fact families from a part-whole model and identify what each number within a calculation represents.

COMMON MISCONCEPTIONS

Children may calculate a total from a pictorial representation without considering what the pictures represent (for example, given a part and the whole, they may add in an attempt to find the unknown part). Ask:

• *Does the picture show the total number of items?*

Children may put the numbers the wrong way around either in the part-whole model or in the scaffold for addition or subtraction calculations. Similarly, they may believe subtraction is commutative. Ask:

• *Which two numbers are the parts? Which number is the whole? If you subtract the whole from a part will you be left with a part?*

Children may incorrectly interpret the part-whole model and as a result may not understand what the number sentence is telling them. Ask:

• *What does each number represent? Where is that number found in the part-whole model or pictorial representation?*

STRENGTHENING UNDERSTANDING

Reinforce learning by encouraging children to make the representations shown using concrete manipulatives. Children can then move the parts and wholes onto part-whole models and into subtraction and addition calculation scaffolds.

GOING DEEPER

Encourage children to record all possible number sentences from a given part-whole model. This could include situations where all numbers are given and those involving an unknown quantity which children can represent using a '?' in their number sentences. Challenge children to write number sentences with the equals sign at the beginning as well as at the end.

KEY LANGUAGE

In lesson: addition, subtraction, +, –, =, **fact family**, number sentence, in total, number bond, altogether

Other language to be used by the teacher: calculation, unknown, equals, equivalent

STRUCTURES AND REPRESENTATIONS

Part-whole model, addition and subtraction calculation scaffold

RESOURCES

Mandatory: cubes or counters, blank part-whole model, blank addition and subtraction calculation scaffolds

Optional: Base 10 equipment, digit cards, physical resources to make the parts and wholes represented in questions

 In the eTextbook of this lesson, you will find interactive links to a selection of teaching tools.

Before you teach

• Based on teaching of the part-whole model in Year 1, are there any additional misconceptions that need to be addressed?

• How will you support children to understand the differences between addition and subtraction when recording numbers in calculation scaffolds?

Discover

WAYS OF WORKING Pair work

ASK

- Question **1** a): *Which numbers are the parts? What do they represent?*
- Question **1** a): *Does it matter if the 7 is in the top or bottom part?*
- Question **1** b): *Does the order that the numbers are placed in the addition and subtraction sentences matter?*

IN FOCUS Question **1** presents children with a real-life problem to help them understand what the different parts and the whole represent in a part-whole model.

ANSWERS

Question **1** a):

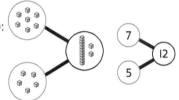

The number 7 represents 🍎 in the tree.

The number 5 represents 🍎 on the ground.

The number 12 represents 🍎 in total.

Question **1** b): 7 + 5 = 12, 5 + 7 = 12
These number sentences tell you how many 🍎 there are altogether.

12 − 5 = 7
This number sentence tells you how many 🍎 are in the tree.

12 − 7 = 5
This number sentence tells you how many 🍎 are on the ground.

Share

WAYS OF WORKING Whole class teacher led

ASK

- Question **1** a): *Which part of the part-whole model represents the number of apples in the tree?*
- Question **1** a): *Which part of the part-whole model represents the number of apples on the ground?*
- Question **1** b): *What are you finding out when you subtract?*

IN FOCUS Question **1** b) requires children to identify what each number within the addition and subtraction sentences represents. Encourage them to explain in full sentences what is being calculated each time.

DEEPEN Challenge children to explain what is the same and what is different about the addition and subtraction sentences. Ask them to write the same number sentences with the equals sign at the beginning (for example, 12 = 7 + 5).

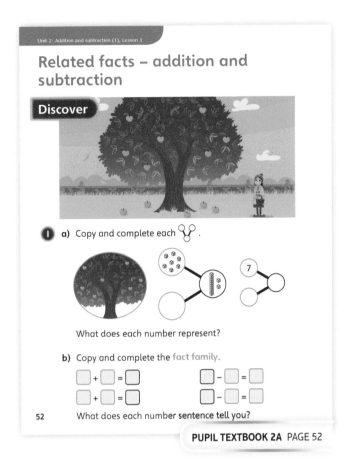

PUPIL TEXTBOOK 2A PAGE 52

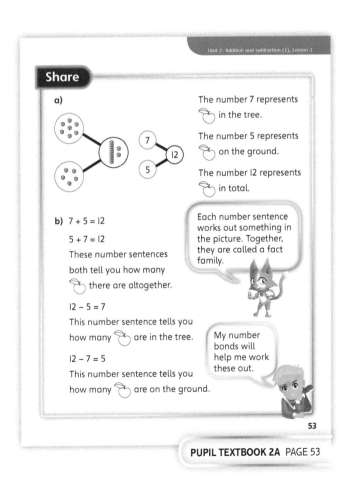

PUPIL TEXTBOOK 2A PAGE 53

Think together

Whole class teacher led (I do, We do, You do)

ASK

- *What does each number within the part-whole model represent?*
- *What does each number within each number sentence represent?*
- *Is the position of the whole within subtraction sentences important?*

IN FOCUS Question **2** requires children to identify what each number within the part-whole model represents and what the result of each number sentence shows within the context of the question.

STRENGTHEN To strengthen understanding of the equals sign and the order of numbers within subtraction sentences, provide children with separate pieces of paper, with parts of a number sentence written on each piece, to move around. For example, write 8 – 5 on one piece of paper, = on another, and 3 on a third piece of paper.

Alternatively, provide children with number cards and blank addition and subtraction sentence scaffolds to help them understand that the three numbers do not change; only their location changes.

DEEPEN Question **3** requires children to write number sentences with the equals sign at the beginning as well as at the end. Ask children to write eight additional sentences where 16 is still the whole, but the parts are different values.

ASSESSMENT CHECKPOINT Assess how children are calculating the number of objects in each part. Are they counting in ones or are they substituting and seeing numbers within each number? Do they start from 0 each time and count each part, or are they capable of starting from one of the parts and counting on? Are they using known addition facts to calculate the whole?

ANSWERS

Question **1** :

2 + 9 = 11, 9 + 2 = 11, 11 – 2 = 9, 11 – 9 = 2

Question **2** : 1) 5 + 3 = 8 matches with C) The number of balloons altogether.

2) 8 – 5 = 3 matches with B) The number of long yellow balloons.

3) 8 – 3 = 5 matches with A) The number of round red balloons.

Question **3** : 6 + 10 = 16, 10 + 6 = 16, 16 = 10 + 6, 16 = 6 + 10, 16 – 10 = 6, 16 – 6 = 10, 6 = 16 – 10, 10 = 16 – 6

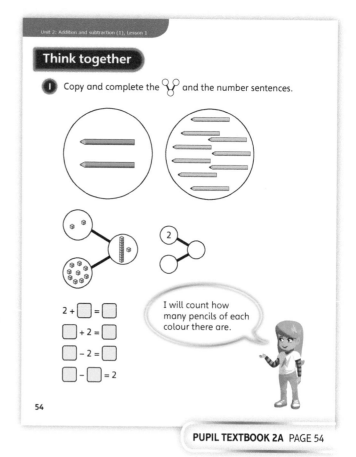

PUPIL TEXTBOOK 2A PAGE 54

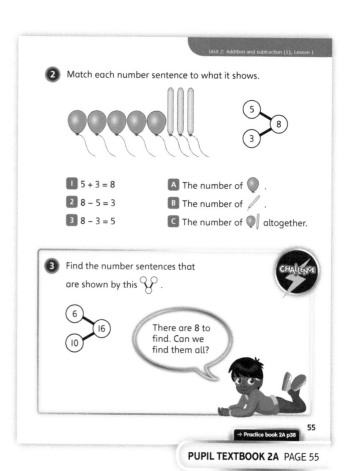

PUPIL TEXTBOOK 2A PAGE 55

Practice

WAYS OF WORKING Independent thinking

IN FOCUS Throughout these questions, children are exposed to different part-whole models and number sentences with the equals sign in different places. There are different levels of scaffold within questions. In question ❷, the equals sign is at the start of the calculation and this may lead to misconceptions for subtraction calculations.

STRENGTHEN Provide children with scaffolds to help them determine the location of the different digits within subtraction calculations; for example, whole – part = part and part = whole – part.

DEEPEN Question ❺ illustrates that parts can themselves be broken down; explain to children that this may be a useful calculation strategy in the future. Challenge them to extend the model, breaking down all the parts into smaller parts in as many different ways as possible.

ASSESSMENT CHECKPOINT Assess whether children can justify their choices of incorrect calculations in question ❷ b). Can they state whether each number within a calculation is a part or a whole and how they know they are correct?

ANSWERS Answers for the **Practice** part of the lesson appear in the separate **Practice and Reflect answer guide**.

Reflect

WAYS OF WORKING Independent thinking

IN FOCUS By the **Reflect** part of the lesson, children should be able to write four number sentences (two addition and two subtraction) with the equals sign at the end of the calculation. Encourage them to write four number sentences with the equals sign at the start of the calculation as well.

ASSESSMENT CHECKPOINT Assess whether children can verbalise how they know they have found all the possible number sentences. Can they use the language of parts and whole to describe their sentences (for example, can they read 9 + 8 = 17 as part + part = whole)?

ANSWERS Answers for the **Reflect** part of the lesson appear in the separate **Practice and Reflect answer guide**.

After the lesson

- Are children confident recording four number sentences for each part-whole model?
- Are children confident recording eight number sentences for each part-whole model?
- Do children understand the importance of the location of the parts and the wholes within addition and subtraction calculations?

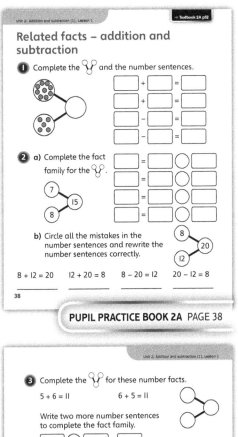

PUPIL PRACTICE BOOK 2A PAGE 38

PUPIL PRACTICE BOOK 2A PAGE 39

PUPIL PRACTICE BOOK 2A PAGE 40

Using number facts to check calculations

Learning focus

In this lesson, children build on what they learned in the previous lesson to determine whether number sentences are correct or incorrect. Children understand that they can do a subtraction calculation to check addition and vice versa.

Small steps

→ Previous step: Related facts – addition and subtraction
→ **This step: Using number facts to check calculations**
→ Next step: Comparing number sentences

NATIONAL CURRICULUM LINKS

Year 2 Number – Addition and Subtraction

- Recall and use addition and subtraction facts to 20 fluently, and derive and use related facts up to 100.
- Recognise and use the inverse relationship between addition and subtraction and use this to check calculations and solve missing number problems.
- Show that addition of two numbers can be done in any order (commutative) and subtraction of one number from another cannot.

ASSESSING MASTERY

Children can complete a subtraction to check an addition and vice versa. Children can use their understanding from the previous lesson to explain their findings and select more than one way to check their original calculation.

COMMON MISCONCEPTIONS

Children may restrict themselves to using the same method to check their answer that they used within their original calculation. Ask:
- *Can you use a different method to check your answer?*

STRENGTHENING UNDERSTANDING

Provide children with completed fact families relevant to the questions. Children can then use these to find and check answers, rather than counting on or back in ones using their fingers.

GOING DEEPER

Children should be able to use more than one method to check and calculate unknown values. Provide a number line to encourage children to make the link between addition and subtraction.

KEY LANGUAGE

In lesson: check, total, subtraction, addition, calculation, fact family

Other language to be used by the teacher: whole, part, strategy, minus, take away, add, plus, number facts

STRUCTURES AND REPRESENTATIONS

Ten frame, part-whole model, number line

RESOURCES

Mandatory: counters, printed ten frames, empty part-whole models

Optional: completed fact families, any physical resources to make the parts and wholes represented in questions (£1 coins, apples, sweets)

 In the eTextbook of this lesson, you will find interactive links to a selection of teaching tools.

Before you teach

- Based on teaching of the part-whole model and creating fact families in Lesson 1, are there any remaining misconceptions that need to be addressed?
- How will you encourage children to use more than one method to calculate and check the answers to each question?

Discover

WAYS OF WORKING Pair work

ASK

• *Which value represents the whole? Which values represent the parts?*

• *What is the link between addition and subtraction? How can one operation help with the other?*

IN FOCUS Question ❶ presents children with a real-life context involving money. Encourage children to make links to the previous lesson and create all possible number sentences from the given parts and whole.

ANSWERS

Question ❶ a): £9 + £5 = £14

The total cost is £14.

Question ❶ b): £14 − £5 = £9

£14 − £9 = £5

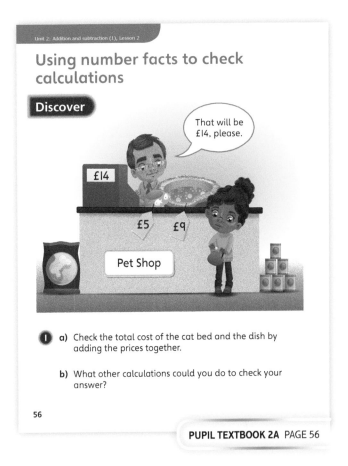

Unit 2: Addition and subtraction (1), Lesson 2

Using number facts to check calculations

Discover

That will be £14, please.

£14

£5   £9

Pet Shop

❶ a) Check the total cost of the cat bed and the dish by adding the prices together.

b) What other calculations could you do to check your answer?

56

PUPIL TEXTBOOK 2A PAGE 56

Share

WAYS OF WORKING Whole class teacher led

ASK

• *Why do you need a different method to check your answer?*

• *Question ❶ a): Why did Flo jump 1 then 4 on the number line?*

• *Question ❶ b): What other ways could you suggest to Flo to check the answer?*

IN FOCUS Question ❶ b) encourages children to think about how to check their answer and how they know if their answer is correct. Flexibility of number is important to suggest other relevant ways to check their work.

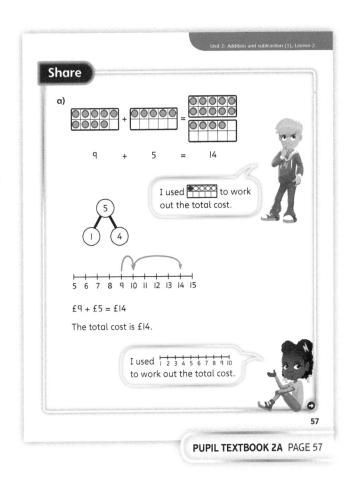

Unit 2: Addition and subtraction (1), Lesson 2

Share

a)

9   +   5   =   14

I used ●●●●● to work out the total cost.

5
1   4

5 6 7 8 9 10 11 12 13 14 15

£9 + £5 = £14

The total cost is £14.

I used 1 2 3 4 5 6 7 8 9 10 to work out the total cost.

57

PUPIL TEXTBOOK 2A PAGE 57

Think together

ASK

- Question **1** : *What is the starting point? What number do you need to start with for subtraction?*
- Question **1** : *Is there more than one subtraction sentence that you could complete to check the total price?*

IN FOCUS Question **1** presents children with a situation where the two parts do not equal the whole. They should be able to explain, using subtraction, how they know the total price (whole) is incorrect.

STRENGTHEN Use £1 coins (real or cut-outs) to represent the total price (£19) in question **1** . Remove the parts representing the cost of the T-shirt (£6) and trousers (£12) to show that there is still something left over (£1), and that therefore the whole was not correct.

DEEPEN Challenge children to explain question **1** using 'less than' or 'greater than' rather than 'equals' for the different number sentences; for example, 19 – 12 is greater than 6.

ASSESSMENT CHECKPOINT Use question **1** to assess whether children can use more than one subtraction sentence to prove that the whole is not correct, and whether they can explain what their findings show.

ANSWERS

Question **1** : £19 – £12 = £7

£19 – £6 = £13

Question **2** :

12 + 6 = 18

6 + 12 = 18

Question **3** : 13 – 5, 13 – 8, 8 + 5

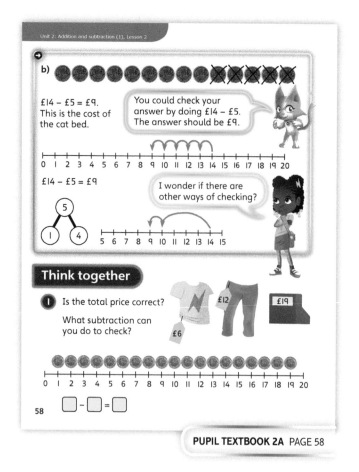

PUPIL TEXTBOOK 2A PAGE 58

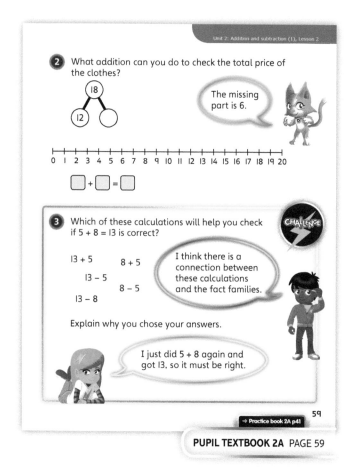

PUPIL TEXTBOOK 2A PAGE 59

Practice

WAYS OF WORKING Independent thinking

IN FOCUS Questions **1**, **3** and **4** require children to check whether the answer to an addition or subtraction calculation is correct, using different methods; this should strengthen their understanding of the link between addition and subtraction.

Question **2** presents the information in a different way: children are given the whole and asked to check one of the parts, but the information is not given in the form of a number sentence.

STRENGTHEN Strengthen understanding by encouraging children to use concrete manipulatives like cubes or counters to count backwards from the whole. These counters could be placed on the part-whole model to strengthen children's understanding further.

DEEPEN The calculations in question **4** can be checked in several different ways; encourage children to write all the calculations they could use. You could also challenge them to think of different ways in which they could change the incorrect calculation. For example, ask: *Could you change one of the parts instead of the whole?*

ASSESSMENT CHECKPOINT Assess whether children are counting back in ones when subtracting, or if they are using known number facts to calculate unknown quantities.

ANSWERS Answers for the **Practice** part of the lesson appear in the separate **Practice and Reflect answer guide**.

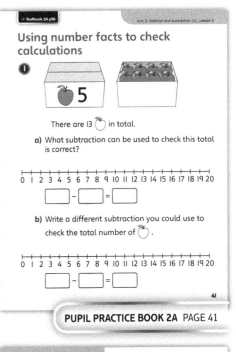

PUPIL PRACTICE BOOK 2A PAGE 41

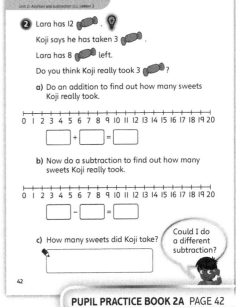

PUPIL PRACTICE BOOK 2A PAGE 42

Reflect

WAYS OF WORKING Independent thinking

IN FOCUS The **Reflect** part of the lesson asks children to choose their own numbers to make a calculation (keeping the whole within 20). They then need to choose an alternative calculation to check that their original calculation is correct. Ask children to share their original calculations with the class and see how many checking calculations can be generated.

ASSESSMENT CHECKPOINT Assess whether children have the confidence to use the inverse operation to check a calculation, or if they are simply swapping the parts around using the same operation. Can children explain how the second calculation links to and checks the initial calculation?

ANSWERS Answers for the **Reflect** part of the lesson appear in the separate **Practice and Reflect answer guide**.

After the lesson ⏸

- Are children confident at using the inverse operation to check calculations?
- Are children using known number facts within calculations rather than counting in ones?
- What resources could you use to increase children's use of known facts?

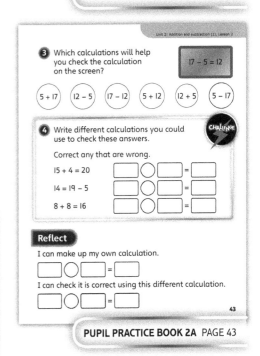

PUPIL PRACTICE BOOK 2A PAGE 43

Comparing number sentences

Learning focus

In this lesson, children make links between numbers in sets of number sentences and compare addition and subtraction facts within 20.

Small steps

→ Previous step: Using number facts to check calculations
→ **This step: Comparing number sentences**
→ Next step: Finding related facts

NATIONAL CURRICULUM LINKS

Year 2 Number – Addition and Subtraction

- Solve problems with addition and subtraction: using concrete objects and pictorial representations, including those involving numbers, quantities and measures.
- Recall and use addition and subtraction facts to 20 fluently, and derive and use related facts up to 100.

ASSESSING MASTERY

Children can compare addition and subtraction statements without working out the calculation and use this understanding to work out missing numbers to satisfy particular equalities and inequalities.

COMMON MISCONCEPTIONS

Children may calculate both sides of the number sentence rather than make links between the numbers within both sides. Ask:
- *What is the most efficient way to complete the inequality?*

Children may compare the number of groups rather than the number of items in each group. Ask:
- *How many objects does each child have in total?*

STRENGTHENING UNDERSTANDING

Provide children with a visual showing the < and > signs and the terms 'less than' and 'greater than'.

Encourage children to represent numbers using different coloured counters to help them see which numbers appear on both sides of the number sentences and therefore which numbers they need to compare.

GOING DEEPER

Encourage children to represent number sentences in as many ways as possible. For example, if they say that $7 + 6 > 7 + 4$, can they also say $7 + 4 < 7 + 6$? Deepen understanding further by asking children to find as many ways as possible to satisfy an inequality such as $7 + 6 > 7 + ?$.

KEY LANGUAGE

In lesson: compare, <, >, =, more, greater than, fewer, smallest

Other language to be used by the teacher: inequality, less than, the same, equal, unequal

STRUCTURES AND REPRESENTATIONS

Number line, part-whole model

RESOURCES

Mandatory: counters

Optional: number lines, blank part-whole models, definitions of < and >, different coloured counters, digit cards

 In the eTextbook of this lesson, you will find interactive links to a selection of teaching tools.

Before you teach

- What resources will you provide to ensure children are confident at using the < and > signs?
- How will you encourage children to make links between the numbers in the number sentences, rather than simply calculating different solutions?

Discover

WAYS OF WORKING Pair work

ASK

- *What is the same and what is different about the three children's trays of cookies?*
- *What number sentences can you form for each character?*

IN FOCUS Question **1** allows children to make a visual comparison before they start thinking about number sentences. In particular, encourage children to identify what is the same about the children's trays of cookies: one of Ola's trays and one of Abbie's trays each holds 7 cookies. This will help them complete the inequalities in the most efficient way possible.

ANSWERS

Question **1** a): Ben baked more cookies than Ola.

Question **1** b): Abbie baked more cookies than Ola.

PUPIL TEXTBOOK 2A PAGE 60

Share

WAYS OF WORKING Whole class teacher led

ASK

- *What is the most efficient way to find out who has baked more cookies?*
- *Does the number of trays that are used affect the answer?*
- *Question **1** b): Can you find a way to compare the number of cookies without working out the calculations?*

IN FOCUS Encourage children to explain how they worked out each answer to question **1** and why their method is the most efficient method.

STRENGTHEN Ask children to represent Ola's and Abbie's trays using counters of two colours: one colour for the first tray (7 cookies in each case) and one for the second tray. This will highlight the fact that children need to focus on the number of cookies on the second trays in order to find which girl baked more cookies.

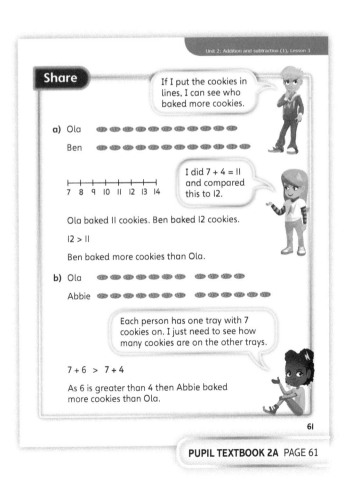

PUPIL TEXTBOOK 2A PAGE 61

Think together

Whole class teacher led (I do, We do, You do)

ASK

- Question **1** : *Does it matter which number you begin with when you are adding?*
- Questions **1** and **2** : *What is the same and what is different about the numbers of objects each child has?*

IN FOCUS In question **2** , the whole is the same, rather than one of the parts. This is the first time children are asked to compare number sentences involving subtraction: ensure children look at the effect the removal of a part will have on the whole, rather than continuing to compare the parts.

STRENGTHEN In question **3** , encourage children to make the number that is the same on both sides of the first inequality using the same coloured counters. They can then make the other given number using a different colour. What can they say about the missing number?

DEEPEN Question **3** has many possible answers; children are then asked to find the smallest possible whole number in each case. Ask children to explain how they know they have found the smallest possible whole number. Can they explain why their method was efficient?

ASSESSMENT CHECKPOINT Assess whether children can explain their choice of inequality sign in question **2** .

Check whether they have made links between the numbers, or simply calculated the number of items each character has.

ANSWERS

Question **1** : 4 + 8 > 4 + 5

Tim has more flowers.

Question **2** : 10 − 2 > 10 − 4

Shaan has fewer tissues left.

Question **3** : Any number greater than or equal to 9 could go in the first box; 9 is the smallest whole number that works.

Any number greater than or equal to 11 could go in the second box; 11 is the smallest whole number that works.

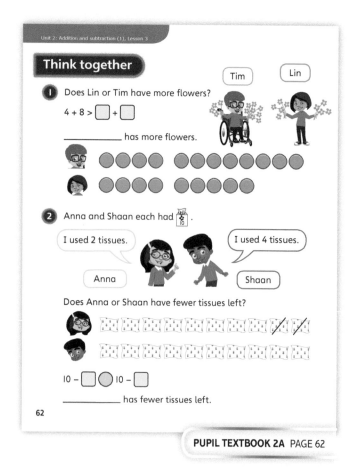

PUPIL TEXTBOOK 2A PAGE 62

PUPIL TEXTBOOK 2A PAGE 63

Practice

WAYS OF WORKING Independent thinking

IN FOCUS Questions ❶ and ❷ require children to complete inequalities, choosing the correct inequality sign in each case. Comparing the numbers that are the same on each side of the inequality will help them make their choices efficiently.

Question ❸ encourages children to reason more deeply, as the similarities between the two sides of the calculations are less explicit.

STRENGTHEN Continue to ask children to make the different number sentences with counters, using the same colour for elements that are the same on both sides.

DEEPEN Each of the four inequalities in question ❹ a) has more than one possible answer. Challenge children to find all the possible missing numbers (noting that for 12 + 6 < 11 + ? the answer is any number greater than or equal to 8). You could also ask them to rewrite each completed inequality using the other inequality sign (for example, rewrite 3 + 7 > 3 + 6 as 3 + 6 < 3 + 7).

ASSESSMENT CHECKPOINT Assess whether children can explain what they used to make their decisions and how they ensured they were being as efficient as possible.

Use question ❸ to assess children's flexibility of number. How many number sentences could they complete without working out the answers on both sides? For example, did they see that for 10 + 4 ◯ 18 they could compare the ones? Did they reason that 8 + 8 > 7 + 7 because 8 > 7?

ANSWERS Answers for the **Practice** part of the lesson appear in the separate **Practice and Reflect answer guide**.

Reflect

WAYS OF WORKING Independent thinking

IN FOCUS In the **Reflect** part of the lesson, children are asked to create their own number sentences using given digits. They should be able to make reasoned choices, rather than using trial and error.

STRENGTHEN Give children digit cards that they can place in the calculation scaffolds. Alternatively, they could use images of 4, 5, 6 and 7 counters in a row to check their number sentences.

ASSESSMENT CHECKPOINT Assess whether children can explain the choices they made, making specific links to the locations of the different numbers.

ANSWERS Answers for the **Reflect** part of the lesson appear in the separate **Practice and Reflect answer guide**.

After the lesson

- Did children make links between the numbers and understand that they did not need to work out and compare the solutions to both sides of the number sentences?
- Are children secure in their understanding of the < and > signs?

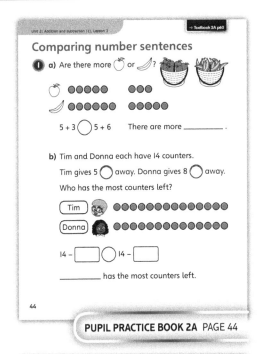

PUPIL PRACTICE BOOK 2A PAGE 44

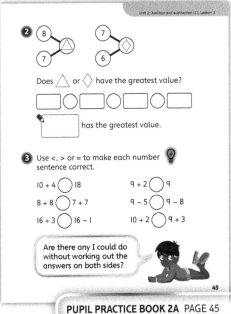

PUPIL PRACTICE BOOK 2A PAGE 45

PUPIL PRACTICE BOOK 2A PAGE 46

Finding related facts

Learning focus

In this lesson, children use known facts to determine other facts.

Small steps

→ Previous step: Comparing number sentences
→ **This step: Finding related facts**
→ Next step: Making number bonds to 100

NATIONAL CURRICULUM LINKS

Year 2 Number – Addition and Subtraction

Recall and use addition and subtraction facts to 20 fluently, and derive and use related facts up to 100.

ASSESSING MASTERY

Children can use number bonds within 20 to determine other facts, rather than calculating these facts as a result of using addition or subtraction in an inefficient way. Children can identify the fact that they have chosen to use and explain why it helps with the calculation.

COMMON MISCONCEPTIONS

Children may not see the purpose of using known facts and may find alternative ways to calculate the answer. Ask:
• *What fact did you use to help with this calculation?*

STRENGTHENING UNDERSTANDING

Ask children to make the numbers using concrete manipulatives alongside the abstract calculations. They should explain the parts that they have made and describe how the known fact relates to the unknown fact (for example, 2 ones + 3 ones = 5 ones so 2 tens + 3 tens = 5 tens).

GOING DEEPER

Encourage children to describe more than one fact that they could use to help them find the solution to a new problem. This will highlight their flexibility and fluency of number facts.

KEY LANGUAGE

In lesson: facts, number sentence, signs, digits, ones, tens

Other language to be used by the teacher: number bonds, addition, subtraction, link, relate

STRUCTURES AND REPRESENTATIONS

Part-whole model, bar model

RESOURCES

Mandatory: Base 10 equipment, bead string

Optional: blank number sentence scaffold

 In the eTextbook of this lesson, you will find interactive links to a selection of teaching tools.

Before you teach

• Can children think of number facts that they could use independently?
• How will you encourage children to make links with known facts?

Discover

WAYS OF WORKING Pair work

ASK

- *What do you know about 2 + 3?*
- *What other facts can you work out from this?*
- *Can you write seven other number sentences based on this one?*

IN FOCUS The numbers in question ❶ allow children to make simple links between the number of pencils Paul and Mr Abbot each have. Encourage children to make these links by asking them to draw both sets of pencils or make both sets of numbers with resources.

ANSWERS

Question ❶ a):

 + =

2 + 3 = 5

Paul has 5 pencils.

Question ❶ b): Mr Abbot has 50 pencils.

The signs and some of the digits are the same.

Some of the numbers are ones. Some of the numbers are tens.

Share

WAYS OF WORKING Whole class teacher led

ASK

- Question ❶ b): *What is the same and what is different about the number of pencils Paul and Mr Abbot each have?*
- Question ❶ b): *How many parts do Paul and Mr Abbot each have?*
- Question ❶ b): *Is there anything the same about the number sentences you can write for the total number of pencils each has?*

IN FOCUS When tackling question ❶ b), children should be able to make links between the number of pencils that Paul and Mr Abbot have: they should be able to see that the number of ones that Paul has is the same as the number of tens that Mr Abbot has.

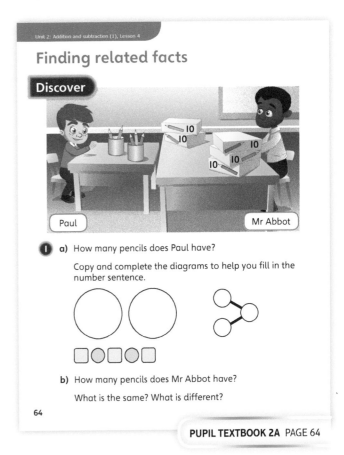

PUPIL TEXTBOOK 2A PAGE 64

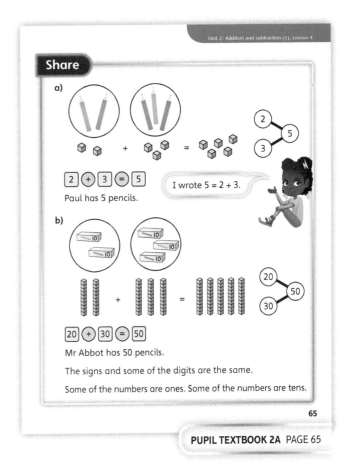

PUPIL TEXTBOOK 2A PAGE 65

Think together

Whole class teacher led (I do, We do, You do)

ASK

- Question **1** : *How does 4 + 3 = 7 help you to know that 40 + 30 = 70?*
- Question **2** : *Can you use known subtraction facts to help you, or does it only work for addition facts?*
- Question **3** : *Whose strategy is more efficient, Astrid's or Flo's?*

IN FOCUS Question **1** is similar to the **Discover** question, while question **2** introduces the idea that known facts can also help with subtraction. Encourage children to verbalise how the known fact helps them with the unknown fact.

Question **3** builds on work from the previous lesson as well as requiring children to use a known fact to help with the calculations. The fourth calculation also tests children's understanding of '=' as meaning 'equal to' rather than indicating that an answer follows it.

STRENGTHEN Making the known and unknown facts using Base 10 equipment will strengthen children's understanding of how the facts are linked. Encourage them to explain the facts (for example, 5 ones + 1 one = 6 ones, so 5 tens + 1 ten = 6 tens).

DEEPEN Ask children to write 16 calculations for each question, applying their understanding of fact families to both the known fact and the unknown fact in each case.

ASSESSMENT CHECKPOINT Children should be able to explain the links between the calculations in questions **1** to **3** . Use their explanations to assess whether children are using known facts or if they are simply calculating each answer.

ANSWERS

Question **1** : 4 + 3 = 7

There are 7 pencils.

40 + 30 = 70

Question **2** :

8 − 6 = 2

80 − 60 = 20

Question **3** : 50 + 10 = 60

60 − 10 = 50

10 = 60 − 50

50 + 10 = 10 + 50

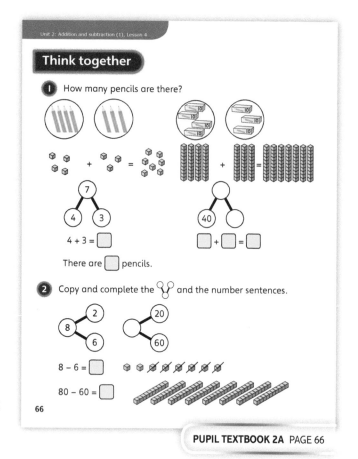

PUPIL TEXTBOOK 2A PAGE 66

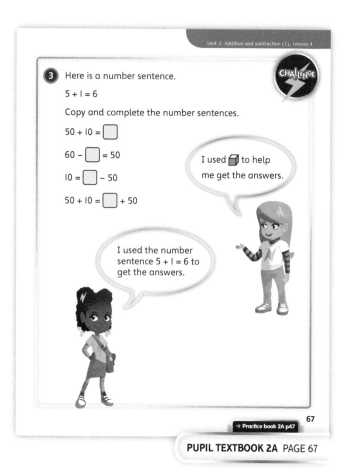

PUPIL TEXTBOOK 2A PAGE 67

Practice

WAYS OF WORKING Independent thinking

IN FOCUS All the **Practice** questions require children to make links to known facts in order to calculate unknown facts. In question ❶ the known and unknown facts are displayed alongside each other, but this support is gradually withdrawn throughout the later questions, to test children's understanding further.

STRENGTHEN If children are finding the concept difficult, they should continue to use concrete resources alongside the abstract calculations they are required to complete. Encourage them to describe the parts and the wholes they are making and to explain what is the same and what is different about the known and unknown facts.

DEEPEN Question ❹ challenges children to make links from given facts. They need to select the appropriate fact to help them with each number sentence and also use their previous learning to make links between numbers within the number sentences. Note that the second number sentence ($10 - ? = 1 + ?$) can be completed in several different ways: encourage children to find more than one answer, and ask them to explain how their completed number sentence is linked to the given fact they have used in each case.

ASSESSMENT CHECKPOINT Assess whether children can justify how the known fact helps them calculate the unknowns. Ask them to explain the link in full sentences.

ANSWERS Answers for the **Practice** part of the lesson appear in the separate **Practice and Reflect answer guide**.

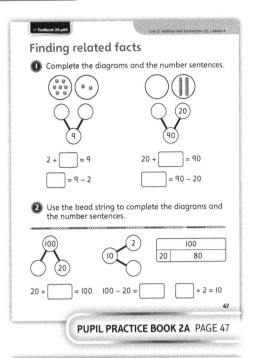

PUPIL PRACTICE BOOK 2A PAGE 47

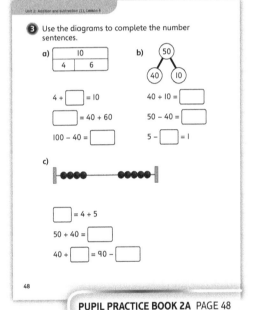

PUPIL PRACTICE BOOK 2A PAGE 48

Reflect

WAYS OF WORKING Independent thinking

IN FOCUS The **Reflect** part of the lesson allows children to show what they have learnt in this and previous lessons. Encourage them to include one number fact involving a minus sign and one involving tens numbers in their three number facts. Alternatively, you could challenge them to write 15 number facts related to the given fact. This will show whether they fully understand how to derive unknown facts from one calculation.

ASSESSMENT CHECKPOINT Assess whether children can explain how they know their number facts are correct, based on the number fact they have been given.

ANSWERS Answers for the **Reflect** part of the lesson appear in the separate **Practice and Reflect answer guide**.

After the lesson ⏸

• What were the most common misconceptions that arose during the lesson?
• How will you address these misconceptions before the next lesson?

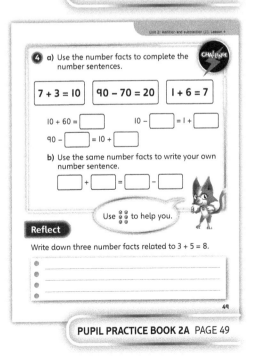

PUPIL PRACTICE BOOK 2A PAGE 49

Making number bonds to 100

Learning focus

In this lesson, children make number bonds to 100 using a 100 square to help them visualise.

Small steps

→ Previous step: Finding related facts
→ **This step: Making number bonds to 100**
→ Next step: Adding and subtracting 1s

NATIONAL CURRICULUM LINKS

Year 2 Number – Addition and Subtraction

- Solve problems with addition and subtraction: using concrete objects and pictorial representations, including those involving numbers, quantities and measures.
- Recall and use addition and subtraction facts to 20 fluently, and derive and use related facts up to 100.

ASSESSING MASTERY

Children can make links to other known facts, such as number bonds to 10, and work out unknown quantities using these facts rather than simply calculating the unknown value. Children can make number bonds to 100 using a 100 square.

COMMON MISCONCEPTIONS

Children may miscount how many squares there are until 100 when using the 100 square to calculate. Ask:
- *Can you use your knowledge of number bonds to 10 to check the number of ones that you have added?*

Children may confuse the game board used in the lesson with a 100 square. Ask:
- *What is the same and what is different between this board and a 100 square?*

STRENGTHENING UNDERSTANDING

Give children a list of number bonds to 10 and multiples of 10 that make 100. This will encourage them to use these known facts rather than simply counting the number of squares to 100 each time. You could ask children to identify which facts helped them calculate the answer to each question.

A bead string (with tens in alternating colours) may help children see how many ones are needed to make the next multiple of 10 and subsequently how many tens there are until 100.

GOING DEEPER

Make links with previous lessons by asking children to complete fact families for each calculation they complete. Encourage them to explain which known facts they used for each calculation.

KEY LANGUAGE

In lesson: number bond, +, number sentence, tens, ones, how many more, bar model

Other language to be used by the teacher: 100 square, multiples of 10, count on, add

STRUCTURES AND REPRESENTATIONS

Part-whole model, 100 square, bar model

RESOURCES

Mandatory: 100 square, counters

Optional: Base 10 equipment, bead string, blank part-whole model, blank addition scaffold

 In the eTextbook of this lesson, you will find interactive links to a selection of teaching tools.

Before you teach

- Are children secure with number bonds to 10?
- How will you ensure children do not make both tens and ones total 10?

Discover

Making number bonds to 100

Discover

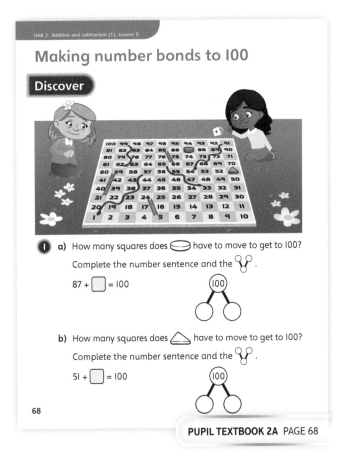

WAYS OF WORKING Pair work

ASK

- *What numbers are the counters on?*
- *How many more squares before the next multiple of 10?*
- *How many tens until 100?*

IN FOCUS For each part of question ❶, encourage children to use known facts to calculate how many more squares there are to 100. They should first consider what square each counter is on, then how many ones are needed to make the next multiple of 10, and then finally how many tens there are to 100.

ANSWERS

Question ❶ a): 87 + 13 = 100

⬭ has to move 13 squares.

Question ❶ b): 51 + 49 = 100

△ has to move 49 squares.

❶ a) How many squares does ⬭ have to move to get to 100?

Complete the number sentence and the 𝖸.

87 + ☐ = 100

b) How many squares does △ have to move to get to 100?

Complete the number sentence and the 𝖸.

51 + ☐ = 100

68

PUPIL TEXTBOOK 2A PAGE 68

Share

Share

WAYS OF WORKING Whole class teacher led

ASK

- *Who counted in ones to get to 100? Was this an efficient strategy to use?*
- *Who calculated the answer in a more efficient way?*
- *Can you write your own number sentence to make 100?*
- *How do you know 87 + 12 is not correct?*

IN FOCUS Use question ❶ b) to highlight that counting in ones is not an efficient strategy, even though doing so can lead to the right answer: it is a slow method and mistakes may result from miscounting. Agree that the 'make 10' strategy – using number bonds to 10 to reach the next multiple of 10, and then counting the number of rows of 10 to 100 – is more efficient.

STRENGTHEN Strengthen understanding by using Base 10 equipment to make the representations in this part of the lesson. This will help children see how many more are needed to make 100.

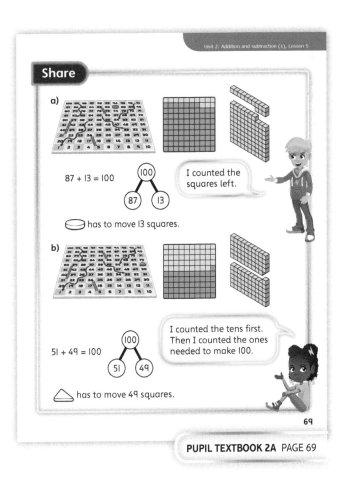

a) 87 + 13 = 100

I counted the squares left.

⬭ has to move 13 squares.

b) 51 + 49 = 100

I counted the tens first. Then I counted the ones needed to make 100.

△ has to move 49 squares.

69

PUPIL TEXTBOOK 2A PAGE 69

Think together

WAYS OF WORKING Whole class teacher led (I do, We do, You do)

ASK

- Question ❷ : *What known fact can you use to calculate 30 + ? = 100?*
- *Is counting in ones an efficient strategy?*

IN FOCUS Question ❶ provides a further opportunity to practise what has been discussed in the **Share** section.

STRENGTHEN If children are confused by the make-up of the game board compared to a traditional 100 square, encourage them to colour in a 100 square to show the 65 squares the counter has already moved through in question ❶ ; this will help them see how many more squares the counter needs to move to get to 100. Alternatively, they could make 65 using Base 10 equipment and place the result on top of a 100 square to see how many more ones are needed to make 10 and then how many tens need to be added.

DEEPEN In question ❸ b), children should be able to explain what mistake has been made, realising that both digits do not total 10. If they find the concept easy, ask, for example: *If 35 + ? = 110, what is the missing number?* (the target number should be a multiple of 10 other than 100). This will allow children to apply their understanding in a different way.

ASSESSMENT CHECKPOINT Assess whether children can tell you how they found the answers, referring to number bonds to 10 and explaining how they helped them complete the calculation. They should be able to make 10 and then count on in tens to 100, and to count in tens until they reach ninety-something and then state how many ones are needed to make 100.

ANSWERS

Question ❶ : 65 + 35 = 100

🟤 has to move 35 squares.

Question ❷ :

100	
70	30

30 + 70 = 100

70 is the number missing from the bar model.

Question ❸ a):

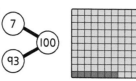

93 is the missing number.

Question ❸ b): Ash has made 110 not 100. He made both digits total 10 rather than adding 6 ones to 44 and then adding 5 more tens to 50 to make 100.

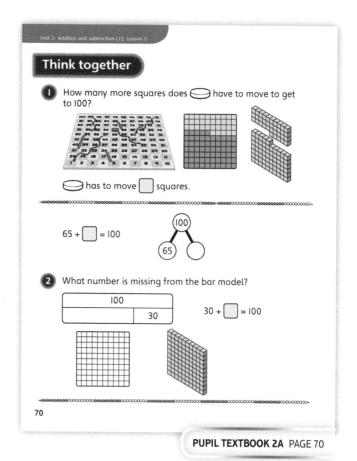

Think together

❶ How many more squares does 🟤 have to move to get to 100?

🟤 has to move ☐ squares.

65 + ☐ = 100

❷ What number is missing from the bar model?

100	
	30

30 + ☐ = 100

70

PUPIL TEXTBOOK 2A PAGE 70

❸ a) Find the missing number.
Copy and complete the ✲.

7 — 100

I used the ▦ and ▮ to help me get the answer.

b) What mistake has been made?

44 + 66 = 100

I know that 4 and 6 make 10. This could help me find the answer.

71

→ Practice book 2A p50

PUPIL TEXTBOOK 2A PAGE 71

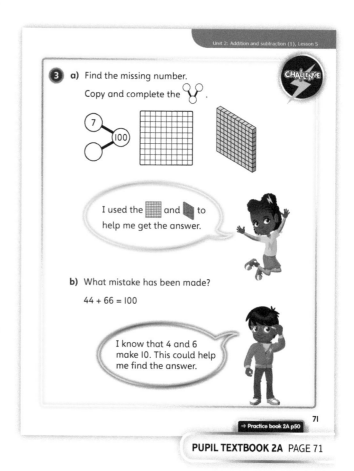

Practice

WAYS OF WORKING Independent thinking

IN FOCUS In question **②**, the first part of the number sentence has been shown on the 100 square vertically rather than horizontally.

In questions **③** and **④**, no 100 square is shown, although a bead string is included in question **③** to support children.

Question **⑥** will challenge children as they are not given the starting number, meaning they cannot simply count on to 100. They will need to use their understanding of place value, recognising, for example, that in part a) the 3 represents 3 tens and the 4 represents 4 ones.

STRENGTHEN Children should use a bead string or Base 10 equipment to strengthen their understanding of the strategies used to make 100. They could work with a partner and comment on what they are doing and which facts they are using as they work through the calculation.

In question **⑤**, check children understand that both circles in the number sentence represent the same number; they cannot find any two numbers that add to 100.

DEEPEN Challenge children to complete the calculation ? + ☐ = 100 (where ? and ☐ are different values). Encourage them to work systematically to begin with and then predict how many different possible answers they think there are. Can they justify their prediction?

ASSESSMENT CHECKPOINT Children should be able to explain the steps that they have completed mentally and which known number facts they have used.

ANSWERS Answers for the **Practice** part of the lesson appear in the separate **Practice and Reflect answer guide**.

Reflect

WAYS OF WORKING Independent thinking

IN FOCUS The **Reflect** part of the lesson requires children to combine what they have learnt in the lesson with known facts in order to find different ways to complete the calculation. Challenge children to work systematically and find all the possibilities.

ASSESSMENT CHECKPOINT Assess whether children are working systematically. Do they understand the concept of both parts having 0 ones? Ask: *What do the two zeros represent? How many ones are in both numbers?*

ANSWERS Answers for the **Reflect** part of the lesson appear in the separate **Practice and Reflect answer guide**.

After the lesson

- Are children confident at counting in tens from any number?
- How many children were able to use their knowledge of number bonds to 10 to count to the nearest multiple of 10?

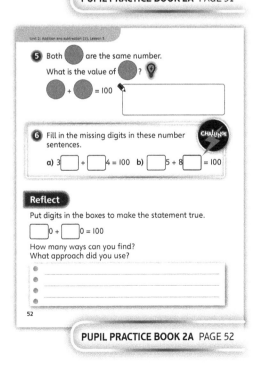

PUPIL PRACTICE BOOK 2A PAGE 50

PUPIL PRACTICE BOOK 2A PAGE 51

PUPIL PRACTICE BOOK 2A PAGE 52

Adding and subtracting 1s

Learning focus

In this lesson, children will add and subtract 1s to or from a 2-digit number without exchanging, using number bonds to help them.

Small steps

→ Previous step: Making number bonds to 100
→ **This step: Adding and subtracting 1s**
→ Next step: Finding 10 more and 10 less

NATIONAL CURRICULUM LINKS

Year 2 Number – Addition and Subtraction

- Add and subtract numbers using concrete objects, pictorial representations, and mentally, including: a 2-digit number and 1s.
- Solve problems with addition and subtraction: using concrete objects and pictorial representations, including those involving numbers, quantities and measures.

ASSESSING MASTERY

Children can identify the number of tens and ones in a number, can add and subtract an additional number of ones without exchange and notice that only the digit in the ones column changes. Children can verbalise the changes that occur and use known number bonds to calculate the answer, rather than counting on or back in ones.

COMMON MISCONCEPTIONS

Children may not know their number bonds and may resort to counting on or back, perhaps incorrectly. Ask:
- *What number bond could you use for this calculation?*

Children may set their work out in columns incorrectly and so add the incorrect values. Ask:
- *Have you made sure the ones digits in each number are above each other?*

Similarly, children may place the incorrect number on top when setting out their work in columns and therefore subtract incorrectly. Ask:
- *Is the number that you are starting from always on top?*

Children may add the ones onto the tens of another number when calculating mentally. Ask:
- *Can you explain to me in words what you are doing?*

STRENGTHENING UNDERSTANDING

Give children a list of number bonds and encourage children to use and memorise them. Ask them to identify the fact they are using each time to help them see the link between the known fact and the calculation they are doing.

GOING DEEPER

Challenge children to record any calculation that they write in as many different ways as possible, practising skills that they have learned in previous lessons. For example, can they use the commutative law and change the location of the equals sign?

KEY LANGUAGE

In lesson: adding, subtracting, +, −, =, ones, in total, number sentence, count on, columns, tens

Other language to be used by the teacher: digit, altogether, take away

STRUCTURES AND REPRESENTATIONS

Number line, place value chart, column method

RESOURCES

Mandatory: place value charts, Base 10 equipment

 In the eTextbook of this lesson, you will find interactive links to a selection of teaching tools.

Before you teach

- Can children confidently recall number bonds?
- Which misconception do you think will be the most likely?

Discover

WAYS OF WORKING Pair work

ASK

- *What does the box of burgers represent?*
- *Is there more than one way to write the addition number sentence?*

IN FOCUS Question ① requires children to differentiate between a box of burgers, representing 10 burgers, and an individual burger, representing one burger, in order to successfully create number sentences.

ANSWERS

Question ① a): There are 39 burgers in total.

$$34 + 5 = 39$$

Question ① b): There are 36 burgers left.

$$39 - 3 = 36$$

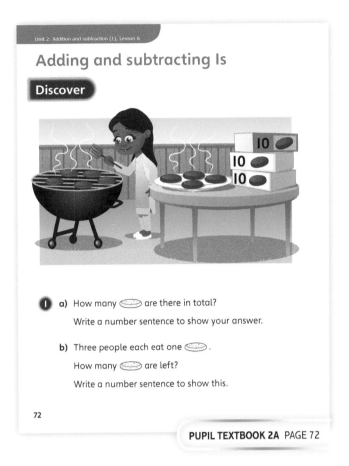

Adding and subtracting 1s

Discover

① a) How many 🍔 are there in total?

Write a number sentence to show your answer.

b) Three people each eat one 🍔.

How many 🍔 are left?

Write a number sentence to show this.

72

PUPIL TEXTBOOK 2A PAGE 72

Share

WAYS OF WORKING Whole class teacher led

ASK

- *What resources could you use to represent the burgers? What is the most efficient way to make the correct number?*
- *Is there a quicker way to calculate the total than just counting on?*

IN FOCUS Ask children to share how they calculated the number of burgers in both parts of question ①. Discuss both methods in each case. What is the same and what is different about the methods? Which method is more efficient?

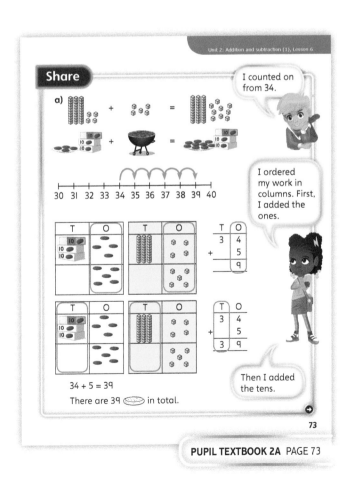

Share

I counted on from 34.

I ordered my work in columns. First, I added the ones.

Then I added the tens.

$$34 + 5 = 39$$

There are 39 🍔 in total.

73

PUPIL TEXTBOOK 2A PAGE 73

101

Think together

ASK

• *How many tens are there in each number? How many ones?*
• *What is the most efficient way to calculate the solution?*

IN FOCUS Question ❸ exposes two common misconceptions that can cause children to make mistakes when using the column method. Ask children to explain why the incorrect workings are incorrect.

STRENGTHEN Encourage children to make each number of objects using concrete manipulatives. They should use their knowledge of number bonds to help them carry out the calculations, and use the manipulatives to check their answers.

DEEPEN Ask children to write as many different number sentences that match the pictorial representation in question ❶ as they can (for example, 40 + 1 + 6 = 47, 20 + 20 + 1 + 6 = 47, and so on).

ASSESSMENT CHECKPOINT Assess whether children can identify the number fact they can use to calculate each solution. Children should also be able to verbalise the steps they are completing mentally (for example, 2 ones plus 5 ones is equal to 7 ones).

ANSWERS

Question ❶ : 41 + 6 = 47

There are 47 crayons in total.

Question ❷ : 26 – 5 = 21

There are 21 doughnuts left.

Question ❸ a): 42 + 5 = 47

Callie is correct; Romesh has incorrectly placed the 5 ones in the tens column.

Question ❸ b): 65 – 3 = 62

Romesh is correct; Callie has not put the largest number on top.

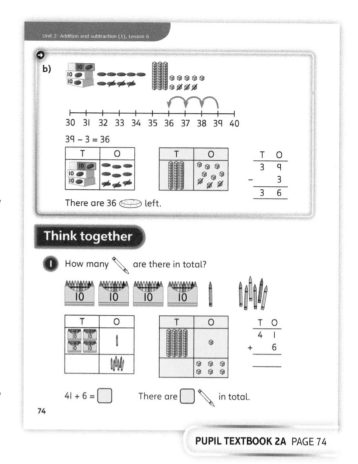

PUPIL TEXTBOOK 2A PAGE 74

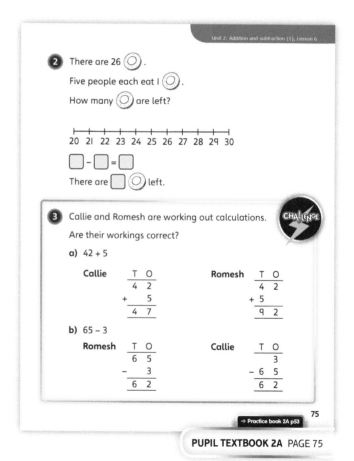

PUPIL TEXTBOOK 2A PAGE 75

Practice

WAYS OF WORKING Independent thinking

IN FOCUS Question **1** encourages the use of a number line and question **2** shows the number represented using Base 10 equipment; both questions set the calculations within a context, with pictorial support, to encourage understanding.

Question **5** again requires children to identify a mistake. As before, encourage them to explain what has been done wrong as well as writing the correct number sentence.

STRENGTHEN Encourage children to make concrete representations of the abstract representations in questions **3** and **4** . Provide number lines and Base 10 equipment and discuss what is the same and what is different about two representations.

DEEPEN Provide children with a number sentence such as 2? + ? = 27 and ask them to explore all the different ways that this question could be answered. Encourage children to work systematically to find all possible ways.

ASSESSMENT CHECKPOINT Assess whether children are able to identify how many tens and ones there are in a number. Can children instantly recall number bonds within 10 and relate them to the starting number or are they relying on counting on or counting back in ones?

ANSWERS Answers for the **Practice** part of the lesson appear in the separate **Practice and Reflect answer guide**.

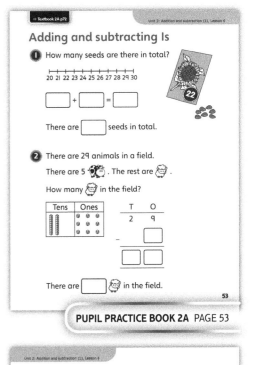

PUPIL PRACTICE BOOK 2A PAGE 53

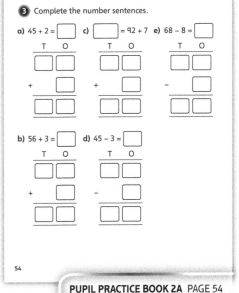

PUPIL PRACTICE BOOK 2A PAGE 54

Reflect

WAYS OF WORKING Pair work

IN FOCUS In the **Reflect** part of the lesson, children verbalise to their partner different ways to work out an addition and a subtraction. They could use resources to help them if required.

ASSESSMENT CHECKPOINT Assess whether children can confidently explain more than one way to answer each question. Do they use accurate mathematical language? Can they tell you which of the methods their partner explained was the more efficient, and why?

ANSWERS Answers for the **Reflect** part of the lesson appear in the separate **Practice and Reflect answer guide**.

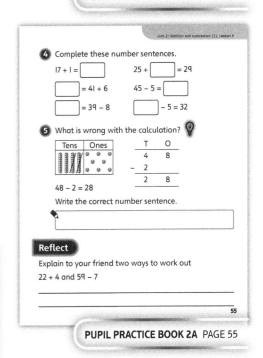

PUPIL PRACTICE BOOK 2A PAGE 55

After the lesson ⏸

- Did children link the use of number bonds to becoming more efficient?
- Can children confidently and accurately explain how they calculated their solutions?

Finding 10 more and 10 less

Learning focus

In this lesson, children will find 10 more and 10 less than a number and notice which digit changes during this process.

Small steps

→ Previous step: Adding and subtracting 1s
→ **This step: Finding 10 more and 10 less**
→ Next step: Adding and subtracting 10s

NATIONAL CURRICULUM LINKS

Year 2 Number – Addition and Subtraction

- Count in steps of 2, 3, and 5 from 0, and in tens from any number, forward and backward.
- Solve problems with addition and subtraction: using concrete objects and pictorial representations, including those involving numbers, quantities and measures.

ASSESSING MASTERY

Children can mentally add or subtract 10 to or from a 2-digit number (staying within 100) and can identify that only the digit in the tens column changes during this process. Children can show this visually on a variety of different representations and explain what each shows.

COMMON MISCONCEPTIONS

Children may add or subtract to or from the ones digit rather than the tens digit of a number. Ask:
- *What is the total number of tens? Have you added/subtracted a ten to/from the tens column?*

Use the sentence scaffold: *? tens + 1 ten = ? tens or ? tens – 1 ten = ? tens.*

STRENGTHENING UNDERSTANDING

Encourage children to use concrete resources. Ask them to work in pairs, commenting on what they are doing during the calculation to their partner. Using the sentence scaffold above will help in this process.

GOING DEEPER

Children should notice that only the tens digit changes when you add or subtract 10. Ask: *Is this always true, or only sometimes true?* Children might be able to see that if you add 10 to a number with 9 tens the digit in the hundreds column will also change (or will become 1).

KEY LANGUAGE

In lesson: 10 more, 10 less

Other language to be used by the teacher: digit, tens, ones, pattern, above, below, count on, count back

STRUCTURES AND REPRESENTATIONS

100 square, number line, number track

RESOURCES

Mandatory: 100 square, number line, Base 10 equipment

Optional: completed number track (increasing in tens)

 In the eTextbook of this lesson, you will find interactive links to a selection of teaching tools.

Before you teach

- Which representation do you think children will find hardest to use or understand?
- How will you support children in explaining the use of this representation?

Discover

WAYS OF WORKING Pair work

ASK

- *What is the same as yesterday's lesson? What is different?*
- *Who can explain what is happening in this game?*

IN FOCUS Question ❶ introduces children to the concept of finding 10 more or 10 less than a number, using the context of a game. Encourage children to see the similarities between this concept and the previous lesson's work.

ANSWERS

Question ❶ a): ◡ player now has 50 points.

Question ❶ b): ◯ player now has 47 points.

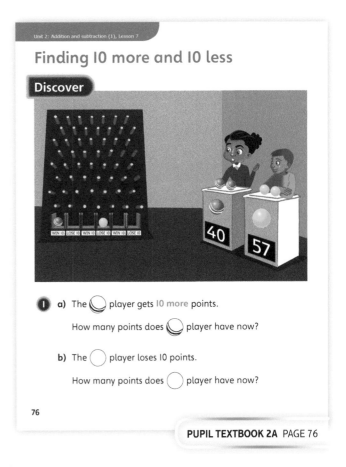

PUPIL TEXTBOOK 2A PAGE 76

Share

WAYS OF WORKING Whole class teacher led

ASK

- *Where is 10 more or less than a number found on a 100 square? Is this always the case?*
- *What digit changes when you find 10 more or 10 less than a number? Is this always the case?*
- *What is 10 more than …? What is 10 less than …?*

IN FOCUS Encourage children to explain how they know how many points each player now has, using different resources and representations to illustrate their reasoning.

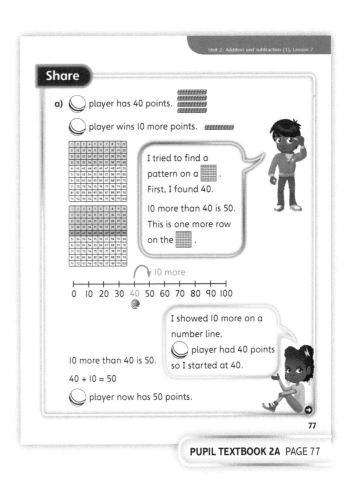

PUPIL TEXTBOOK 2A PAGE 77

Think together

WAYS OF WORKING Whole class teacher led (I do, We do, You do)

ASK
- *What digit changes when you add or subtract 10 to or from a number?*
- *What patterns can you spot in the arrangement of the numbers in the 100 square?*

IN FOCUS Question ❶ revisits the game context used in **Discover** and **Share**, while questions ❷ and ❸ use different ways of asking children to find 10 more or 10 less than given numbers. It is important that children continue to use a variety of different resources, rather than just the one that is clearest to them, in order to increase their understanding of this key concept.

In question ❸, the second and fourth sentences require children to work counterintuitively. For example, to complete '35 is 10 more than ?' they actually need to find 10 less than 35. Encourage them to think carefully about what the sentence is saying, perhaps rearranging it to read '10 more than ? is 35'.

STRENGTHEN If children make the starting number incorrectly, using resources such as Base 10 equipment, this will need to be addressed at another time. In order to keep the focus of this lesson on finding 10 more or 10 less than a number, give children a pictorial representation of the starting number and ask them to draw another 10 items, or cross 10 out, as the question requires.

DEEPEN If children can calculate 10 more than a number, can they then also say the inverse? For example, '10 more than 33 is 43, so I know 10 less than 43 is 33'. Encourage children to verbalise or write down the inverse for each of the calculations they have completed.

ASSESSMENT CHECKPOINT Assess whether children can predict what 10 more or 10 less than a number will be before using resources. Can they explain how they know they are correct? Encourage them to prove it using a variety of different resources.

ANSWERS

Question ❶: 10 more than 76 is 86.

76 + 10 = 86.

◑ player has 86 points.

Question ❷ a): | 20 | 30 | 40 | 50 | 60 | 70 | 80 | 90 | 100 |

Question ❷ b): | 84 | 74 | 64 | 54 | 44 | 34 | 24 | 14 | 4 |

Question ❸: 10 more than 73 is 83.

35 is 10 more than 25.

10 less than 99 is 89.

60 is 10 less than 70.

On a ▦, 10 more than a number is on the line below.

On a ▦, 10 less than a number is on the line above.

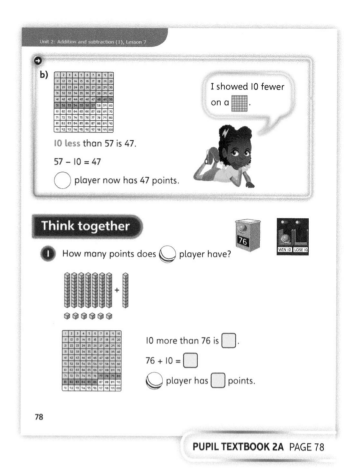

PUPIL TEXTBOOK 2A PAGE 78

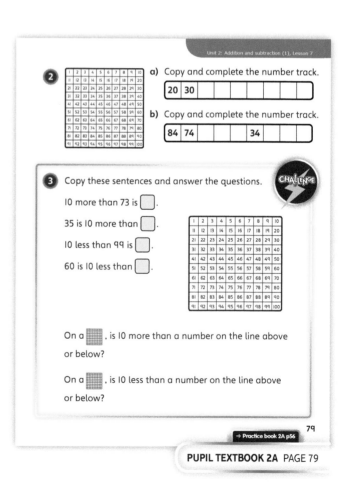

PUPIL TEXTBOOK 2A PAGE 79

Practice

WAYS OF WORKING Independent thinking

IN FOCUS In questions ❶ and ❷, children are required to interpret numbers represented in different ways, using different resources and representations. This variation will help strengthen children's understanding of the topic.

STRENGTHEN Encourage children to continue working with concrete resources. Asking them to explain what they are doing will strengthen their understanding.

DEEPEN In question ❹, children should be able to make links between '10 more' and '+ 10'. Challenge them to write both types of number sentence for each part of the question. For example, when they have completed '10 more than 25 is 35', they should also be able to write '10 + 25 = 35'. You could further challenge them to write the calculation in as many different ways as they can (for example, 25 + 10 = 35, 35 = 25 + 10, or 35 = 10 + 25).

ASSESSMENT CHECKPOINT Check whether children can explain how they know their answer is correct. They should be able to explain why the digit in the tens column changes and why the digit in the ones column does not change.

Use questions ❸ to ❺, which have no pictorial support, to determine whether children understand the concept of 10 more and 10 less, or if they still need to make the numbers in order to see the answer.

ANSWERS Answers for the **Practice** part of the lesson appear in the separate **Practice and Reflect answer guide**.

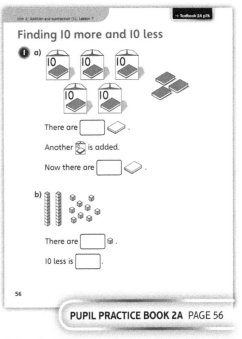

PUPIL PRACTICE BOOK 2A PAGE 56

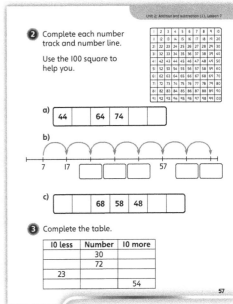

PUPIL PRACTICE BOOK 2A PAGE 57

Reflect

WAYS OF WORKING Pair work

IN FOCUS In the **Reflect** part of the lesson, children create their own questions for their partner to complete. They should choose one of the numbers shown and write it in one of the empty boxes in the first number sentence, leaving the other blank for their partner to complete. They then do the same with the second number sentence.

ASSESSMENT CHECKPOINT Assess what children say they would do to check their partner's answer. Can they use their knowledge of the inverse? Can they accurately describe the digit in the tens column and how and why it changes as a result of the calculation?

ANSWERS Answers for the **Reflect** part of the lesson appear in the separate **Practice and Reflect answer guide**.

After the lesson ⏸

- Are children confident finding 10 more and 10 less?
- What resource did children find most or least easy to use?

PUPIL PRACTICE BOOK 2A PAGE 58

107

Adding and subtracting 10s

Learning focus

In this lesson, children will build on what they learned in the previous lesson, but will now focus on addition and subtraction of more than one ten to a 2-digit number.

Small steps

→ Previous step: Finding 10 more and 10 less
→ **This step: Adding and subtracting 10s**
→ Next step: Adding a 2-digit number and a 1-digit number (1)

NATIONAL CURRICULUM LINKS

Year 2 Number – Addition and Subtraction

- Add and subtract numbers using concrete objects, pictorial representations, and mentally, including: a 2-digit number and tens.
- Solve problems with addition and subtraction: using concrete objects and pictorial representations, including those involving numbers, quantities and measures.

ASSESSING MASTERY

Children can make links to previous learning and identify that only the digit in the tens column changes when they add or subtract a multiple of 10. Children can recognise that the method they use and visualise is similar to the method for adding ones to a 2-digit number.

COMMON MISCONCEPTIONS

Children may add tens to the ones column. Ask:
- *Have you added or subtracted tens to or from the tens column?*

Children may forget to write the 0 in the ones column when they record their working in columns (this may increase the likelihood of them adding tens to the ones column). Ask:
- *How many ones are there in 20, 30, 40 …?*

Children may also forget what operation they are using and may add when they should be subtracting and vice versa. Ask:
- *What operation does this question require? How do you know?*

STRENGTHENING UNDERSTANDING

Encourage children to work in pairs, with one child using the manipulatives and the other recording how many tens and ones there are at different points. Working in this way will help children conceptualise the numbers within the column method and strengthen their understanding of what the numbers recorded represent.

GOING DEEPER

Ask children to apply their understanding of adding and subtracting tens to and from a number by representing or writing a calculation in as many different ways as possible. You could also ask them to make a whole in as many different ways as possible, with the restriction that one of the parts is always a multiple of 10.

KEY LANGUAGE

In lesson: adding, subtraction, +, −, =, total, ones, tens, columns, number line, calculation

Other language to be used by the teacher: digit, multiple of 10, method, altogether, take away, minus

STRUCTURES AND REPRESENTATIONS

Column method, part-whole model, number line, bar model, number wall

RESOURCES

Mandatory: Base 10 equipment, place value chart

Optional: blank number tracks

 In the eTextbook of this lesson, you will find interactive links to a selection of teaching tools.

Before you teach

- How will you promote the use of number bonds within this lesson?
- How can you help children critique each other's methods to see which is most efficient?

Discover

ASK

• *What is the same as yesterday's lesson? What is different?*
• *Can you use number bonds to work in an efficient way?*

IN FOCUS To answer question ❶ , children need to identify the number of tens and ones in the given numbers and add or subtract more than one ten to or from this number.

ANSWERS

Question ❶ a): There are 46 🍬 in total.

Question ❶ b): There are 25 children at the fireworks.

Adding and subtracting 10s

Discover

❶ a) How many 🍬 are there in total?

b) There are 65 people at the fireworks.
40 of the people are adults.
How many of the people are children?

80

PUPIL TEXTBOOK 2A PAGE 80

Share

ASK

• *How can you organise your work and the resources you are using? Have you organised your work in this way before?*
• *Question ❶ a): Is the process similar to when you added ones to a 2-digit number?*

IN FOCUS In both parts of question ❶ , encourage children to make links between what they are doing in this lesson and what they did when they added or subtracted ones to or from a 2-digit number. Lead them towards arranging the resources to reflect the column method, using a place value chart to help them. Help children make links between the different representations, highlighting how the same information is recorded in different ways.

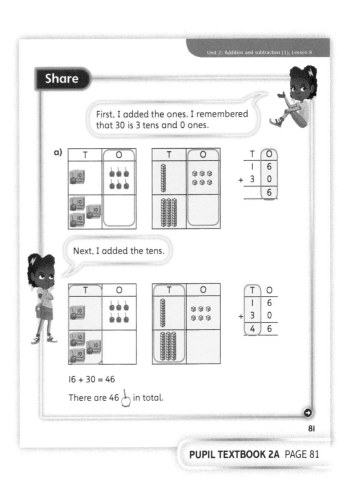

Share

First, I added the ones. I remembered that 30 is 3 tens and 0 ones.

a)

Next, I added the tens.

16 + 30 = 46

There are 46 🍬 in total.

81

PUPIL TEXTBOOK 2A PAGE 81

Think together

Whole class teacher led (I do, We do, You do)

ASK

- *How do you know which operation to use in each question?*
- *Does the digit in the ones column change in any of these questions?*

IN FOCUS Encourage children to think about each question in different ways. How could it be represented using different resources? For example, in question ①, use Flo's comment to prompt children to consider how the calculation could be represented on a number line.

STRENGTHEN Allow children to continue to use resources to calculate the answers. This will help them understand the concept of adding and subtracting a number of tens from a given number.

DEEPEN Present children with some incorrect calculations and challenge them to explain how they know the given answers are not possible. For example, ask: *How do you know that 38 – 20 = 36 is not correct?*

ASSESSMENT CHECKPOINT Assess whether children can verbalise what they are doing with the resources and what they are doing mentally using the appropriate vocabulary. They should also be able to explain why the digit in the ones column does not change.

ANSWERS

Question ① : 27 + 50 = 77

There are 77 🎆 in total.

Question ② : 51 – 40 = 11

There are 11 pieces of toffee left.

Question ③ : The first child has added the 2 digits in the tens column, rather than using subtraction.

The second child has forgotten to write the 0 in 20 and as a result has subtracted the 2 tens from the ones digits by mistake.

35 – 20 = 15

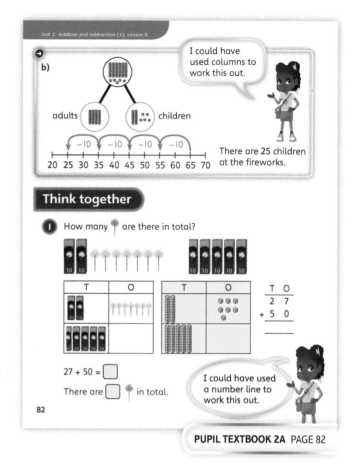

PUPIL TEXTBOOK 2A PAGE 82

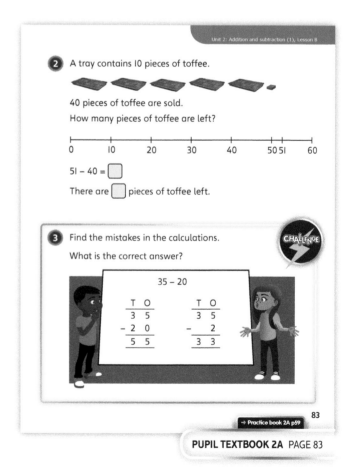

PUPIL TEXTBOOK 2A PAGE 83

110

Practice

WAYS OF WORKING Independent thinking

IN FOCUS Question ③ uses the part-whole model and bar model to represent addition and subtraction of multiples of 10. For all questions, allow children to use a different resource from that shown to check their answer.

STRENGTHEN Encourage children to record 'skip counting' on a number track. For example, for 35 + 40, children would write 35 first, then 45, 55, 65, 75 in the next boxes. Doing this at the same time as using a resource such as Base 10 equipment will help them understand how each 10 affects the total number.

DEEPEN Challenge children to choose a number and represent it on a number wall, as in question ⑤, finding as many different ways to make it as possible. Note that one of the parts should always be a multiple of 10. For example, if children chose 74 as the whole, their number wall would show 10 + 64, 20 + 54, 30 + 44, and so on.

ASSESSMENT CHECKPOINT Children should be able to verbalise the steps that they are completing using the correct mathematical vocabulary. They should also be able to explain what each number they record represents.

ANSWERS Answers for the **Practice** part of the lesson appear in the separate **Practice and Reflect answer guide**.

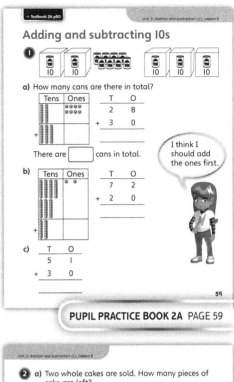

PUPIL PRACTICE BOOK 2A PAGE 59

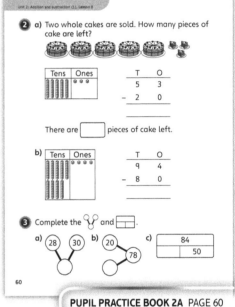

PUPIL PRACTICE BOOK 2A PAGE 60

Reflect

WAYS OF WORKING Independent thinking

IN FOCUS The **Reflect** part of the lesson requires children to find two tens digits that add to 7(0) and two tens digits with a difference of 3(0), and to explain their reasoning. Children could be challenged to find all the possible solutions for each calculation.

ASSESSMENT CHECKPOINT Assess whether children can explain how they found suitable numbers to complete the calculations. Can they tell you if more than one answer is possible, and why or why not?

ANSWERS Answers for the **Reflect** part of the lesson appear in the separate **Practice and Reflect answer guide**.

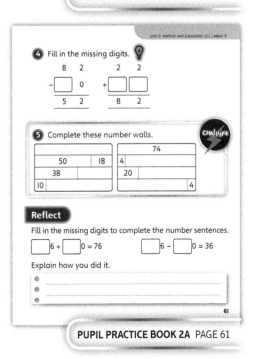

PUPIL PRACTICE BOOK 2A PAGE 61

After the lesson ⏸

- Did all children understand the concept that the column method elicits, or were some children simply following a procedure for easier questions?

Adding a 2-digit number and a 1-digit number ①

Learning focus

In this lesson, children will add 2-digit and 1-digit numbers together, with the focus on bridging 10. They will represent this using ten frames and relate the calculation to the part-whole model.

Small steps

→ Previous step: Adding and subtracting 10s

→ **This step: Adding a 2-digit number and a 1-digit number (1)**

→ Next step: Adding a 2-digit number and a 1-digit number (2)

NATIONAL CURRICULUM LINKS

Year 2 Number – Addition and Subtraction

- Add and subtract numbers using concrete objects, pictorial representations, and mentally, including: a 2-digit number and ones.
- Solve problems with addition and subtraction: using concrete objects and pictorial representations, including those involving numbers, quantities and measures.

ASSESSING MASTERY

Children can make links to previous lessons and concepts and recognise that 10 ones is the same as one ten. Children understand how this is represented when writing numbers in digits and when using resources to make different numbers.

COMMON MISCONCEPTIONS

Children may count on in 1s from a starting number, rather than using their understanding of number. Ask:
- *Is there a more efficient way to calculate the answer? Can you use what you know about numbers to calculate the answer?*

Children may try to partition the 1-digit number in a way that is not helpful to aid their mental calculation. Ask:
- *How does the way that you have partitioned the 1-digit number help with your mental calculation?*

STRENGTHENING UNDERSTANDING

Children should be encouraged to use the 'make 10' strategy, as this will help them understand how to use number bonds to calculate the answers; using ten frames throughout the lesson will highlight this strategy. Using counters of one colour to make the starting number, and counters of another colour to make 10 and then count on to the final answer, will clearly highlight the partitioning of the 1-digit number.

GOING DEEPER

Encourage children to record calculations in as many different ways as possible, to show the different methods that they could use to find the answers, and to consolidate learning from previous lessons in this unit.

KEY LANGUAGE

In lesson: adding, +, =, digit, total, whole, parts, number sentence

Other language to be used by the teacher: ones, tens, partition

STRUCTURES AND REPRESENTATIONS

Ten frames, part-whole model, number line

RESOURCES

Mandatory: counters (double-sided or two colours, if possible), ten frames, blank part-whole models

Optional: 1–100 number line, pictures of completed ten frames

 In the eTextbook of this lesson, you will find interactive links to a selection of teaching tools.

Before you teach

- Are children confident adding and subtracting tens?
- Are children secure using the 'make 10' strategy?

Discover

WAYS OF WORKING   Pair work

ASK

- *What number does four complete ten frames represent?*
- *Question ❶ b): How many more do you need to fill the ten frame?*
- *Question ❶ b): How could you represent the different parts on a part-whole model?*

IN FOCUS   Question ❶ a) requires children to make a 2-digit number (45) using counters and ten frames. This will help them see how many complete tens and how many ones make 45. They then build on this in question ❶ b), which is designed to encourage them to use the 'make 10' strategy to add on a further 7. It is important that children see that five of the additional chairs can be used to fill the fifth ten frame from question ❶ a).

ANSWERS

Question ❶ a): There are 45 stacked chairs.

Question ❶ b): 45 + 7 = 45 + 5 + 2 = 52

There are 52 chairs in total.

Adding a 2-digit number and a 1-digit number ❶

Discover

❶ a) Use ◯ and ⊞ to show the chairs that are stacked. How many stacked chairs are there?

   b) How many chairs are there in total?

84

PUPIL TEXTBOOK 2A PAGE 84

Share

WAYS OF WORKING   Whole class teacher led

ASK

- *Question ❶ b): Would it be useful to partition the 1-digit number?*
- *Question ❶ b): Why is it better not to count on in ones 7 times?*

IN FOCUS   Make sure children understand what the three different representations used in question ❶ b) each show, and how they are linked. In particular, children need to understand how the ten frames can help them see how to partition the 1-digit number.

Share

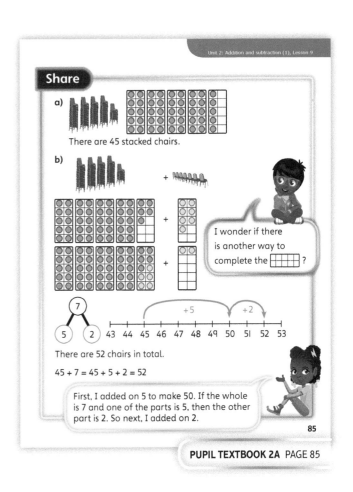

a) There are 45 stacked chairs.

b) *I wonder if there is another way to complete the ⊞?*

There are 52 chairs in total.

45 + 7 = 45 + 5 + 2 = 52

First, I added on 5 to make 50. If the whole is 7 and one of the parts is 5, then the other part is 2. So next, I added on 2.

85

PUPIL TEXTBOOK 2A PAGE 85

Think together

Think together

WAYS OF WORKING Whole class teacher led (I do, We do, You do)

ASK

• Question ❶ : *What is the same and what is different about the ten frames and the number line?*
• *How can you decide what to partition the 1-digit number into?*

IN FOCUS As before, make sure children understand what the three different representations used in question ❶ each show and how they are linked. Can children explain why 8 is partitioned into 6 and something?

Question ❸ tests children's understanding of the '=' sign. Check they know that it means 'the same as' and does not simply indicate than an answer follows it. This is particularly important here because each number sentence contains two equals signs: children need to understand that all three parts within each number sentence are equal.

STRENGTHEN Children can continue to use ten frames to see how many more they need to add on to the starting number to make 10. To save time, you could give them pictures of completed ten frames to represent the tens in the starting number, but children should make the ones themselves before adding on the 1-digit number.

DEEPEN Challenge children to write several number sentences to represent a calculation, partitioning the 1-digit number in as many different ways as possible (for example, 42 + 9 can be written as 42 + 8 + 1 = 51, but also 42 + 7 + 2 = 51, 42 + 6 + 3 = 51, and so on). Doing this will both highlight and increase children's flexibility of number.

ASSESSMENT CHECKPOINT Ask children if they can explain why they have chosen to partition the 1-digit number as they have. This will allow you to assess their recall of number bonds and their ability to apply them to different concepts.

ANSWERS

Question ❶ : 14 + 8 = 14 + 6 + 2 = 22
There are 22 ▯▯ in total.

Question ❷ : 27 + 8 = 27 + 3 + 5 = 35
There are 35 ☆ in total.

Question ❸ a): 42 + 9 = 42 + 8 + 1 = 51

Question ❸ b): 48 + 7 = 48 + 2 + 5 = 55

Question ❸ c): 29 + 7 = 29 + 1 + 6 = 36

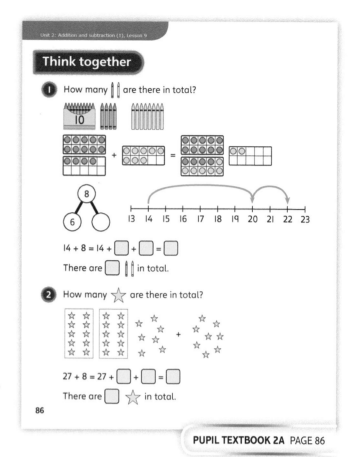

PUPIL TEXTBOOK 2A PAGE 86

PUPIL TEXTBOOK 2A PAGE 87

Practice

WAYS OF WORKING Independent thinking

IN FOCUS The **Practice** questions provide progressively less scaffolding for children. Question ② requires children to identify for themselves how to partition the number 5, given that they need to add it to 18. Question ③ requires them to decide first which number they need to partition and then how to partition it.

STRENGTHEN Encourage children to continue to use ten frames to help them see what to partition the 1-digit number into. They might be able to draw a pictorial representation of the ten frames as a step on from using concrete resources to make the number.

DEEPEN Present children with a number sentence with one unknown, such as 67 + ? = 75. Can children apply what they have learnt in this lesson to calculate the unknown? Can they work backwards to see that 75 − 5 = 70 and 70 − 3 = 67, and therefore that the missing number is 8? Help children make the link by encouraging them to show their working on a number line.

ASSESSMENT CHECKPOINT Assess whether children can explain why they have chosen to partition the 1-digit number in the way that they have and how this helps their mental calculation. Ensure children are not simply counting on in 1s to find the solution.

ANSWERS Answers for the **Practice** part of the lesson appear in the separate **Practice and Reflect answer guide**.

Reflect

WAYS OF WORKING Independent thinking

IN FOCUS By the **Reflect** part of the lesson, children should be able to visualise the ten frames and identify that 6 needs to be added to 54 to 'make 10'; the remaining 2 can then be added to 60. If any children struggle with this, ask: *If you visualise the number 54, what can you see? How can this help you with your mental calculation?*

ASSESSMENT CHECKPOINT Check to see what explanations children give and how comfortable they are at describing them.

ANSWERS Answers for the **Reflect** part of the lesson appear in the separate **Practice and Reflect answer guide**.

After the lesson ⏸

- Were children able to identify the correct way to partition the 1-digit number?
- Did children continue to count in 1s on their fingers to calculate the answer?
- Do they understand the limitations this method will have when they start working with larger numbers?

115

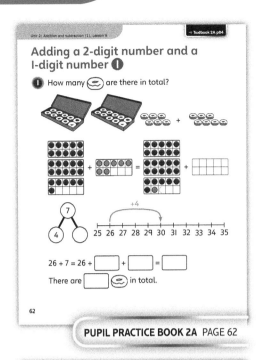

PUPIL PRACTICE BOOK 2A PAGE 62

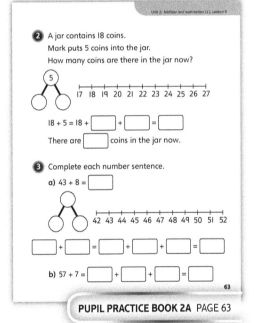

PUPIL PRACTICE BOOK 2A PAGE 63

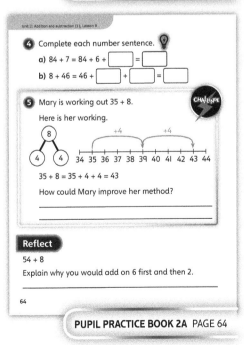

PUPIL PRACTICE BOOK 2A PAGE 64

Adding a 2-digit number and a 1-digit number ❷

Learning focus

In this lesson, children build on what they learned in the previous lesson, comparing different methods for addition and focusing on the column method.

Small steps

→ Previous step: Adding a 2-digit number and a 1-digit number (1)

→ **This step: Adding a 2-digit number and a 1-digit number (2)**

→ Next step: Subtracting a 1-digit number from a 2-digit number (1)

NATIONAL CURRICULUM LINKS

Year 2 Number – Addition and Subtraction

- Add and subtract numbers using concrete objects, pictorial representations, and mentally, including: a 2-digit number and ones.
- Solve problems with addition and subtraction: using concrete objects and pictorial representations, including those involving numbers, quantities and measures.

ASSESSING MASTERY

Children can see similarities and differences between different methods to calculate the same answer. Children can use their knowledge of number bonds to help them reach their answer, and can describe the steps that are represented pictorially, or that they are completing with resources.

COMMON MISCONCEPTIONS

As in the previous lesson, children may count on in 1s rather than using their understanding of number to find the answer, or they may partition the 1-digit number in a way that does not aid their mental calculation. Challenge these misconceptions by asking children to explain what they are doing in full sentences.

When using the column method, children may set their work out incorrectly and so add the incorrect values. Ask:
- *Have you made sure the ones digits in each number are above each other?*

STRENGTHENING UNDERSTANDING

Provide ten frames to consolidate the previous lesson's learning and highlight the concept of bridging 10 clearly. Display sets of complementary numbers for each number within 20 to strengthen children's understanding of number bonds within 20.

GOING DEEPER

Encourage children to make links between addition and subtraction and begin to see them as inverse operations. The use of the number line will help to highlight this concept. Ask children what moving in the opposite direction on a number line would show.

KEY LANGUAGE

In lesson: adding, +, =, digit, ones, exchange, tens, number line, total, columns, subtract, bonds

Other language to be used by the teacher: partition

STRUCTURES AND REPRESENTATIONS

Ten frames, column method, bar model, part-whole model, number line

RESOURCES

Mandatory: counters (double-sided or two colours, if possible), ten frames, Base 10 equipment, place value charts

Optional: sets of complementary numbers for each number within 20, 1–100 number line, pictures of completed ten frames

 In the eTextbook of this lesson, you will find interactive links to a selection of teaching tools.

Before you teach

- Did you observe any misconceptions in the previous lesson that need to be addressed during this lesson?

Discover

WAYS OF WORKING Pair work

ASK

- *What calculation(s) did you complete mentally?*
- *Did these additions require exchange?*
- *What resource could you use to highlight that you needed to exchange?*

IN FOCUS Question ① requires children to carry out three additions, each involving a 2-digit number and a 1-digit number. You could begin by reviewing the 'make 10' strategy covered in the previous lesson, and explain that in this lesson you are going to focus on the column method.

ANSWERS

Question ① a): △ team now has 32 points.

Question ① b): 31 + 4 = 35, 27 + 6 = 33

▢ scored most points.

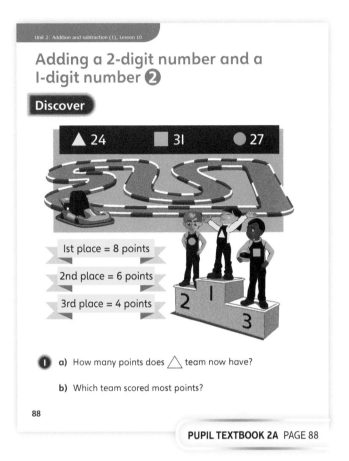

Share

WAYS OF WORKING Whole class teacher led

ASK

- *Question ① a): The calculation is represented using ten frames and Base 10 equipment. What is the same and what is different about the two representations?*
- *Question ① a): Which representation more clearly shows that exchange is needed?*
- *What do the digits in the column method represent?*

IN FOCUS Discuss what is the same and what is different about the two types of representation used in question ① a). Children should understand that both show that exchange is needed, but in different ways. Make sure they also understand how each method links to the numbers written within the column method.

DEEPEN Ask children to compare the scores of the different teams using > and < (or ask them to complete ? > ? > ?). They could use the team names and/or numbers.

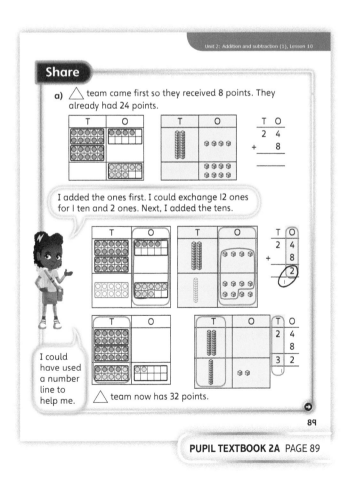

Think together

WAYS OF WORKING Whole class teacher led (I do, We do, You do)

ASK

- Question **1** : *Why does Dexter start with the ones?*
- Question **2** : *What operation do you need to use to find the unknown quantities in the bar model and part-whole model?*

IN FOCUS Talk through the use of the column method in question **1** with children. Agree that it is important to follow Dexter's advice and discuss why it is not possible to start with the tens.

Question **3** looks in detail at different ways of adding on numbers. You could use it as the basis of a discussion about which is the most efficient method and when you might choose not to use a place value grid.

STRENGTHEN Children who are finding this concept difficult should continue to use concrete resources to increase their understanding.

DEEPEN When children have completed the bar model and part-whole representations in question **2** , they could write all the possible calculations shown by each representation, consolidating their work from Lesson 2.

ASSESSMENT CHECKPOINT Check whether children are counting on in 1s or using known number facts to find the total number of 1s. Also check to see if children can explain why 14 ones is the same as 1 ten and 4 ones.

ANSWERS

Question **1** :

```
    T   O
    3   7
+       6
_____
        3
        ₁
```

There are 43 🖼 in total.

Question **2** a): 56

Question **2** b): 82

Question **3** : There will be a variety of answers here depending on children's own explanations.

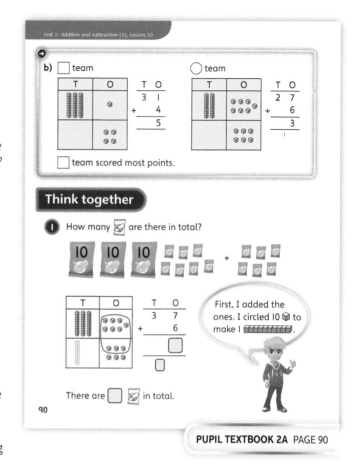

PUPIL TEXTBOOK 2A PAGE 90

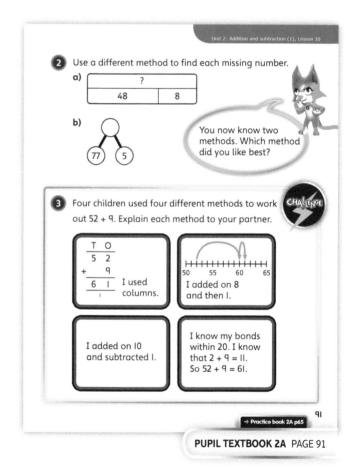

PUPIL TEXTBOOK 2A PAGE 91

Practice

WAYS OF WORKING Independent thinking

IN FOCUS Question **4** requires children to think carefully about what the incomplete column method shows and to work backwards. Draw children's attention to the carried '1' in part a) and ask: *What do you need to add to 4 to make 11?*

STRENGTHEN Encourage children to use concrete resources if they need them to understand what they are doing. Some children may benefit from using a number line to check the results of the column method.

You could also give children sentence scaffolds to help them verbalise the key steps needed to calculate the answer (for example: ? ones + ? ones = ? ones. Ten ones is the same and 1 ten, so ? ones = 1 ten and ? ones).

DEEPEN Before children tackle question **5**, ask: *What combinations of numbers require exchange? What combinations of numbers do not require exchange? How do you know?*

ASSESSMENT CHECKPOINT Check whether children are simply following a procedure to calculate the unknown quantities within the column method or if they fully understand the concept of what they are doing. Children should be able to explain key steps (for example: 6 ones + 7 ones = 13 ones. 10 ones is the same as 1 ten, so 13 ones is the same as 1 ten and 3 ones).

ANSWERS Answers for the **Practice** part of the lesson appear in the separate **Practice and Reflect answer guide**.

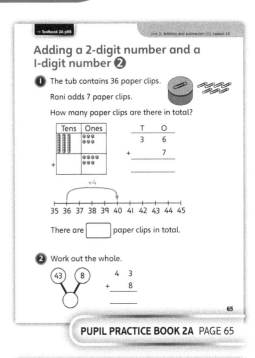

PUPIL PRACTICE BOOK 2A PAGE 65

PUPIL PRACTICE BOOK 2A PAGE 66

Reflect

WAYS OF WORKING Independent thinking

IN FOCUS Children should independently complete the calculation in the **Reflect** part of the lesson, using both the 'make 10' strategy (using the number line to help them) and the column method. You could then ask them to explain the two different methods to their partner or the whole class. Which method do they think is more efficient?

ASSESSMENT CHECKPOINT Assess the quality of children's explanations, noticing whether they are more confident using one method than the other. Children who have mastered the key concepts will have the flexibility to use either method and explain the merits of each.

ANSWERS Answers for the **Reflect** part of the lesson appear in the separate **Practice and Reflect answer guide**.

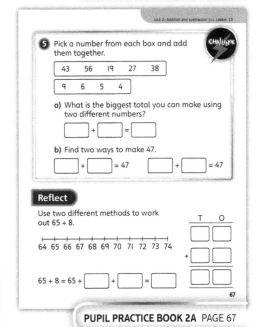

PUPIL PRACTICE BOOK 2A PAGE 67

After the lesson

- Are children secure with the concepts within the column method?
- Are children confident using known number facts within this process?

Subtracting a 1-digit number from a 2-digit number

Learning focus

In this lesson, children will subtract a 1-digit number from a 2-digit number, building on what they learned when subtracting ones, and extending their understanding to bridge 10. Children will use ten frames to understand this concept.

Small steps

→ Previous step: Adding a 2-digit number and a 1-digit number (2)

→ **This step: Subtracting a 1-digit number from a 2-digit number (1)**

→ Next step: Subtracting a 1-digit number from a 2-digit number (2)

NATIONAL CURRICULUM LINKS

Year 2 Number – Addition and Subtraction

- Add and subtract numbers using concrete objects, pictorial representations, and mentally, including: a 2-digit number and ones.
- Solve problems with addition and subtraction: using concrete objects and pictorial representations, including those involving numbers, quantities and measures.

ASSESSING MASTERY

Children can subtract ones from a 2-digit number, making links to previous learning and applying number bonds to bridge 10. Children can choose the appropriate way to partition the 1-digit number.

COMMON MISCONCEPTIONS

Children may confuse addition from the previous lessons with subtraction in this lesson. As a result, they may simply add the number of 1s rather than subtract them. Discuss the context of each question to help children understand the concept of subtraction, and make sure they identify the subtraction sign in each calculation.

Children may count back in 1s to find the solution rather than applying their understanding of number bonds. Ask:
- *Have you used the most efficient method to find the answer?*

STRENGTHENING UNDERSTANDING

Give children double-sided counters and ten frames. They can turn over counters as they 'subtract' them to clearly see the partitioned parts of the 1-digit number within the previously complete ten frame and the partially filled frame.

GOING DEEPER

Building on the **Going deeper** task in the previous lesson, children could write calculations that are the inverse of each other, including the parts of the partitioned number. For example, if children have written 35 – 5 – 1 = 29, they can also write 29 + 1 + 5 = 35. Challenge them to explain the links between the two calculations, using a number line to help them.

KEY LANGUAGE

In lesson: subtracting, –, =, digit, whole, part, number sentence

Other language used to be by the teacher: partition, ones, exchange, tens

STRUCTURES AND REPRESENTATIONS

Ten frames, number line, part-whole model

RESOURCES

Mandatory: counters (double-sided, if possible), ten frame, Base 10 equipment, blank part-whole model

Optional: number cards

 In the eTextbook of this lesson, you will find interactive links to a selection of teaching tools.

Before you teach

- How can you improve children's fluency within this lesson?
- Could you reward children who use their knowledge of number bonds rather than counting back in 1s?

Discover

Unit 2: Addition and subtraction (1), Lesson 11

WAYS OF WORKING Pair work

ASK

- Question **1** b): *What could you use to represent the numbers in the calculation?*

IN FOCUS Question **1** a) requires children to represent the 35 children using ten frames and counters, and using Base 10 equipment. In question **1** b), they then subtract 6 children: this is more easily done using the ten frames, as children can take one counter from an initially completed ten frame; using the Base 10 equipment requires children to exchange a ten for 10 ones.

ANSWERS

Question **1** a):

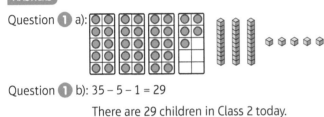

Question **1** b): 35 – 5 – 1 = 29

There are 29 children in Class 2 today.

Subtracting a 1-digit number from a 2-digit number **1**

Discover

1 a) Represent the 35 children in Class 2 using ⬤◯◯◯◯ and 🪵 .

b) Today 6 children are away.

How many children are in Class 2 today?

☐ – ☐ = ☐

92

Share

WAYS OF WORKING Whole class teacher led

ASK

- Question **1** b): *How does the procedure completed with the ten frames link to the number line?*
- Question **1** b): *Why has 6 been partitioned into 5 and 1?*
- Question **1** b): *Which number bonds are being used within this question?*

IN FOCUS Use question **1** b) to discuss with children different ways in which they could complete the calculation. Make sure children understand the links between the ten frames and how the stages of the calculation are shown on the number line. You could also discuss how they would subtract 6 from the Base 10 equipment, and how this is the same as and different from using the ten frames.

Share

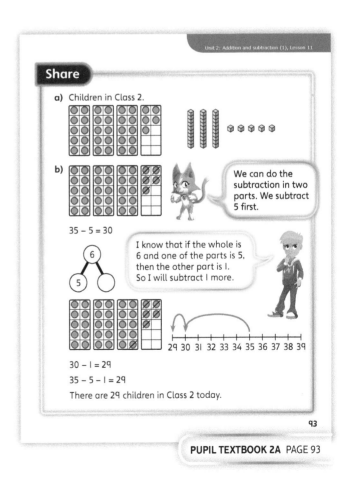

a) Children in Class 2.

b) We can do the subtraction in two parts. We subtract 5 first.

35 – 5 = 30

I know that if the whole is 6 and one of the parts is 5, then the other part is 1. So I will subtract 1 more.

30 – 1 = 29

35 – 5 – 1 = 29

There are 29 children in Class 2 today.

93

Think together

WAYS OF WORKING Whole class teacher led (I do, We do, You do)

ASK
- *What decisions are you making when deciding how to partition the 1-digit number?*
- *Are you ensuring that you are being efficient with your calculations?*

IN FOCUS Question ③ requires children to subtract 7 from four different starting numbers. This means they need to partition 7 in four different ways, subtracting a different number each time to get back to a multiple of 10. Discuss what is the same and what is different about the four calculations, and help children see the link between the starting number and how they partition the 7.

STRENGTHEN Children who find the concept difficult should continue to work using ten frames as well, as this clearly shows why one ten needs to be exchanged for 10 ones.

DEEPEN Ask children to explain in writing what is the same and what is different about the four calculations in question ③. This will allow them to demonstrate their deepening understanding using correct mathematical vocabulary.

ASSESSMENT CHECKPOINT Assess whether children can explain the strategy that they are using, how this uses their knowledge of number bonds and why their method is efficient.

ANSWERS

Question ① :

 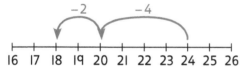

$24 - 6 = 24 - 4 - 2 = 18$

There are 18 children with their hand still up.

Question ② :

 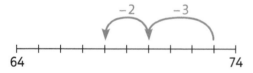

$73 - 3 - 2 = 68$

$73 - 5 = 68$

Question ③ a): $34 - 7 = 34 - 4 - 3 = 27$

Question ③ b): $46 - 7 = 46 - 6 - 1 = 39$

Question ③ c): $55 - 7 = 55 - 5 - 2 = 48$

Question ③ d): $41 - 7 = 41 - 1 - 6 = 34$

PUPIL TEXTBOOK 2A PAGE 94

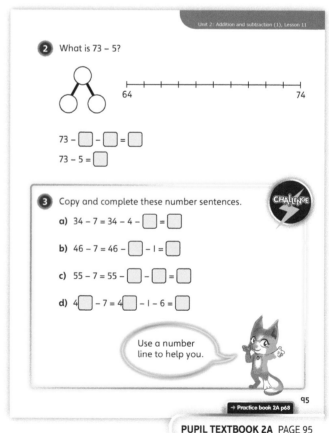

PUPIL TEXTBOOK 2A PAGE 95

Practice

WAYS OF WORKING Independent thinking

IN FOCUS Question **1** represents the starting number using ten frames, but this support is removed in later questions.

In question **2** , the scaffold within the part-whole model is also gradually removed.

Question **3** is presented in the abstract and requires children to apply their understanding to complete the missing values.

STRENGTHEN Children who find the concept difficult should continue to work with concrete resources. If they are struggling to identify how many 1s they need to subtract to get to the nearest 10, give them practice by showing them number cards and asking them to quickly recall how many more 1s the number has than the nearest 10.

DEEPEN In question **4** , Tim works out 27 – 9 by subtracting 10 and then adding 1. Children could explore whether this works in other situations (such as with different starting numbers). Can they explain why it works?

ASSESSMENT CHECKPOINT Question **3** will highlight whether children understand the choices that they have been making. As the missing values are in different locations within the number sentences, children need to be flexible about the order in which they work. Ask children to explain what they did in order to assess the depth of their understanding.

ANSWERS Answers for the **Practice** part of the lesson appear in the separate **Practice and Reflect answer guide**.

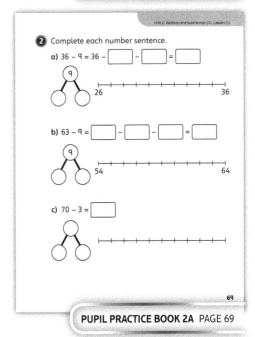

PUPIL PRACTICE BOOK 2A PAGE 68

Reflect

WAYS OF WORKING Whole class

IN FOCUS In the **Reflect** part of the lesson, discuss what Hanna has partitioned 9 into and how effective this is. Hanna gets the correct answer, but children should see that it is not an effective strategy. Hanna's method is likely to result in mistakes as the nearest 10 has not been made and therefore the mental calculation is more difficult.

ASSESSMENT CHECKPOINT Assess children's ability to reflect on the method used, including its efficiency and effectiveness. Can they suggest a more suitable method?

ANSWERS Answers for the **Reflect** part of the lesson appear in the separate **Practice and Reflect answer guide**.

After the lesson

- Did children recognise when their method was not efficient? Were they able to use a more efficient method after this reflection?
- Are there any underlying misconceptions that should be addressed before the next lesson?

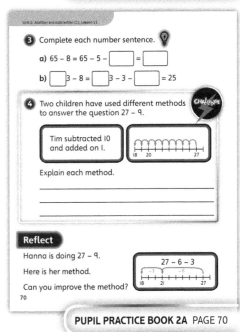

PUPIL PRACTICE BOOK 2A PAGE 70

Subtracting a 1-digit number from a 2-digit number ②

Learning focus

In this lesson, children will again subtract a 1-digit number from a 2-digit number, but will focus on using the column method.

Small steps

→ Previous step: Subtracting a 1-digit number from a 2-digit number (1)

→ **This step: Subtracting a 1-digit number from a 2-digit number (2)**

→ Next step: Adding two 2-digit numbers (1)

NATIONAL CURRICULUM LINKS

Year 2 Number – Addition and Subtraction

- Add and subtract numbers using concrete objects, pictorial representations, and mentally, including: a 2-digit number and ones.
- Solve problems with addition and subtraction: applying their increasing knowledge of mental and written methods.

ASSESSING MASTERY

Children can make links between the number line and ten frame and the column method. Children can verbalise and explain the steps taken within the column method.

COMMON MISCONCEPTIONS

Children may write the number they are subtracting above the starting number. Prompt children to always write the larger number at the top.

Children may write the 1-digit number in the tens column, rather than the ones column. Ask:
- *Have you checked that each digit is in the correct column, based on its place value?*

Faced with a subtraction that requires exchange, children may instead incorrectly subtract the smaller number of ones from the larger number of ones. Give children plenty of practice in making the starting number using concrete resources, and physically exchanging a ten for 10 ones.

STRENGTHENING UNDERSTANDING

To strengthen understanding of the concept of exchange, ask children to make a 2-digit number (for example, 50) using Base 10 equipment. Then ask them to roll a dice, and take away each number they roll from their equipment. When they do not have enough ones they will need to exchange a ten for 10 ones so they can take the correct amount away.

GOING DEEPER

Ask children to predict whether calculations require exchange or not and to justify their opinion. Similarly, ask children to write all the possible subtractions for a given starting number that do and do not require exchange. (For example, give them the calculation $17 - ? = ?$. Can they identify the seven possibilities that do not require exchange and the two that do?)

KEY LANGUAGE

In lesson: subtracting, –, =, digit, one, exchange, tens

Other language to be used by the teacher: larger

STRUCTURES AND REPRESENTATIONS

Column method, ten frames

RESOURCES

Mandatory: Base 10 equipment, place value chart

Optional: dice, ten frames, double-sided counters, digit cards

 In the eTextbook of this lesson, you will find interactive links to a selection of teaching tools.

Before you teach

- Are children able to access this learning, or would it be more worthwhile to re-teach the previous lesson to consolidate the content?
- How can you help children make the best links between the different resources used?

Discover

ASK

- Question ❶ a): *Are there enough single straws to share between all of the cups?*
- Question ❶ a): *What does Amy need to do in order to give the teddy bears a straw each?*

IN FOCUS Question ❶ requires children to carry out two subtractions, each time subtracting a 1-digit number from a 2-digit number. You could begin by reviewing the strategies covered in the previous lesson, and explaining that in this lesson you are going to focus on using Base 10 equipment and the column method.

ANSWERS

Question ❶ a): Amy has 18 ⟍⟍ left.

Question ❶ b): Amy gave 9 ⟍⟍ to Liam.

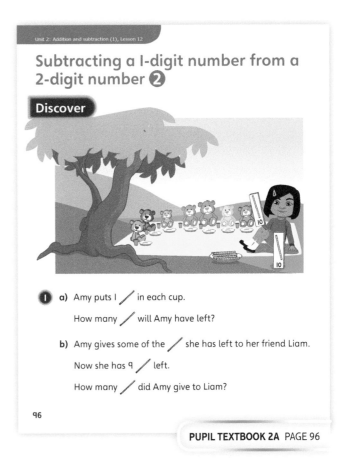

Subtracting a 1-digit number from a 2-digit number ❷

Discover

❶ a) Amy puts 1 ⟍ in each cup.

How many ⟍ will Amy have left?

b) Amy gives some of the ⟍ she has left to her friend Liam.

Now she has 9 ⟍ left.

How many ⟍ did Amy give to Liam?

96

PUPIL TEXTBOOK 2A PAGE 96

Share

WAYS OF WORKING Whole class teacher led

ASK

- *What is 1 ten the same as?*
- *Why do you need to exchange 1 ten for 10 ones to be able to subtract 7 from the total number of straws?*

IN FOCUS Question ❶ a) makes explicit links between what children do with the resources and what is recorded in the column method. Encourage children to notice what is the same about both representations.

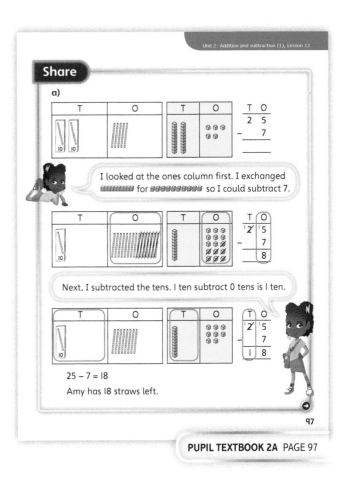

Share

a)

I looked at the ones column first. I exchanged ▭ for ▭▭▭▭▭▭▭▭▭ so I could subtract 7.

Next, I subtracted the tens. 1 ten subtract 0 tens is 1 ten.

25 − 7 = 18
Amy has 18 straws left.

97

PUPIL TEXTBOOK 2A PAGE 97

Think together

WAYS OF WORKING Whole class teacher led (I do, We do, You do)

ASK

• *What number bond did you use to help you with this calculation?*
• *Was the method you used efficient? Why / why not?*

IN FOCUS Question ❶ guides children through a subtraction, again using Base 10 equipment and the column method, while question ❷ allows them to choose their own method. Encourage children to verbalise the steps of their working out in both cases.

STRENGTHEN Put children in pairs: give one child Base 10 equipment and the other a pencil and paper. Ask the first child to carry out a subtraction using the equipment: at each stage, the first child should explain to their partner what they are doing and the second child should then write down what has been done.

DEEPEN Give children three different digit cards and ask them to use them to make as many different subtraction sentences as possible. Then sort the calculations into two groups: those that require exchange and those that do not. (For example, using the digit cards 3, 4 and 5, children can make six different subtraction sentences; three, such as 34 – 5, require exchange and three, such as 35 – 4, do not.)

ASSESSMENT CHECKPOINT Use questions ❶ and ❷ to assess the security of children's verbal explanations, and hence their understanding.

ANSWERS

Question ❶ : 43 – 8 = 35

There are 35 bread rolls left.

Question ❷ : 65 – 9 = 56

Question ❸ : The digits in the calculations are the same and both calculations are subtractions.

The starting number (the whole) is different and the amount subtracted is also different, so they give different answers.

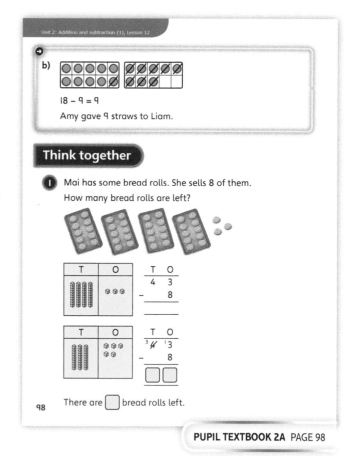

PUPIL TEXTBOOK 2A PAGE 98

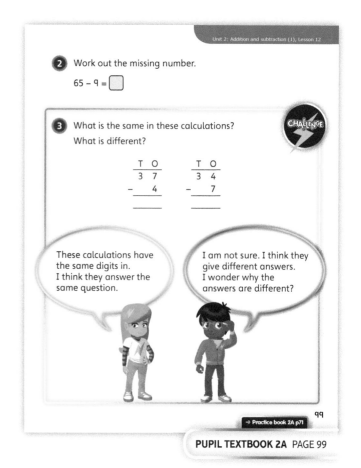

PUPIL TEXTBOOK 2A PAGE 99

126

Practice

WAYS OF WORKING Independent thinking

IN FOCUS Questions ❶ and ❷ are modelled using pictorial representations of Base 10 equipment, to support children in continuing to make links between the resources and the column method. In question ❸ a) only the starting number is represented, and in subsequent questions this support is withdrawn.

STRENGTHEN Encourage children to use resources, working in pairs, to strengthen their understanding of the concepts. Some children may benefit from using ten frames and counters to consolidate their understanding of subtraction without the column method.

DEEPEN Display a number sentence with several unknowns, such as ?4 – 7 = ?. Ask children to complete it in as many different ways as possible. Agree that there is only one possible answer for one of the boxes and discuss why this is.

ASSESSMENT CHECKPOINT Assess whether children are making links between the representations and the column method. They should be able to explain what every number represents, why they cross numbers out and what this represents.

ANSWERS Answers for the **Practice** part of the lesson appear in the separate **Practice and Reflect answer guide**.

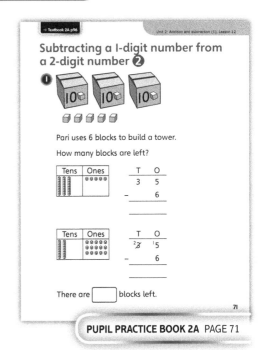

PUPIL PRACTICE BOOK 2A PAGE 71

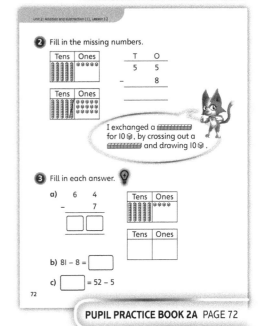

PUPIL PRACTICE BOOK 2A PAGE 72

Reflect

WAYS OF WORKING Whole class

IN FOCUS In the **Reflect** part of the lesson, children should demonstrate the different methods they have learned to answer the question. They should listen to each other's responses and assess the efficiency of each method suggested.

ASSESSMENT CHECKPOINT Assess children on their ability to use a variety of different methods to answer the same question and to critique the methods presented by others.

ANSWERS Answers for the **Reflect** part of the lesson appear in the separate **Practice and Reflect answer guide**.

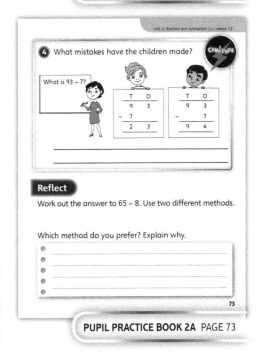

PUPIL PRACTICE BOOK 2A PAGE 73

After the lesson

- Which resource did children find easiest to link to the column method?
- Are children secure in their knowledge of the column method?

End of unit check

> **Don't forget the Power Maths Unit Assessment Grid on p26.**

WAYS OF WORKING Group work – adult led

IN FOCUS These questions assess the links that children can make between numbers and how they can use known facts to calculate unknowns. Children must understand the links between addition and subtraction and when each operation is needed as a result of the context that they are provided with.

Think!

WAYS OF WORKING Pairs or small groups

IN FOCUS This question allows children to identify errors that have been made within an addition calculation.

Children should be able to use mathematical language to describe where the errors have occurred, rather than just stating what the correct answer is.

Children's ability to explain the mistake that each child has made will ascertain children's security in the different methods that could be used for addition calculations.

ANSWERS AND COMMENTARY Children who have mastered this unit will be able to relate each number in a calculation to what it represents within a given context. Children will be able to use a variety of manipulatives to represent addition and subtraction and use these alongside the column method. Children will also be fluent at recalling and applying their number bonds within 20 to addition and subtraction calculations.

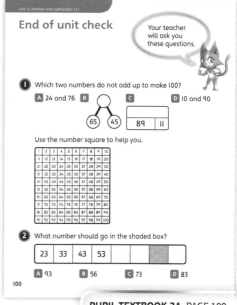

PUPIL TEXTBOOK 2A PAGE 100

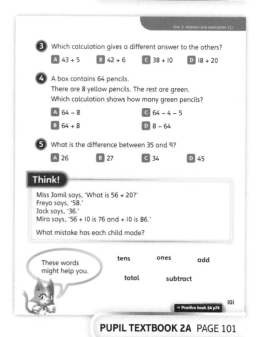

PUPIL TEXTBOOK 2A PAGE 101

Q	A	WRONG ANSWERS AND MISCONCEPTIONS	STRENGTHENING UNDERSTANDING
1	B	Children should be able to use the 100 square to prove why A, C and D are correct.	Children who are still finding it difficult to identify which operation links with the context that they are provided with should be given the opportunity to create their own maths stories for the different operations, or sort problems into either subtraction or addition categories. Children should also practise writing all possible calculations from a complete part-whole diagram (fact family), understanding that the equals sign can occur in different places and means 'is the same as'.
2	D	A suggests they have counted on too many tens. B suggests they have not understood that the numbers increase by 10 each time and have instead counted on in ones .	
3	D	Children should recognise that all answers have 8 ones, but that the total of 1 ten and 2 tens is 3 tens so D is different to the others which all have 4 tens.	
4	A	C suggests they have identified the make 10 strategy, counting back from 64 to 60 by subtracting 4, but have then subtracted the incorrect second amount.	
5	A	C and D both suggest that the child does not understand the concept of difference and its link to subtraction.	

My journal

WAYS OF WORKING Independent thinking

ANSWERS AND COMMENTARY The mistake that Freya has made is that she has added on 2 more ones rather than 2 more tens. The mistake that Jack has made is he has subtracted 2 tens from 56, rather than adding them. The mistake that Mira has made is that 56 + 10 does not equal 76. She should have added 10 to make 66 and another 10 to make 76, or should have added 20 in one step: 56 + 20 = 76.

Encourage children to use the mathematical vocabulary they have been provided with to explain the mistake that each child has made, rather than simply saying 'Freya is wrong because 56 + 20 is 76 and she said 58.'

PUPIL PRACTICE BOOK 2A PAGE 75

Power check

WAYS OF WORKING Independent thinking

ASK

- *How well do you know your number bonds within 20?*
- *How confidently do you use these within additions and subtractions?*

Power puzzle

WAYS OF WORKING Pair work or small group

IN FOCUS It is possible to complete the Power puzzle by working sequentially through the problems. Children should be encouraged to record what they have calculated as they work, rather than trying to store this mentally. Children should also be encouraged to not complete the final stage until they have calculated all shapes.

ANSWERS AND COMMENTARY Children should count on from 63 to 68 to calculate 63 + **5** = 68. This could be shown on a number line.

Children then must apply what they have just calculated to form the calculation 5 + ? = 100. They should then count back from 100 to calculate 5 + **95** = 100.

22 + 50 = ?. Children could start from 22 and count on 5 jumps of 10 (22, 32, 42, 52, 62, **72**), or start at 50, count on 2 and then count on 2 jumps of 10 (this will be explored as a strategy in the next unit, but some children may already see how this is possible using their understanding of commutativity, place value and the 100 square).

72 – 5 = ?. Children should partition 5 into 2 and 3 and count back from 72 to 70 and then 70 to 67. This could be displayed on a number line.

Shapes from smallest to largest: star (5), triangle (67), square (72), diamond (95).

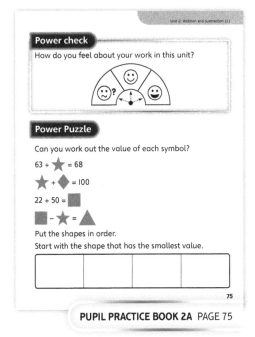

PUPIL PRACTICE BOOK 2A PAGE 75

After the unit ⏸

- Could children spot the deliberate mistakes? Were they able to identify if they make similar mistakes in their own work?
- What are the most common misconceptions that still remain in the class that must be addressed before the content becomes more difficult in Unit 3?

Strengthen and **Deepen** activities for this unit can be found in the *Power Maths* online subscription.

Unit 3
Addition and subtraction ②

Mastery Expert tip! "It is important for children to make links between different areas of maths and understand the progression of what they are learning. Children should view this unit as an opportunity for them to build on what they have previously learnt and extend their thinking to new content."

Don't forget to watch the Unit 3 video!

WHY THIS UNIT IS IMPORTANT

This unit directly builds upon what children have learnt in Unit 2 and provides an opportunity for what they have understood to be applied to larger numbers. Children must understand this progression and see the importance of applying this learning, rather than seeing larger numbers as a different area of maths and therefore using inefficient methods as a result.

Within this unit children will progress to addition and subtraction involving two 2-digit numbers, again representing the steps within these calculations visually with different resources. Children will use the column method as a way to represent the mental calculation steps, but not see this as the only method for calculation.

Children continue to use known number facts within mental calculations and use their understanding of the inverse as a way to check their calculations. The final stage of children's learning allows the bar model to be used to represent a word problem, to allow children to self-identify the operation needed to complete the calculation.

WHERE THIS UNIT FITS

→ Unit 2: Addition and subtraction (1)

→ **Unit 3: Addition and subtraction (2)**

→ Unit 4: Money

This unit directly builds upon the content of the previous unit and exposes children to addition and subtraction involving two 2-digit numbers, where the tens boundary is crossed and regrouping and exchange is required.

Before they start this unit, it is expected that children:

- know how to partition 2-digit numbers into tens and ones and place these onto a place value table
- understand the value of each digit within a 2-digit number and how these will change as a result of addition and subtraction
- know number bonds within 10 and 20 and how to apply these to mental addition and subtraction calculations.

ASSESSING MASTERY

Children who have mastered this unit will be able to differentiate between addition and subtraction problems, understanding how to represent the numbers provided within the context in different ways, using different resources. Children should be flexible with the methods they can use to calculate different problems depending on their complexity in order to work efficiently.

COMMON MISCONCEPTIONS	STRENGTHENING UNDERSTANDING	GOING DEEPER
Children may confuse addition and subtraction and find it difficult to change between the two operations.	Children should have increased opportunity to make numbers using different resources, and then be required to add and take away different quantities explaining the changes that occur to the number.	Use subtraction to check addition calculations and vice versa.
Children may try to complete problems using the column method procedurally and therefore make mistakes within the process because of a lack of understanding.	Providing children with number facts that are useful to complete equations will increase the likelihood of children understanding the importance of memorisation.	Challenge children to calculate unknown quantities in the most efficient way possible and justify how they have been efficient and accurate.

Unit 3: Addition and subtraction ❷

WAYS OF WORKING

Use these pages to introduce the unit focus to children as a whole class. You can use the characters to explore different ways of working.

STRUCTURES AND REPRESENTATIONS

Part-whole model: This model helps children understand that a number can be partitioned in different ways and how changing the ways that it is partitioned suits different mental calculations.

Number line: This model helps children to count on and back from a number. It is used to show jumps of different amounts to help children understand the 'make 10' strategy and the steps completed in the column method.

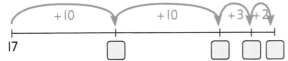

Column method: This column method shows a number broken down into parts based on the place value of its digits and how these digits change as a result of another number being added or subtracted to or from it.

```
  T O
  3 2
+ 1 4
  ———
```

Ten frame: The ten frame helps children make links to their number bonds to 10 and helps children to recognise the structure of numbers and what happens to this structure during addition and subtraction calculations.

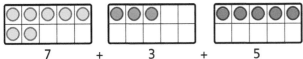

KEY LANGUAGE

There is some key language that children will need to know as a part of the learning in this unit:

→ part, whole and part-whole, partition

→ add, added, plus, total, altogether, sum, calculation, (+)

→ count, count on, count back, left, difference

→ subtract, take away, minus, (−)

→ exchange, compare, greater than, less than, more, less, (>), (<), regroup, represent

→ ones, tens, 10 more, 10 less, place value, column, 1-digit number, 2-digit number, bar model

→ number sentence, number bonds, known fact, fact family

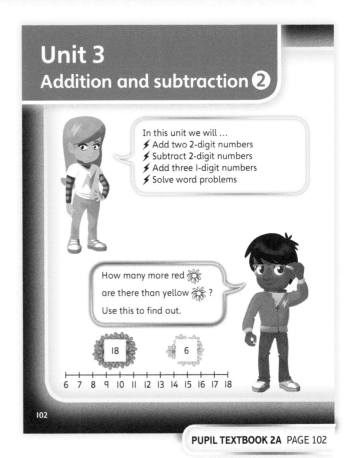

PUPIL TEXTBOOK 2A PAGE 102

PUPIL TEXTBOOK 2A PAGE 103

Adding two 2-digit numbers ❶

Learning focus

In this lesson, children will add together two 2-digit numbers using two different methods.

Small steps

→ Previous step: Subtracting a 1-digit number from a 2-digit number (2)
→ **This step: Adding two 2-digit numbers (1)**
→ Next step: Adding two 2-digit numbers (2)

NATIONAL CURRICULUM LINKS

Year 2 Number – Addition and Subtraction

- Add and subtract numbers using concrete objects, pictorial representations, and mentally, including: two 2-digit numbers.
- Solve problems with addition and subtraction: applying their increasing knowledge of mental and written methods.

ASSESSING MASTERY

Children can mentally add two 2-digit numbers in different ways and explain the merits of different methods. Children can use concrete manipulatives and pictorial representations to show their mental calculations and make links to previous answers to help calculate new ones where appropriate.

COMMON MISCONCEPTIONS

If children confuse the values of the digits within a number, ask:
- *What is the value of each digit in the number?*

When using the column method, children may have difficulty setting out the numbers. Throughout the lesson, highlight the importance of lining up the numbers based on their place value. Ask:
- *What is the value of each digit in the number?*

STRENGTHENING UNDERSTANDING

To strengthen children's place value understanding, provide opportunities for them to make 2-digit numbers with different resources, such as straws and Base 10 equipment. Ask children to compare what is the same and what is different. To consolidate the processes within the column method, place two numbers made using resources on a large place value grid and move them downwards into the large equal sign.

GOING DEEPER

Children may find different ways to complete additions with unknown digits, but a known sum. Challenge them to find all possible ways to satisfy the calculation.

KEY LANGUAGE

In lesson: add, +, =, total, more, tens, ones, exchange

Other language to be used by the teacher: column, sum, partition, is equal to, altogether

STRUCTURES AND REPRESENTATIONS

Place value grid, column method, part-whole model, number line

RESOURCES

Mandatory: Base 10 equipment, place value grid

Optional: straws, elastic bands, pictures of numbers made with Base 10 equipment, place value counters

 In the eTextbook of this lesson, you will find interactive links to a selection of teaching tools.

Before you teach ❶❶

- Can all children in the class partition 2-digit numbers into tens and ones?
- How can you ensure that children are using known number facts rather than simply counting in 1s?

Discover

WAYS OF WORKING Pair work

ASK

• Question **1** a): *Can you start with either number?*
• Question **1** a): *Which number would you choose to start with?*

IN FOCUS Question **1** a) allows children to explore different ways to find the total score, building on their prior learning. Ensure children understand that there are many different ways to find the total, but the answer is always the same. The different ways that children pose should be discussed, critiqued and celebrated.

ANSWERS

Question **1** a): The total score for the team wearing red checks is 46.

Question **1** b): The other plain green ▱ lands on 42.

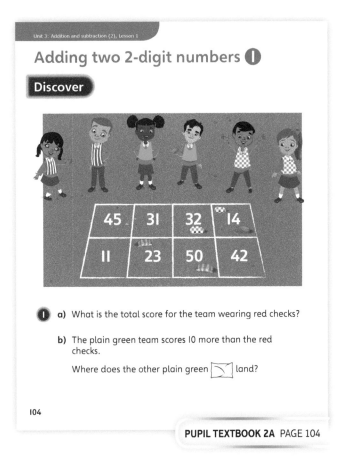

PUPIL TEXTBOOK 2A PAGE 104

Share

WAYS OF WORKING Whole class teacher led

ASK

• Question **1** a): *Who did it the same way as Flo? Who did it the same way as Astrid?*
• Question **1** a): *Can I start with 14 instead of 32?*
• Question **1** a): *Which method is more efficient?*

IN FOCUS Question **1** allows children to explore the commutative (addition can be done in any order) and associative (numbers can be split into different parts) properties of addition without explicitly using these terms. Discuss which way is more efficient, but ensure children understand both main methods as presented by Flo and Astrid.

DEEPEN Allowing children to see addition on a number line alongside the two methods will help secure their understanding of why the order the numbers are added, the choice of the starting number and the size of the parts that are added will not affect the total.

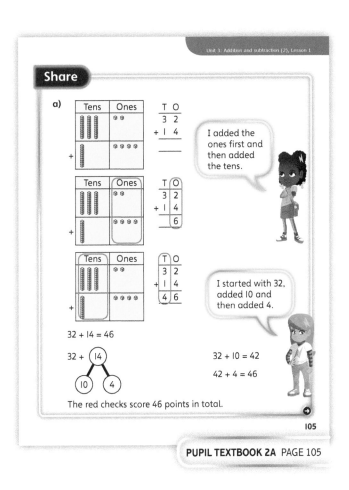

PUPIL TEXTBOOK 2A PAGE 105

Think together

Whole class teacher led (I do, We do, You do)

ASK

- Question ❶ : *How do you make the starting number 50 with Base 10 equipment? How many tens, how many ones?*
- Question ❶ : *Do you need to write the zero in the column method?*
- Question ❸ : *How is question 2 similar to question 3?*

IN FOCUS In question ❶ it is important to highlight the role of the zero in 50 as a place holder. Without necessary discussion, children may write the 5 tens in the ones column by mistake.

STRENGTHEN Use straws alongside the Base 10 equipment to help children understand the 'ten-ness' of the ten block. Asking children to bunch ten straws together to make the tens will consolidate their understanding that 10 ones are the same as one ten. This is important for future lessons where exchange is required.

DEEPEN Question ❸ allows children to make links to what they already know and become more efficient mathematicians as a result. Show the calculations from question ❷ and question ❸ alongside each other, in the abstract, as 31 + 11 = 42 and 32 + 11 = 43. Ask: *What is the same? What is different?* You can then ask further questions to assess deeper understanding, for example *What is 33 + 11?*

ASSESSMENT CHECKPOINT In question ❶ , check whether children are saying 5 + 2 = 7 or 5 tens + 2 tens = 7 tens. 5 + 2 = 7 may indicate a misconception that will hinder their progress. Ask children to repeat key number statements together to embed this key concept.

ANSWERS

Question ❶ : 50 + 23 = 73
The total score is 73.

Question ❷ : 31 + 10 = 41
41 + 1 = 42
31 + 11 = 42
The total score is 42.

Question ❸ : 32 + 10 = 42
42 + 1 = 43
The total score is 43.

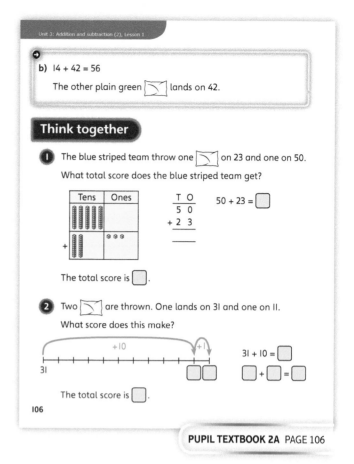

PUPIL TEXTBOOK 2A PAGE 106

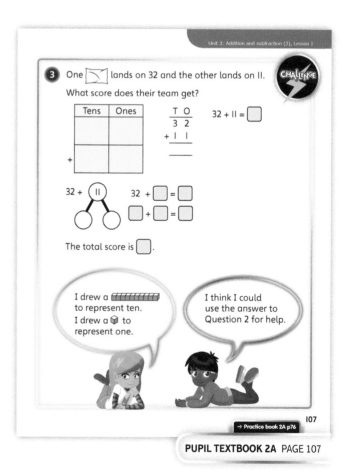

PUPIL TEXTBOOK 2A PAGE 107

Practice

WAYS OF WORKING Independent thinking

IN FOCUS In question ❶ the digits 5 and 3 are repeated but they have different values in each number. Ensure children can differentiate between the values of each digit. Question ❸ c) and ❸ f) require children to use their number sense and allow you to see if they are making links between the numbers they are given or just following a procedure to work each calculation out.

STRENGTHEN Strengthen understanding by continuing to work in the concrete alongside the abstract. Children could work in pairs, with one manipulating the Base 10 equipment and the other writing the abstract simultaneously.

DEEPEN Challenge children to find all possible answers to question ❺. Encourage them to work in a systematic way to ensure they find all the possibilities.

ASSESSMENT CHECKPOINT Assess whether children are successfully partitioning each 2-digit number and making or writing it correctly.

Check whether children are using the resources to calculate the answer rather than to understand the concept. Children should be using their number bonds to 10 rather than repeatedly counting the Base 10 blocks in ones.

ANSWERS Answers for the **Practice** part of the lesson appear in the separate **Practice and Reflect answer guide**.

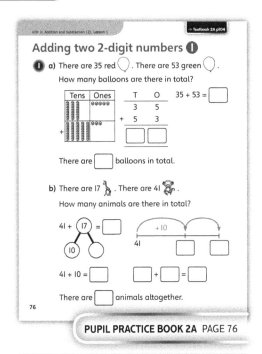

PUPIL PRACTICE BOOK 2A PAGE 76

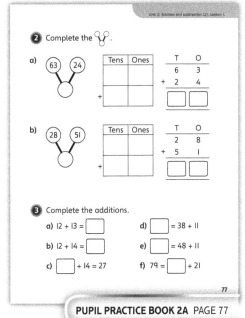

PUPIL PRACTICE BOOK 2A PAGE 77

Reflect

WAYS OF WORKING Independent thinking

IN FOCUS The **Reflect** part of the lesson requires children to explain how they would work out 25 + 62. Challenge them to justify their choice of method and discuss with the class which method is more efficient.

ASSESSMENT CHECKPOINT By this point in the lesson children should be confident explaining, either pictorially or orally, how to partition a 2-digit number. Children should be using their knowledge of number bonds within 10 to calculate the addition steps, rather than relying on using their fingers at each stage.

ANSWERS Answers for the **Reflect** part of the lesson appear in the separate **Practice and Reflect answer guide**.

After the lesson

- Did children rely on the concrete manipulatives throughout the lesson in order to calculate the correct answer?
- Did children use known number bonds or counting in 1s to calculate the answer?
- How confident were children at verbally explaining the method they chose, using appropriate mathematical vocabulary at each stage?

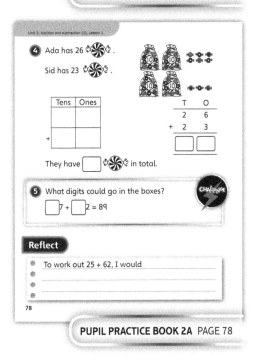

PUPIL PRACTICE BOOK 2A PAGE 78

135

Adding two 2-digit numbers ②

Learning focus

In this lesson, children will build on their previous knowledge of adding two 2-digit numbers and extend to where exchange is required.

Small steps

→ Previous step: Adding two 2-digit numbers (1)
→ **This step: Adding two 2-digit numbers (2)**
→ Next step: Subtracting a 2-digit number from another 2-digit number (1)

NATIONAL CURRICULUM LINKS

Year 2 Number – Addition and Subtraction

- Add and subtract numbers using concrete objects, pictorial representations, and mentally, including: two 2-digit numbers.
- Solve problems with addition and subtraction: applying their increasing knowledge of mental and written methods.

ASSESSING MASTERY

Children can mentally add two 2-digit numbers in different ways, where exchange is required, and explain the merits of different methods. Children can use concrete manipulatives and pictorial representations to show their mental calculations and make links to previous answers to help calculate new ones where appropriate.

COMMON MISCONCEPTIONS

Children may simply find the total number of ones, rather than exchanging, for example 1**4** + 1**7** = 2**11**. Ask:
- *What is the total number of ones? How many tens and ones is this equal to?*

Children may reach 9 ones and not add any more on. Ask:
- *What is 1 more than 9?*

Children may attempt to exchange, but then forget to add on the additional ten when finding the final total. Ask:
- *Have you included the ten that you exchanged for ones?*

STRENGTHENING UNDERSTANDING

Children should continue to work with concrete manipulatives to understand the concept of partitioning and exchanging. A place value grid that has the ones section within the equals sign split into nine parts (a reduced ten frame) may be useful to help children understand that 9 is the maximum digit that can be placed in this section.

GOING DEEPER

Encourage children to think about what number to start with when working mentally (the commutative law). They can also begin to split the ones of the second number into smaller parts, using the make 10 strategy, to simplify the mental calculations.

KEY LANGUAGE

In lesson: add, +, =, total, tens, ones, exchange

Other language to be used by the teacher: exchange, is equal to, partition, place value, is the same as, equivalent, sum, altogether

STRUCTURES AND REPRESENTATIONS

Place value grid, column method, number line, part-whole model

RESOURCES

Mandatory: Base 10 equipment, place value grid, empty number lines

Optional: straws and elastic bands, place value grid (with the ones section within the equal sign split into 9 sections), pictures of numbers made with Base 10 equipment

 In the eTextbook of this lesson, you will find interactive links to a selection of teaching tools.

Before you teach

- How will you ensure that children are using their knowledge of number bonds effectively?
- How can you scaffold questioning to explain the key processes within exchange?

Discover

WAYS OF WORKING Pair work

ASK

- Question **1** a): *Is this question easier or harder than the questions you answered in the previous lesson?*
- Question **1** a): *What is 15 ones the same as?*

IN FOCUS Question **1** a) will be the first time children encounter a problem where the total of the ones column exceeds 9. They will therefore need to exchange 10 ones for one ten when adding. Allow children to try to calculate the total, then ask what is different compared to the previous lesson.

In question **1** b), children may choose the 50 peg as they are told 50 is the total. This provides an excellent opportunity to recap and consolidate their understanding of 'total'. In this instance, knowledge of doubles could be discussed within the mental process that children use to calculate the total.

ANSWERS

Question **1** a): Asha scored 65 points in total.

Question **1** b): Sol's other ⭕ also lands on 25.

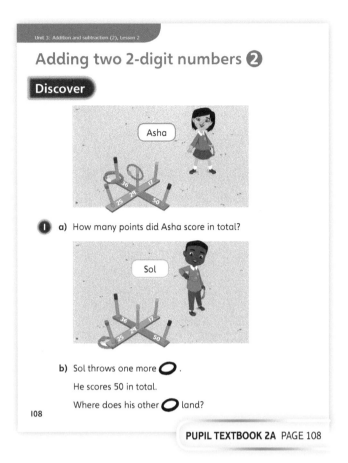

PUPIL TEXTBOOK 2A PAGE 108

Share

WAYS OF WORKING Whole class teacher led

ASK

- Question **1** a): *Who can explain in their own words what Dexter means?*
- *If you throw 2 hoops, what is the smallest or greatest score you could get?*

IN FOCUS When exploring question **1** a), discuss with children the fact that 36 + 29 is equivalent to 5 tens and 15 ones, and also to 6 tens and 5 ones. Give children ample time to understand this key concept. Use the part-whole model to help them visualise this.

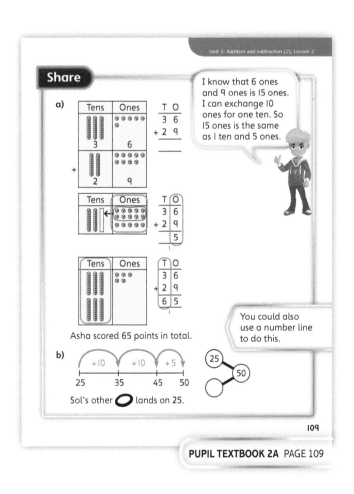

PUPIL TEXTBOOK 2A PAGE 109

Think together

Think together

WAYS OF WORKING Whole class teacher led (I do, We do, You do)

ASK

- *Which number would you choose to start with?*
- *Which total score will be the highest or smallest?*
- *Question ③: Why has Dexter chosen to use a number line starting from 29 when the first hoop landed on 17?*

IN FOCUS When children are working on question ③, encourage them to use their answer to question ② to help them predict the total. Ask them to explain why the answer to Ash's question is 'Yes'.

STRENGTHEN Give children concrete experience of exchanging 10 ones for 1 ten to consolidate their understanding of this key concept. Children may benefit from using straws before moving on to Base 10 equipment, as they can physically group 10 single straws together with an elastic band and move this group into the tens column.

DEEPEN Each question has one score in common with a previous question. Help children to recognise this and encourage them to estimate the answer to each question before they begin to work it out. Ask: *Will the answer be greater than or less than the previous answer? How much greater or less?*

ASSESSMENT CHECKPOINT Ensure children use full sentences to explain what they are doing. Assessing the accuracy of these explanations will allow you to determine the extent of children's understanding.

ANSWERS

Question ① : The total score is 61.

Question ② : 17 + 20 = 37
   37 + 3 = 40
   40 + 2 = 42
   The total score is 42.

Question ③ : 17 + 29 = 46
   The total score is 46.

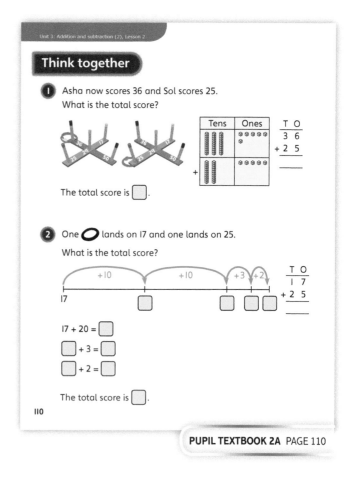

PUPIL TEXTBOOK 2A PAGE 110

PUPIL TEXTBOOK 2A PAGE 111

Practice

WAYS OF WORKING Independent thinking

IN FOCUS In question **4**, children use the answers to two additions to find the answers to other, related additions. The second set of additions requires children to use their understanding of adding multiples of 10 to a number and then extend this to a near multiple of 10. To find the final sum, children should adjust their previous answer by 1 (calculating 48 + 30 – 1).

STRENGTHEN Provide pictures of the numbers made with Base 10 equipment. Additionally, children can draw around 10 ones to consolidate their understanding that 10 ones are equal to 1 ten.

DEEPEN Question **6** provides another opportunity for children to make links with other questions and to find more than one solution to a problem. Tell them the numbers less than 10 if they cannot immediately recall them.

ASSESSMENT CHECKPOINT Question **4** can be used to assess whether children are able to make links between calculations. Ask them to explain how they know the answer to each.

ANSWERS Answers for the **Practice** part of the lesson appear in the separate **Practice and Reflect answer guide**.

Reflect

WAYS OF WORKING Independent thinking

IN FOCUS Children may choose different ways to answer the **Reflect** question, and should justify their choice. They could keep the numbers in the order that they are given and add the ones and exchange, they could choose to start with 18 as it is closest to the next multiple of 10 and complete the addition in steps, or they could add 20 to 35 and then adjust by subtracting 2.

ASSESSMENT CHECKPOINT Assess whether children are able to explain the steps within their calculation and justify their choice of method. If children can present more than one possible way of answering the question their understanding is likely to be more secure.

ANSWERS Answers for the **Reflect** part of the lesson appear in the separate **Practice and Reflect answer guide**.

After the lesson ⏸

- Are children confident in using more than one method to answer the same question?
- Could children recognise a more or less efficient method?
- Could children confidently write the steps of their mental method using the column method and an empty number line?

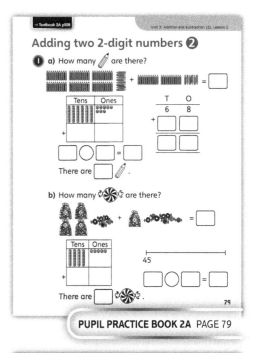

PUPIL PRACTICE BOOK 2A PAGE 79

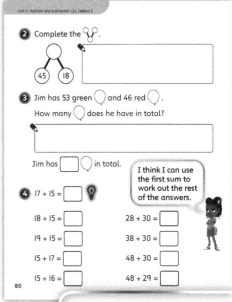

PUPIL PRACTICE BOOK 2A PAGE 80

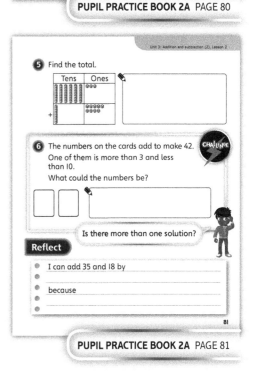

PUPIL PRACTICE BOOK 2A PAGE 81

Subtracting a 2-digit number from another 2-digit number

Learning focus

In this lesson, children will subtract a 2-digit number from another 2-digit number without exchange. They will do this by making the larger number and subtracting the smaller number from it, resulting in the difference.

Small steps

→ Previous step: Adding two 2-digit numbers (2)
→ **This step: Subtracting a 2-digit number from another 2-digit number (1)**
→ Next step: Subtracting a 2-digit number from another 2-digit number (2)

NATIONAL CURRICULUM LINKS

Year 2 – Addition and Subtraction
- Add and subtract numbers using concrete objects, pictorial representations, and mentally, including: two 2-digit numbers.
- Solve problems with addition and subtraction: applying their increasing knowledge of mental and written methods.

ASSESSING MASTERY

Children can make the larger number using different resources, partitioning it into tens and ones and then removing the relevant amount according to the smaller number, resulting in the difference. Children may recognise that this process is the opposite of addition and use addition to check that their answer is correct.

COMMON MISCONCEPTIONS

Children may write the smaller number first when using the column method as they learned that addition could be done in any order. Ask:
- *Have you chosen the largest number as the starting number? Have you only made the largest number?*
Children may forget that they are subtracting and add instead. Ask:
- *What does the – sign mean? What do you need to do during these calculations?*
Children may write the number that they subtract as the number that is left. Ensure children understand the problem's context to help them conceptualise subtraction. Ask:
- *Have you written what is left after subtraction has taken place?*

STRENGTHENING UNDERSTANDING

To eliminate misunderstanding as a result of making the wrong number or making the larger number incorrectly, provide children with pictures of the starting number made with different resources. They can then make the number on top of the picture or cross out ones and tens on the picture.

GOING DEEPER

Ask children to compare what is the same and what is different in the methods used for addition and subtraction, leading to the understanding that subtraction is not commutative. Encourage them to use their understanding of inverse operations to check calculations.

KEY LANGUAGE

In lesson: subtract, –, =, ones

Other language to be used by the teacher: larger number, smaller number, difference, addition, reduce, minus

STRUCTURES AND REPRESENTATIONS

Place value grid, column method, part-whole model, number line

RESOURCES

Mandatory: Base 10 equipment, place value grid

Optional: pictures of numbers made with Base 10 equipment or other resources, for example, eggs, egg boxes and cubes

 In the eTextbook of this lesson, you will find interactive links to a selection of teaching tools.

Before you teach ⏸

- Are there any adaptations you are planning to make to this lesson, to link it to other lessons or curriculum work?
- How can links be made to previous lessons in the unit without confusing addition and subtraction?

Discover

WAYS OF WORKING Pair work

ASK

- *How did you work out the answers?*
- *What similarities and differences are there in the method you used in today's and yesterday's lesson?*
- *Did you all agree with the method your partner used to answer the question?*

IN FOCUS Children have already subtracted a 2-digit number from another 2-digit number, but only within 20. Question ❶ a) requires children to first identify the starting number of eggs, to then recreate this using resources and finally to remove the correct number of eggs. Ensure children understand the concept of subtraction within the context of cooking prior to the lesson. This could provide an opportunity to model drawing the concrete objects and crossing out the tens and ones that represent what has been used.

DEEPEN Challenge children to write one calculation linking the two steps involved in questions ❶ a) and ❶ b), i.e. 45 – 12 – 20 = 13.

ANSWERS

Question ❶ a): There are 33 eggs left.

Question ❶ b): There are 13 eggs left.

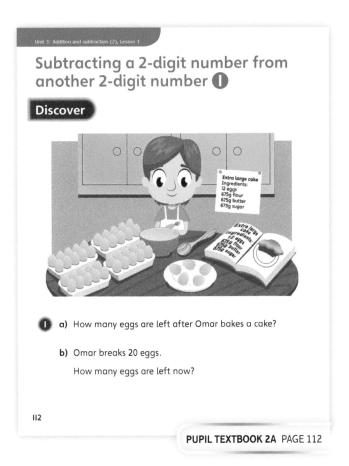

PUPIL TEXTBOOK 2A PAGE 112

Share

WAYS OF WORKING Whole class teacher led

ASK

- Question ❶ a): *Why did Astrid choose to start with the greatest number? Why did she only make this number?*
- *Was question ❶ a) or ❶ b) easier?*

IN FOCUS Use question ❶ a) to emphasise the importance of partitioning the smaller number into tens and ones rather than just counting backwards in 1s: children should cross out two single eggs and one box of 10 eggs. If they were to cross out all five single eggs and the first seven eggs within a box of 10, they would find the correct answer, but may become confused when tackling later questions.

Question ❶ b) requires children to subtract 0 from 3. If they are not secure with the concept of 0 they may think that 3 – 0 = 0. Model 3 – 0 = 3 using resources to allow children to understand that when nothing is subtracted the larger number remains the same.

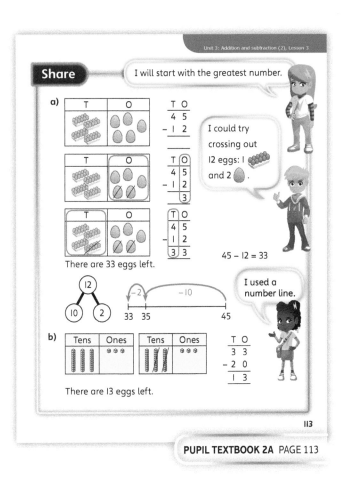

PUPIL TEXTBOOK 2A PAGE 113

Think together

WAYS OF WORKING Whole class teacher led (I do, We do, You do)

ASK
- *How can you draw the eggs to represent the eggs which are in boxes of 10 and those that are not?*
- *How could you check that your answer is correct?*
- *Can you use the answer to any question to write another calculation, using your understanding of fact families?*

IN FOCUS Use a part-whole model with question ❶ to allow children to make links between addition and subtraction, and to enable them to write other number sentences without the need for further calculation. Question ❸ has no scaffolding, so children are required to select the starting number, draw this correctly in the place value grid and cross out the necessary number parts.

STRENGTHEN Provide children with other objects and ask them to create their own subtraction word problem to enhance their understanding of the concept of subtraction.

DEEPEN Give children the difference and challenge them to create their own subtractions that result in this difference. Can they find more than one possible subtraction?

ASSESSMENT CHECKPOINT Ask children to verbalise another word problem to match the abstract calculation in question ❸. This will help you assess their understanding of the concept of subtraction.

ANSWERS

Question ❶ : 38 🥚 – 16 🥚 = 22 🥚

Question ❷ : 64 – 41 = 23
   Eva has 23 eggs left.

Question ❸ : 74 – 41 = 33

PUPIL TEXTBOOK 2A PAGE 114

PUPIL TEXTBOOK 2A PAGE 115

Practice

WAYS OF WORKING Independent thinking

IN FOCUS Question **2** b) will leave children with no ones blocks. Some children may not write the zero if their understanding of the concept of zero is not secure. Question **4** focuses on related subtractions. Writing the information they know on a part-whole diagram will help children to see that they can swap parts from the answer to the question and to recognise fact families.

STRENGTHEN To consolidate the steps involved in subtraction and the mathematical vocabulary used to describe them, ask children to comment on what they are doing with the physical resources as they work through a question. Alternatively, children could work in pairs, with one following instructions given by their partner.

DEEPEN Challenge children to explain the links between the calculations in question **4** and how they can use these links to work out the answers.

Ash's comment in question **6** should help children make links between the numbers in the calculation. Children may initially need to use physical resources to find a solution, but should then be encouraged to try to think of alternative solutions without using resources.

ASSESSMENT CHECKPOINT Use question **3** to assess whether children have a secure understanding of multiples of 10 and their chosen subtraction method. Ask children to explain why the number of ones does not change.

ANSWERS Answers for the **Practice** part of the lesson appear in the separate **Practice and Reflect answer guide**.

Reflect

WAYS OF WORKING Independent thinking

IN FOCUS The **Reflect** part of the lesson requires children to explain how they know the calculation is incorrect. They could use subtraction to prove that 5 – 2 is not 4, and that 6 – 3 is not 4, or they could use addition to check the inverse.

ASSESSMENT CHECKPOINT Assess the confidence and security of children's explanations, and their ability to self-check their own work and identify mistakes.

ANSWERS Answers for the **Reflect** part of the lesson appear in the separate **Practice and Reflect answer guide**.

After the lesson ⏸

- Are children confident subtracting a 2-digit number from another 2-digit number?
- What was the most common misconception that could restrict children's progression to more complex subtraction problems?

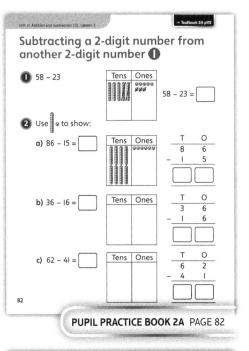

PUPIL PRACTICE BOOK 2A PAGE 82

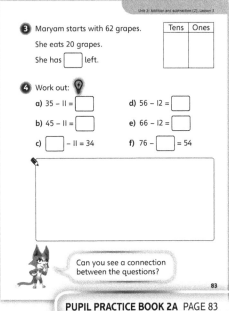

PUPIL PRACTICE BOOK 2A PAGE 83

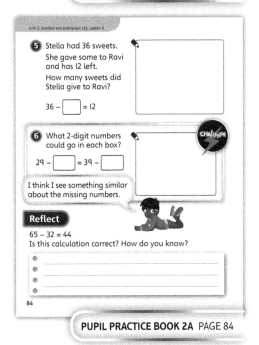

PUPIL PRACTICE BOOK 2A PAGE 84

Subtracting a 2-digit number from another 2-digit number ②

Learning focus

In this lesson, children will subtract a 2-digit number from another 2-digit number without exchange. They will focus on understanding the concept of difference and the methods used to calculate and visually represent difference.

Small steps

→ Previous step: Subtracting a 2-digit number from another 2-digit number (1)

→ **This step: Subtracting a 2-digit number from another 2-digit number (2)**

→ Next step: Subtracting a 2-digit number from another 2-digit number (3)

NATIONAL CURRICULUM LINKS

Year 2 Number – Addition and Subtraction

- Add and subtract numbers using concrete objects, pictorial representations, and mentally, including: two 2-digit numbers.
- Solve problems with addition and subtraction: applying their increasing knowledge of mental and written methods.

ASSESSING MASTERY

Children can calculate the difference between two numbers. They can use a number line to visually represent their calculation, and carefully count on or back in jumps of ten and one to find the answer.

COMMON MISCONCEPTIONS

Children may be unsure when to use subtraction and when to use addition, and may find it difficult to identify where on the number line the answer is found. Ask:

- *Have you re-read the question to ensure you have given the answer that is required?*

Children may find it difficult to position numbers on an empty number line with the appropriate spacing between them. Ask:
- *Have you considered the size of each jump based on what is being subtracted?*

STRENGTHENING UNDERSTANDING

Give children a complete 0–100 number line to support them in drawing and labelling their own number lines. Encourage them to place Base 10 equipment on the number line as they count on or back in 10s and 1s. This will both help them understand the need to add the jumps, and support them in doing so. To support them in calculating 10 more or 10 less than a number, use a 100 square, if children are confident with its structure, or bead strings.

GOING DEEPER

Provide children with a subtraction and challenge them to make comments on what they notice when they increase the starting number but make the difference stay the same (the smaller number has to increase). If they show this on a number line then the space between the largest and smallest number remains the same.

KEY LANGUAGE

In lesson: subtract, + =, tens, ones, **difference**, count on, count back, more

Other language used by the teacher: less, compare, is equal to

STRUCTURES AND REPRESENTATIONS

Number line

RESOURCES

Mandatory: 0–100 number line

Optional: Base 10 equipment, 100 square, bead strings, other manipulatives such as counters

 In the eTextbook of this lesson, you will find interactive links to a selection of teaching tools.

Before you teach

- How can you extend children's ideas of the concept of subtraction to include difference?
- How can you ensure that children differentiate appropriately between addition and subtraction?

Discover

WAYS OF WORKING Pair work

ASK

- *How is this the same as the previous lesson? How is it different?*
- *Can a question be subtraction if nothing is 'taken away'?*

IN FOCUS Question ❶ extends children's knowledge of subtraction by asking them to find the difference. They are comparing two quantities rather than taking one quantity away from another.

STRENGTHEN Help children understand the concept of difference by presenting a simpler scenario before pairs attempt question ❶ . For example, show them five basketballs and three tennis balls and ask: *How many more basketballs than tennis balls are there?*

ANSWERS

Question ❶ a): The 👕 team is winning by 25 points.

Question ❶ b): The 👕 team will have 31 points at the end.

Share

WAYS OF WORKING Whole class teacher led

ASK

- *Who chose to subtract the tens first? Who chose to subtract the ones first?*
- *Question ❶ a): Why is it important that Dexter worked out the numbers in the jumps on the number line?*
- *Could you use addition to check your answer?*

IN FOCUS In question ❶ b) the answer is, as in question ❶ a), found by counting back and adding the jumps. Discuss how the number line relates to the calculation 46 – ? = 15; ensure children understand that 46 represents the red team's score and 15 represents the difference between the two scores. You could use another number line to count back from 46 to 31 and check that the difference is 15.

STRENGTHEN In the context of difference, allowing children to make the larger number and take away from it, or to cross things out, is likely to cause confusion. However, children could make both numbers and compare them. Emphasise that the process used to find the difference is still subtraction.

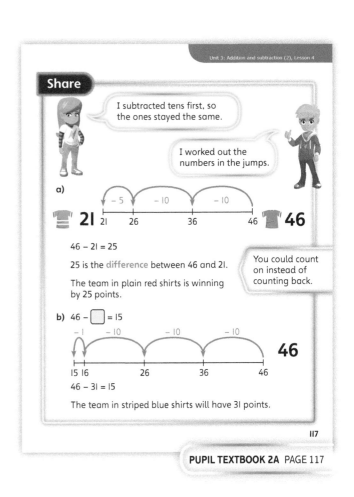

Think together

WAYS OF WORKING Whole class teacher led (I do, We do, You do)

ASK

- Question **1** : *Why has 56 been placed on the right-hand side of the number line? Why has 22 been placed on the left-hand side?*
- *How do you know how many jumps of 10 you can make between two numbers on a number line?*

IN FOCUS In question **1** the scores are listed with the lower score first. Ensure children understand that they need to identify the larger number and count back from it, as shown on the number line: focusing on counting back initially will consolidate children's understanding of difference as the result of subtraction. Question **3** explores different ways of finding the difference between 65 and 31. Spend some time looking at the three number lines and discussing what is the same and what is different.

STRENGTHEN Use a 100 square and/or bead string to strengthen children's ability to fluently recall 10 more or 10 less than a 2-digit number within 100. Remind children that in the previous lesson they saw that only the tens digit changes when a multiple of 10 is subtracted.

DEEPEN In question **2** , children find the difference between 74 and 31. Challenge them to tell you the difference between 54 and 31 without using a number line. In question **3** , challenge children to find as many different sets of jumps to represent the difference as possible.

ASSESSMENT CHECKPOINT Assess whether children are fluent at finding 10 less than a number when completing the missing gaps on the number line. If they are not, provide additional resources such as a bead string or 100 square to assist them.

ANSWERS

Question **1** : 56 – 22 = 34
34 is the difference between the scores.

Question **2** : 74 – 31 = 43
The difference between the scores is 43.

Question **3** : The difference between the scores is 34.

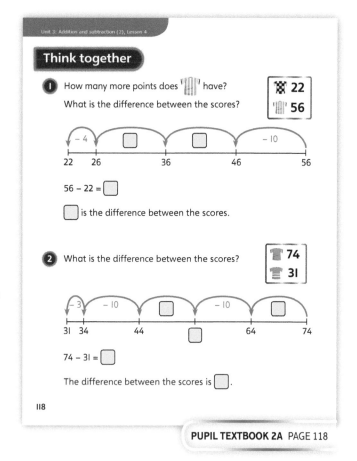

PUPIL TEXTBOOK 2A PAGE 118

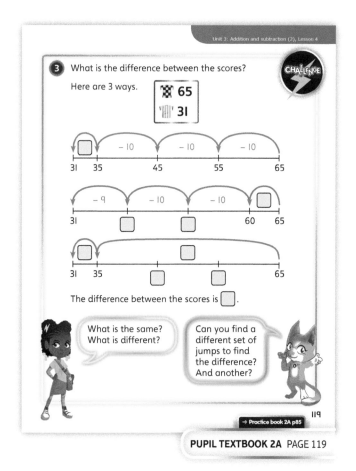

PUPIL TEXTBOOK 2A PAGE 119

Practice

WAYS OF WORKING Independent thinking

IN FOCUS Questions ❶ and ❷ ask 'how many more'. Some children may associate 'more' with addition and add the numbers instead of subtracting as a result. Ensure children understand that 'more' and 'less'/'fewer' can both indicate difference, and therefore subtraction. Say, for example: *The difference is 31. Penny has 31 more sweets than Ali. Ali has 31 fewer sweets than Penny.*

Question ❺ provides an opportunity for children to show the depth of their understanding. Do they realise that the = sign means 'is equal to', rather than indicating that an answer follows it?

STRENGTHEN If children find the mental calculations difficult, allow them to use Base 10 equipment to model the jumps, or to make both the numbers and compare them.

DEEPEN Ask children to use a number line to present different ways of showing the difference of 25. Which starting numbers would suit different initial jumps? For example, if 34 is the starting number, the difference could be jumps of 4, 10, 10 and 1.

ASSESSMENT CHECKPOINT Continue to assess whether children are able to efficiently calculate 10 less than a number. Are children using known number bonds within calculations rather than counting in ones or using their fingers? A confident response to question ❺, using correct mathematical language, is a good indicator of mastery.

ANSWERS Answers for the **Practice** part of the lesson appear in the separate **Practice and Reflect answer guide**.

Reflect

WAYS OF WORKING Independent thinking

IN FOCUS The **Reflect** part of the lesson gives children the opportunity to write two different ways to solve the same calculation. They may find the difference, and take 16 away from 48. Alternatively, they may find the difference using two different sets of jumps on a number line. Whole-class discussion following children's independent work will expose all children to their peers' thoughts.

ASSESSMENT CHECKPOINT Assess whether children are capable of completing the same calculation in different ways. Can they describe what is the same and what is different about the two methods?

ANSWERS Answers for the **Reflect** part of the lesson appear in the separate **Practice and Reflect answer guide**.

After the lesson ⏸

- Can children accurately use the language of difference and recognise difference as the result of subtraction?
- Could children recognise when their method was less efficient than their peers' and see ways that they could become more efficient?

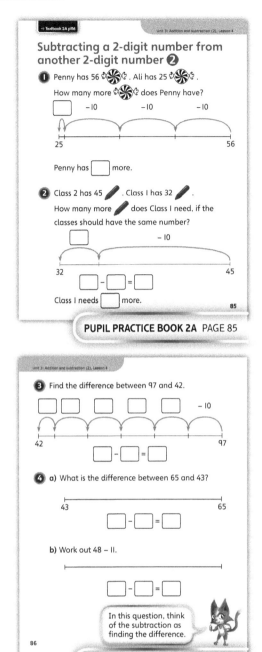

PUPIL PRACTICE BOOK 2A PAGE 85

PUPIL PRACTICE BOOK 2A PAGE 86

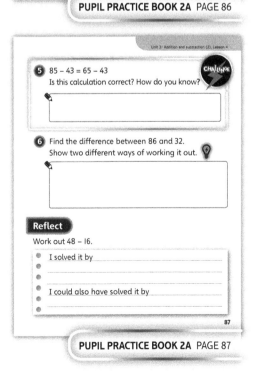

PUPIL PRACTICE BOOK 2A PAGE 87

Subtracting a 2-digit number from another 2-digit number ③

Learning focus

In this lesson, children will subtract a 2-digit number from another 2-digit number using partitioning of the ones to cross ten. They will represent these mental calculations on a number line.

Small steps

→ Previous step: Subtracting a 2-digit number from another 2-digit number (2)

→ **This step: Subtracting a 2-digit number from another 2-digit number (3)**

→ Next step: Subtracting a 2-digit number from another 2-digit number (4)

NATIONAL CURRICULUM LINKS

Year 2 Number – Addition and Subtraction

- Add and subtract numbers using concrete objects, pictorial representations, and mentally, including: two 2-digit numbers.
- Solve problems with addition and subtraction: applying their increasing knowledge of mental and written methods.

ASSESSING MASTERY

Children can identify the largest number. Children can make and justify decisions on how to partition the smaller number to help with their mental calculation and represent these visually on a number line.

COMMON MISCONCEPTIONS

Children may continue to confuse subtraction with addition and may switch from one to the other halfway through a number line. Ask:

- *Have you checked your calculation on your number line?*

STRENGTHENING UNDERSTANDING

Children should continue to use a complete 0–100 number line to support them in drawing and labelling their own number lines. A 100 square or bead strings will help them to accurately and efficiently calculate 10 more or 10 less than a number.

GOING DEEPER

Children will explore partitioning as an efficient method for subtraction. Encourage them to calculate unknown quantities in the most efficient way possible and challenge them to justify the efficiency and accuracy of their choice.

KEY LANGUAGE

In lesson: subtract, −, =, count back

Other language to be used by the teacher: partition, efficient, accurate, smaller number, larger number, tens, ones

STRUCTURES AND REPRESENTATIONS

Number lines, part-whole model

RESOURCES

Mandatory: 0–100 number line

Optional: 100 square, bead strings

 In the eTextbook of this lesson, you will find interactive links to a selection of teaching tools.

Before you teach

- How can you improve the teaching of reasoning through this lesson as children are asked to critique their methods?
- How can you develop and refine children's own representation of the problem on a number line?

Discover

WAYS OF WORKING Pair work

ASK

- *What operation is required to calculate the answer to the question?*
- *Which number should you start with?*
- *Can you complete the calculation mentally?*

IN FOCUS Question ❶ is the first time children will have encountered a subtraction in which the ones digit of the smaller number is larger than the ones digit in the larger number.

ANSWERS

Question ❶ a): Kara needs 28 more 🍓.

Question ❶ b): Ben has 36 🍓.

Subtracting a 2-digit number from another 2-digit number ❸

Discover

❶ a) Kara has 24 🍓 .
She needs 52 to make jam.
How many more does she need to pick?

b) Ben needs 16 more 🍓 to make jam.
How many 🍓 does he have?

120

PUPIL TEXTBOOK 2A PAGE 120

Share

Share

WAYS OF WORKING Whole class teacher led

ASK

- Question ❶ a): *Do you agree or disagree with Ash?*
- Question ❶ a): *Do you agree or disagree with Dexter?*
- *Can you subtract the tens and ones in any order?*

IN FOCUS Use question ❶ to highlight the make 10 strategy, explaining to children that they are less likely to make mistakes if they work to a multiple of 10 within a calculation. It can also be more efficient and accurate to work in this way, as children use their knowledge of number bonds within 10 rather than relying on more complex mental calculations.

STRENGTHEN Partitioning the smaller number using a part-whole model will help ensure that children remember to subtract all partitioned parts from the larger number.

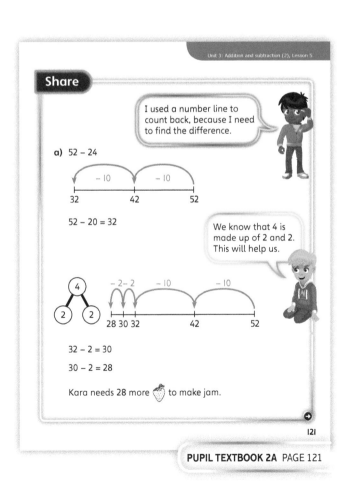

I used a number line to count back, because I need to find the difference.

a) 52 – 24

52 – 20 = 32

We know that 4 is made up of 2 and 2. This will help us.

32 – 2 = 30
30 – 2 = 28

Kara needs 28 more 🍓 to make jam.

121

PUPIL TEXTBOOK 2A PAGE 121

Think together

WAYS OF WORKING Whole class teacher led (I do, We do, You do)

ASK

• Question **1** : *Is there a more efficient way to calculate the answer than doing 5 jumps of 10?*

• Question **3** : *How many different ways do you think Flo can calculate the answer?*

IN FOCUS Questions **2** and **3** require children to choose their own jumps. Encourage them to show their mental calculations in an efficient way. Check that when they subtract the ones they partition them to land on a multiple of 10, to simplify the mental calculation.

STRENGTHEN Providing children with completed number bonds within 10 will increase their confidence and speed in using them within other mental calculations.

DEEPEN Children could explore alternative methods using near multiples of 10 and represent these on the number line. For example, for question **2** , children could subtract 20 from 35, jumping back on the number line, and then adjust by jumping on 2 to show 35 – 18 rather than 35 – 20.

ASSESSMENT CHECKPOINT Ensure children are using their knowledge of number bonds to partition the ones digit appropriately, rather than randomly.

ANSWERS

Question **1** : 71 – 52 = 19
Zeb has 19 left over.

Question **2** : Lan has 17 🍓 left.

Question **3** : There are 47 boys.

PUPIL TEXTBOOK 2A PAGE 122

PUPIL TEXTBOOK 2A PAGE 123

Practice

WAYS OF WORKING Independent thinking

IN FOCUS Question **3** presents the same calculation in different ways. Sam's method may be the first time children see the ones subtracted at different points, before and after subtraction of the tens. This may make subtraction of the tens easier as they will be counting from a multiple of 10.

Question **6** provides an opportunity for children to show the depth of their understanding, based on their learning in this and the previous lesson. Again, it requires them to understand that the = sign means 'is equal to', rather than indicating that an answer follows it, and to make links between the numbers within the calculations in order to answer the questions efficiently.

STRENGTHEN Using a bead string will help children see the number of ones they should subtract at different stages to reach the next multiple of 10.

DEEPEN Provide children with subtractions such as 45 = 92 – ?, 45 = 82 – ?, 45 = 72 – ?. What pattern can they spot in the calculations and the unknown quantity? How many more calculations could be written that continue the same pattern?

ASSESSMENT CHECKPOINT Children should be able to explain what they have chosen to represent on their number line, using appropriate mathematical vocabulary and justifying their choices.

ANSWERS Answers for the **Practice** part of the lesson appear in the separate **Practice and Reflect answer guide**.

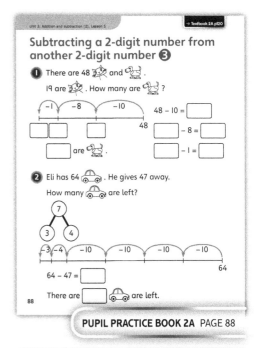

PUPIL PRACTICE BOOK 2A PAGE 88

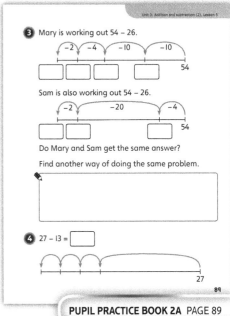

PUPIL PRACTICE BOOK 2A PAGE 89

Reflect

WAYS OF WORKING Independent thinking

IN FOCUS The **Reflect** part of the lesson requires children to make links to previous learning in order to identify how to calculate the value of the missing number. They may refer to the concept of difference, or use a part-whole model.

ASSESSMENT CHECKPOINT Children should be becoming more confident at completing the same calculation in different ways. Can they identify which they think is the best method for this calculation and explain their choice?

ANSWERS Answers for the **Reflect** part of the lesson appear in the separate **Practice and Reflect answer guide**.

After the lesson ⏸

- Were children confident at completing calculations in different ways?
- What was the most common misconception that children were making?

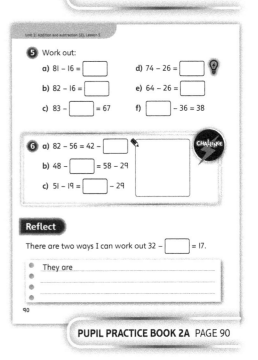

PUPIL PRACTICE BOOK 2A PAGE 90

Subtracting a 2-digit number from another 2-digit number ④

Learning focus

In this lesson, children will subtract a 2-digit number from another 2-digit number with exchange. They will do this by making the larger number and subtracting the smaller number from it, resulting in the difference.

Small steps

→ Previous step: Subtracting a 2-digit number from another 2-digit number (3)

→ **This step: Subtracting a 2-digit number from another 2-digit number (4)**

→ Next step: Adding three 1-digit numbers

NATIONAL CURRICULUM LINKS

Year 2 Number – Addition and Subtraction

- Add and subtract numbers using concrete objects, pictorial representations, and mentally, including: two 2-digit numbers.
- Solve problems with addition and subtraction: applying their increasing knowledge of mental and written methods.

ASSESSING MASTERY

Children can confidently use Base 10 equipment or other resources to exchange when subtracting. They can explain what they have done with concrete resources in combination with mental calculations.

COMMON MISCONCEPTIONS

When subtracting, children may swap the numbers around and subtract the smaller number of ones from the larger; for example, when working out 32 – 16, children may mentally subtract 2 ones from 6 ones. To challenge this misconception, and to help children understand the concept of exchange, it is crucial that all children make the starting number with resources and experience exchanging a ten for 10 ones. Ask:
- *Have you checked whether it is necessary to exchange?*

STRENGTHENING UNDERSTANDING

Children who find the concept of exchange difficult, or follow a procedural method but lack understanding, should continue to work with concrete resources until they have grasped the key concept. For practice, give children 99 in Base 10 equipment (9 tens and 9 ones). Ask them to roll a dice: they should take away each number they roll from their equipment. When they do not have enough ones they will need to exchange a ten for 10 ones so they can take the correct amount away.

GOING DEEPER

Can children explain why we start with the ones in column subtraction? Challenge them to make links with previous work on addition, when they exchanged tens and ones. This will strengthen their understanding of addition and subtraction as inverse operations.

KEY LANGUAGE

In lesson: subtract, –, =, equal to, how many more, difference

Other language to be used by the teacher: exchange, larger number, smaller number, tens, ones, the same as, equivalent, left over

STRUCTURES AND REPRESENTATIONS

Place value grid, column method, number line

RESOURCES

Mandatory: Base 10 equipment, place value grid

Optional: dice, 0–100 number line

 In the eTextbook of this lesson, you will find interactive links to a selection of teaching tools.

Before you teach

- How can you help children to avoid the main misconception regarding exchange within subtraction?
- How can you promote reasoning and explanation to help children understand key concepts?

Discover

WAYS OF WORKING Pair work

ASK

• *What operation do you need to use to find the solution?*
• *What number would you make using concrete resources? Why?*

IN FOCUS Question ① a) does not require exchange, but introduces children to the concept of having zero ones remaining. Question ① b) requires exchange and therefore it is crucial that all children make the starting number with resources in order to understand the concept of exchange and to avoid the main misconception.

ANSWERS

Question ① a): Susie has 30 lengths left.

Question ① b): Kay has 18 lengths left.

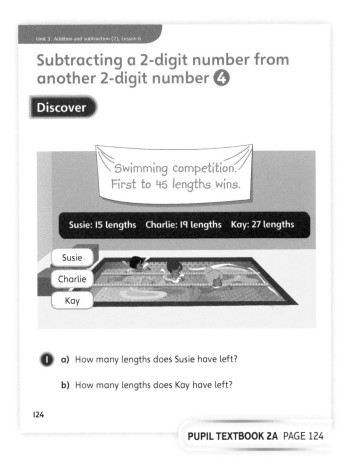

Subtracting a 2-digit number from another 2-digit number ❹

Discover

Swimming competition. First to 45 lengths wins.

Susie: 15 lengths   Charlie: 19 lengths   Kay: 27 lengths

Susie
Charlie
Kay

❶ a) How many lengths does Susie have left?

b) How many lengths does Kay have left?

124

PUPIL TEXTBOOK 2A PAGE 124

Share

WAYS OF WORKING Whole class teacher led

ASK

• *What number did you make to begin the problem?*
• *What was the first difficulty that you encountered? How did you overcome this problem?*
• *Question ① b): Can you think of three other calculations that would require exchange?*

IN FOCUS Question ① b) highlights why it is necessary to start with the ones column when using column subtraction: sometimes the tens column needs to be adjusted so that the ones can be subtracted.

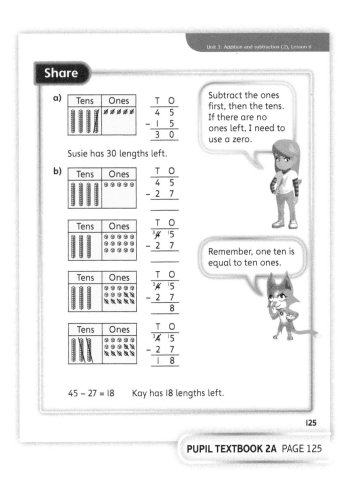

Share

a)

Tens	Ones

T O
4 5
− 1 5
3 0

Susie has 30 lengths left.

b)

Tens	Ones

T O
4 5
− 2 7

T O
³4̷ ¹5
− 2 7

T O
³4̷ ¹5
− 2 7
    8

T O
³4̷ ¹5
− 2 7
1 8

Subtract the ones first, then the tens. If there are no ones left, I need to use a zero.

Remember, one ten is equal to ten ones.

45 − 27 = 18   Kay has 18 lengths left.

125

PUPIL TEXTBOOK 2A PAGE 125

Think together

WAYS OF WORKING Whole class teacher led (I do, We do, You do)

ASK

• *What operation does the question require you to complete?*
• *What information in the question tells you that you need to use this operation?*

IN FOCUS All the **Think together** questions require children to find the difference. The information children are presented with, and the value they need to find, varies for each question. Check children understand the questions and ensure they recognise that they need to subtract in order to answer them.

STRENGTHEN Children who find it difficult to understand that 'how many left' and 'how much more' questions require subtraction could role play a simpler scenario to strengthen their understanding.

DEEPEN Challenge children to create their own word problems that require exchange. This will deepen their understanding of when and why exchange is necessary.

ASSESSMENT CHECKPOINT Ask children to explain why they are using subtraction to answer the questions. Assess whether they can explain the process of exchange accurately, using the correct mathematical language; for example, 'one ten is the same as 10 ones'.

ANSWERS

Question ❶ : Mr Peters has 17 more lengths to swim.

Question ❷ : Miss Stone has 26 more lengths to swim.

Question ❸ : Layla swims 25 more lengths than Oz.

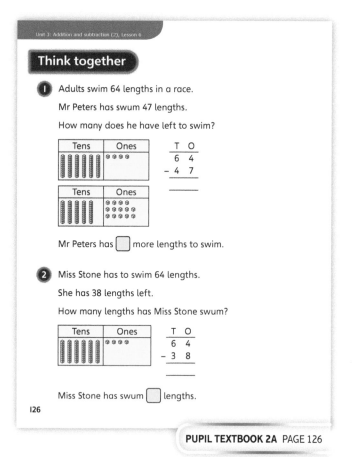

PUPIL TEXTBOOK 2A PAGE 126

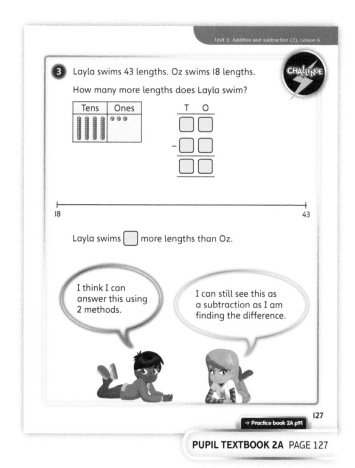

PUPIL TEXTBOOK 2A PAGE 127

Practice

WAYS OF WORKING Independent thinking

IN FOCUS The final three calculations in question **3** encourage children to make links, using what they already know to work out a new unknown. The calculations are also set out differently, with the difference on the left and the subtraction on the right.

STRENGTHEN Children who find the notation associated with exchange within the column method difficult could work in pairs, with one using resources and commentating on what they are doing while their partner writes down what they do using the column method.

DEEPEN Challenge children to explain why the statement in question **5** is true using both addition and subtraction. This will deepen their understanding of the links between the two operations.

ASSESSMENT CHECKPOINT Children may no longer need to use resources to make the numbers. Assess their understanding by asking them to explain the steps they are taking as they complete the column method.

ANSWERS Answers for the **Practice** part of the lesson appear in the separate **Practice and Reflect answer guide**.

Reflect

WAYS OF WORKING Independent thinking

IN FOCUS The **Reflect** part of the lesson requires children to explain how they know when to use subtraction. Encourage them to draw on the different elements of subtraction they have learned about in the previous three lessons, as well as this lesson. They may describe subtraction as 'taking away' or 'finding the difference'.

ASSESSMENT CHECKPOINT Assess the confidence with which children explain the two main structures of subtraction. This will allow you to identify whether they need more exposure to either area, or both.

ANSWERS Answers for the **Reflect** part of the lesson appear in the separate **Practice and Reflect answer guide**.

After the lesson ⏸

- Did children use their reasoning skills to explain the key concept of exchange within the lesson?
- Are children ready to move away from subtraction at this stage or do they need to consolidate their understanding?

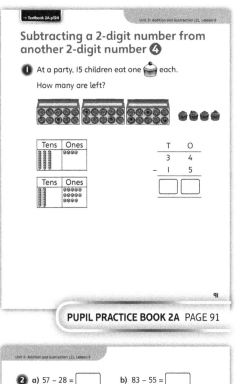

PUPIL PRACTICE BOOK 2A PAGE 91

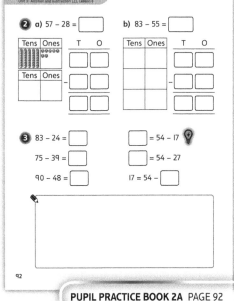

PUPIL PRACTICE BOOK 2A PAGE 92

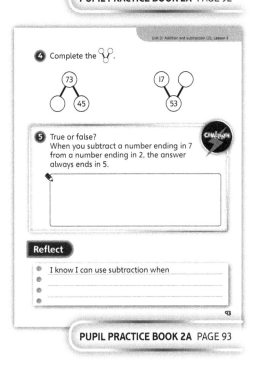

PUPIL PRACTICE BOOK 2A PAGE 93

Adding three I-digit numbers

Learning focus

In this lesson, children will add three numbers presented in a variety of ways, including concrete and pictorial representations. They will select the most appropriate resource to help them and rearrange the numbers to add efficiently.

Small steps

→ Previous step: Subtracting a 2-digit number from another 2-digit number (4)
→ **This step: Adding three 1-digit numbers**
→ Next step: Solving word problems – the bar model (1)

NATIONAL CURRICULUM LINKS

Year 2 Number – Addition and Subtraction

- Add and subtract numbers using concrete objects, pictorial representations, and mentally, including: adding three 1-digit numbers.
- Solve problems with addition and subtraction: applying their increasing knowledge of mental and written methods.

ASSESSING MASTERY

Children can use their knowledge of number bonds to make decisions regarding the order in which to complete mental addition. Children can understand that the order does not affect the final total.

COMMON MISCONCEPTIONS

Children may think the numbers have to be added in the order that they are given. Make each number using cubes and ask:
- *Does the order in which you add the groups of cubes change the total number of cubes?*

Children may confuse addition and subtraction when they are asked to work out a missing number, as in $19 = 8 + 5 + ?$. Ask:
- *Have you read through the completed calculation to check you have not made any mistakes? Do the three parts add up to equal the whole?*

STRENGTHENING UNDERSTANDING

Give children a completed set of number bonds within 20 to increase their confidence and emphasise recall, rather than allowing them to calculate the answer by counting in ones using their fingers.

GOING DEEPER

Challenge children to justify why they have chosen to add numbers in a specific order.

KEY LANGUAGE

In lesson: add, + , =, altogether, number bonds, total

Other language to be used by the teacher: digits, partition, rearrange

STRUCTURES AND REPRESENTATIONS

Ten frame, part-whole model

RESOURCES

Mandatory: ten frames, counters

Optional: number bonds within 20, counters in three different colours

 In the eTextbook of this lesson, you will find interactive links to a selection of teaching tools.

Before you teach

- How secure are children recalling known number facts?
- How can you enable children to critique approaches used by others?

Discover

Pair work

ASK

- Question **1** a): *What number did you choose to start with?*
- *What strategies could you use to effectively add numbers mentally?*

IN FOCUS Encourage children to discuss different ways to calculate the answer to question **1** a). Which way is easiest? Which way is most efficient?

ANSWERS

Question **1** a): 15 fingers are being held up altogether to make the target number.

Question **1** b): Malik should show 7 fingers.

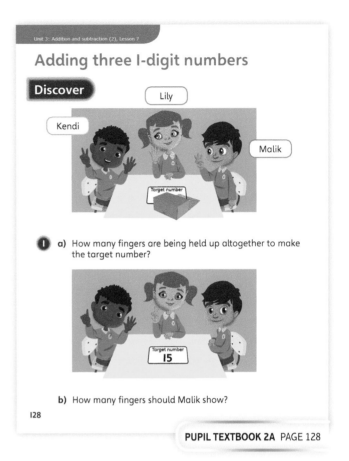

PUPIL TEXTBOOK 2A PAGE 128

Share

WAYS OF WORKING Whole class teacher led

ASK

- Question **1** a): *Who found the answer the same way as Astrid? Who found the answer the same way as Dexter?*
- Question **1** a): *Which method do you think is more efficient? Why?*

IN FOCUS Throughout question **1**, encourage children to use what they know, rather than using their fingers to count on in ones. For example, in question **1** a), they could start by working out 7 + 5 if they are comfortable doing so; if not, they may prefer to look for a number bond to 10 (7 + 3) as their initial strategy.

DEEPEN Challenge children to find three different numbers that make a total of 15. How many different ways can they find?

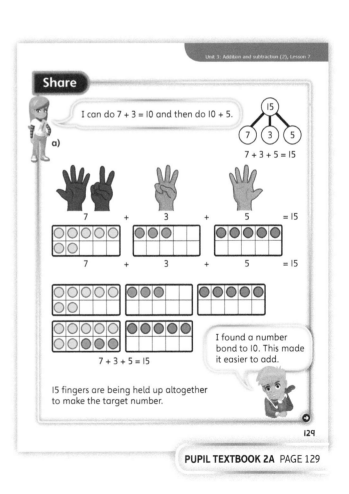

PUPIL TEXTBOOK 2A PAGE 129

Think together

WAYS OF WORKING Whole class teacher led (I do, We do, You do)

ASK

- *What strategies could you use to answer the question?*
- *How can you use resources to help you decide in what order to add the numbers mentally?*
- Question **3**: *Who used Astrid's method to answer the question? Who used Flo's method?*

IN FOCUS In questions **1** and **2**, it is not possible to use number bonds to 10. Encourage children to visualise making 10 to help them partition and add larger numbers, such as 9 + 8. Where appropriate, they could also use doubles or near doubles.

STRENGTHEN Ensure children understand that the order in which the numbers that need to be added are given does not change the total by giving them a part-whole model with three parts and ask them to complete it in as many different ways as possible for a given whole.

DEEPEN The answer to question **3** is 17. Ask children to find as many other possible ways of making 17 with three numbers as they can. Can they put the different ways into categories: those that use number bonds to 10, those that use doubling or near doubling facts, and those that require partitioning?

ASSESSMENT CHECKPOINT Check whether children are using their fingers to count on in ones. If they are, they may need extra practice in using and recalling number bonds within 20.

ANSWERS

Question **1** : 9 + 8 + 6 = 23. There are 23 fingers in total.

Question **2** : 8 + 5 + 6 = 19. The missing number is 6.

Question **3** : There are 17 pencils in total.

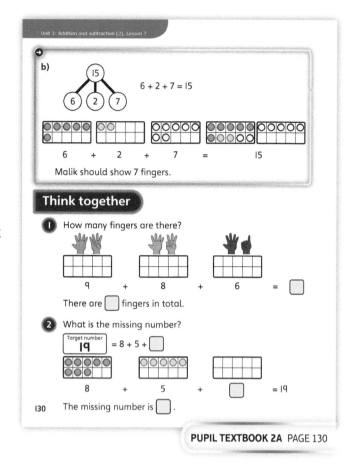

PUPIL TEXTBOOK 2A PAGE 130

PUPIL TEXTBOOK 2A PAGE 131

Practice

WAYS OF WORKING Independent thinking

IN FOCUS Questions ❶ and ❷ a) include numbers that add to 10, while questions ❷ b) and ❷ c) include doubles or near doubles. Children should make clear in what order they chose to add the numbers, for example using different colours in the ten frames, rather than simply drawing each number and then counting in tens and ones to find the total.

STRENGTHEN Using counters in three different colours will help children see which pairs of numbers work well together. Children can also use counters to see how a number can be partitioned to make 10, and to see what remains.

DEEPEN In question ❸, encourage children to find all the different ways of making 12 with three numbers. Can they prove, by the way that they have worked, that they have found all the possible ways?

ASSESSMENT CHECKPOINT Use question ❺ to assess how well children can link different sets of numbers. Some children will find the totals of both sets of numbers and then compare these totals. Other children will compare the numbers on each side of the calculation and make their judgements based on these comparisons.

ANSWERS Answers for the **Practice** part of the lesson appear in the separate **Practice and Reflect answer guide**.

Reflect

WAYS OF WORKING Independent thinking

IN FOCUS The **Reflect** part of the lesson requires children to use different strategies to add combinations of three numbers. Four different totals are possible. If pairs of children have both worked out all four totals correctly, they will find that they both made the biggest number possible. Encourage them to make the link between the size of the numbers they added and the size of the total: adding the three biggest numbers makes the biggest total; adding the three smallest numbers makes the smallest total.

ASSESSMENT CHECKPOINT Assess whether children can explain clearly how they found the different totals. Did they find some combinations easier than others?

ANSWERS Answers for the **Reflect** part of the lesson appear in the separate **Practice and Reflect answer guide**.

After the lesson ⏸

- Did children use known number facts or count on in ones to calculate the answers?
- Did children understand the focus of the lesson, or did they just concentrate on finding the answer to each question?

159

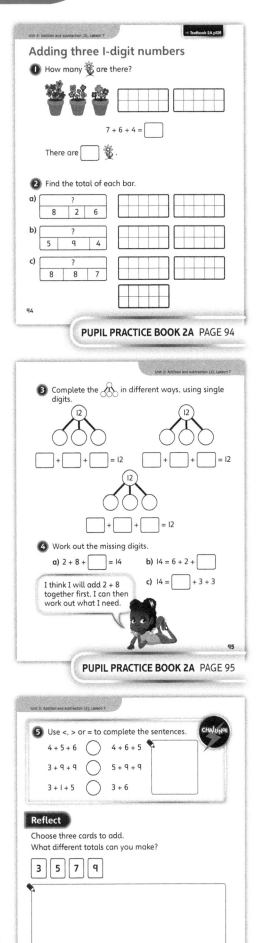

Solving word problems – the bar model ①

Learning focus

In this lesson, children will represent word problems using single bar models. They will use the words 'part' and 'whole' to help them identify whether the calculation is addition or subtraction.

Small steps

→ Previous step: Adding three 1-digit numbers

→ **This step: Solving word problems – the bar model (1)**

→ Next step: Solving word problems – the bar model (2)

NATIONAL CURRICULUM LINKS

Year 2 Number – Addition and Subtraction

Solve problems with addition and subtraction: using concrete objects and pictorial representations, including those involving numbers, quantities and measures.

ASSESSING MASTERY

Children can confidently draw bar models to represent addition and subtraction. They know that you can write the parts on the bar model in any order, but that it is more efficient and systematic to begin at one end.

COMMON MISCONCEPTIONS

The size of the bars should be proportional to the size of the numbers that they represent. Children will initially find this difficult but, in this lesson, the focus is on deciding which number should go in each bar rather than drawing bar models; encourage them to consider the size of the bar when they make their choice. Ask:

• *Is the number with the greatest value represented by the largest bar?*

Children may confuse addition and subtraction until they become familiar with the bar model. To help them decide whether a word problem requires addition or subtraction, encourage them to explain the problem in their own words, using the terms 'part' and 'whole'. Ask:

• *Do you need to add or subtract to answer the question? Can you explain why?*

STRENGTHENING UNDERSTANDING

To help children become familiar with the bar model, give them strips of paper of fixed length to represent the bars within a bar model. Ask children to manipulate the strips to represent addition or subtraction.

GOING DEEPER

When children have completed a bar model, ask them if they agree with the relative size of each bar. Although it is not the focus of the lesson, doing this will deepen children's sense of number and help them be more accurate in future lessons.

KEY LANGUAGE

In lesson: +, −, =, bar model, altogether, left, part, whole, total

Other language to be used by the teacher: proportion, addition, subtraction, relative, accurate, difference, remaining

STRUCTURES AND REPRESENTATIONS

Bar model, column method

RESOURCES

Mandatory: Base 10 equipment

Optional: strips of paper to represent bars, place value grid, counters

 In the eTextbook of this lesson, you will find interactive links to a selection of teaching tools.

Before you teach

• How might you scaffold questioning to help children reflect on their assumptions regarding the size or choice of the bar for each number?

• How can you continue to promote the importance of mental calculation strategies within this lesson?

Discover

Unit 3: Addition and subtraction (2), Lesson 8

Solving word problems – the bar model ❶

Discover

WAYS OF WORKING Pair work

ASK

• *What key words could you look for to help you determine if a question involves addition or subtraction?*

IN FOCUS Question ❶ helps children distinguish between addition and subtraction. Discuss how they know which operation they need to use.

ANSWERS

Question ❶ a): Mr Dean has 87 stickers.

Question ❶ b): Mr Dean has 42 stickers left.

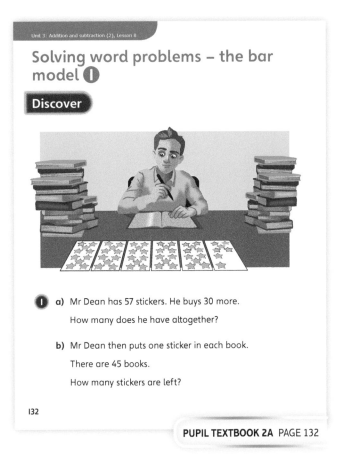

❶ a) Mr Dean has 57 stickers. He buys 30 more.
How many does he have altogether?

b) Mr Dean then puts one sticker in each book.
There are 45 books.
How many stickers are left?

132

PUPIL TEXTBOOK 2A PAGE 132

Share

WAYS OF WORKING Whole class teacher led

ASK

• *Which question does Astrid use 'part + part = whole' for? Which does she use 'whole – part = part' for?*

• *Question ❶ a): What is the same and what is different about the four different representations?*

• *Could you swap the parts of the bar model around? Would it change the whole?*

IN FOCUS In question ❶ a), three different representations of the calculation are given. Identifying what is the same in all three will help children to see that they can all be used to find the answer.

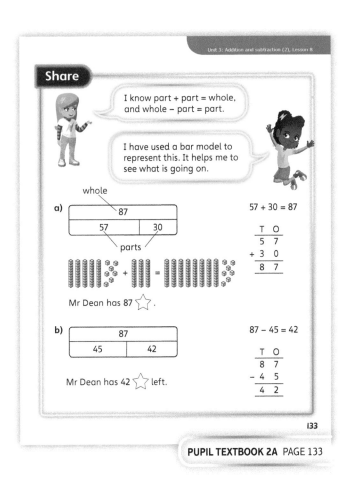

Share

I know part + part = whole, and whole – part = part.

I have used a bar model to represent this. It helps me to see what is going on.

a)

whole
87

57	30

parts

$57 + 30 = 87$

T	O
5	7
+ 3	0
8	7

Mr Dean has 87 ☆.

b)

87

45	42

$87 - 45 = 42$

T	O
8	7
– 4	5
4	2

Mr Dean has 42 ☆ left.

133

PUPIL TEXTBOOK 2A PAGE 133

Think together

Whole class teacher led (I do, We do, You do)

ASK

- *Can the size of the bars help you estimate the size of the parts and/or whole?*
- *Can you think of anything you learned in a previous lesson that will help you find the answers to these problems?*

IN FOCUS Use question ❶ to emphasise that the bar model is used only to represent the problem; it is not a way to calculate the answer. Prompt children to recognise that to answer question ❶ they need to find the difference between 27 and 45, using a method practised in previous lessons.

Question ❸ introduces children to a bar model with three parts. Encourage them to make links to the previous lesson to consolidate their understanding of this representation.

STRENGTHEN Using strips of paper to represent the bars in questions ❶ and ❷ will help children distinguish whether they need to add or subtract to find the solution.

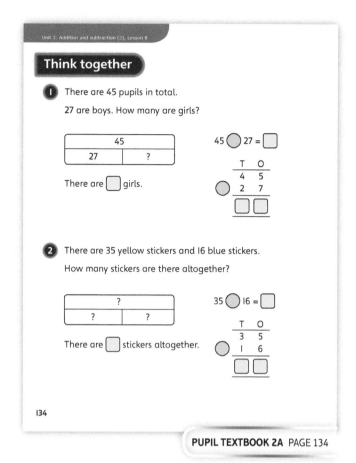

PUPIL TEXTBOOK 2A PAGE 134

DEEPEN From the 3 parts shown on the bar model, how many different ways can the addition equation be written? How many different ways could the whole (the total number of stickers) be made if the quantities changed but the number of parts stayed the same?

ASSESSMENT CHECKPOINT Assess whether children can justify why they have decided to add or subtract, explaining the question in their own words and with reference to the bar model.

ANSWERS

Question ❶ : 45 – 27 = 18. There are 18 girls.

Question ❷ : 35 + 16 = 51. There are 51 stickers altogether.

Question ❸ : 7 + 5 + 9 = 21. Mrs Bell uses 21 stickers altogether.

PUPIL TEXTBOOK 2A PAGE 135

Practice

WAYS OF WORKING Independent thinking

IN FOCUS In question **1** , the different parts, and therefore the bars, are significantly different in size. This will help children decide where each number should be placed in the bar model. Question **3** requires children to explain how they know which bar model represents the word problem given. Children should explain why the model they have chosen does match, as well as why the other two do not match.

STRENGTHEN If children make calculation errors that prevent them understanding the concept of the bar model, give them some completed calculations and ask them to draw them in different ways on an empty bar model. Similarly, you could ask children to create their own word problems based on a complete bar model.

DEEPEN Challenge children to estimate the value of a missing part or whole based on the relative size of the bars in a bar model. After they have calculated the answer, they can assess the accuracy of their estimations.

ASSESSMENT CHECKPOINT Assess children's understanding by asking them to justify their placement of the numbers in a bar model.

ANSWERS Answers for the **Practice** part of the lesson appear in the separate **Practice and Reflect answer guide**.

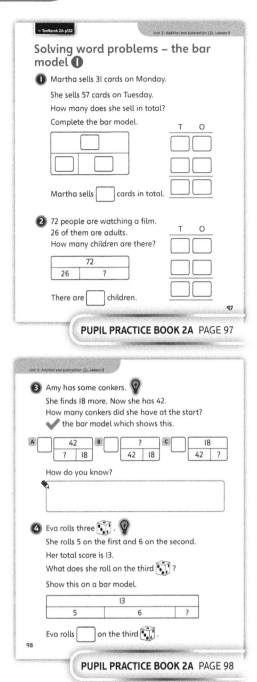

PUPIL PRACTICE BOOK 2A PAGE 97

PUPIL PRACTICE BOOK 2A PAGE 98

Reflect

WAYS OF WORKING Whole class

IN FOCUS The **Reflect** part of the lesson requires children to recognise that the problem must involve subtraction, since the whole is known but one of the parts is unknown.

DEEPEN Challenge children to write two different subtraction problems, one using take away and the other using difference.

ASSESSMENT CHECKPOINT Assess whether children are using the vocabulary 'part' and 'whole'. Do they recognise that this bar model represents a subtraction?

ANSWERS Answers for the **Reflect** part of the lesson appear in the separate **Practice and Reflect answer guide**.

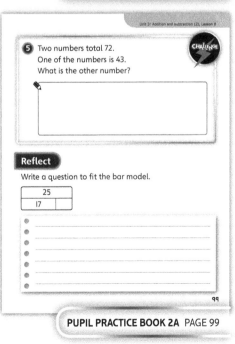

PUPIL PRACTICE BOOK 2A PAGE 99

After the lesson

- Are children confident at identifying whether a bar model represents addition or subtraction?
- Can children create their own word problems that involve addition and subtraction?

Solving word problems – the bar model ②

Learning focus

In this lesson, children will represent word problems using single and comparison bar models. They will use the words 'part' and 'whole' to help them identify whether the calculation is addition or subtraction.

Small steps

→ Previous step: Solving word problems – the bar model (1)
→ **This step: Solving word problems – the bar model (2)**
→ Next step: Counting money – coins

NATIONAL CURRICULUM LINKS

Year 2 Number – Addition and Subtraction

Solve problems with addition and subtraction: using concrete objects and pictorial representations, including those involving numbers, quantities and measures.

ASSESSING MASTERY

Children can use bar models to help them see which operation to use when completing word problems, leading to increased conceptual understanding.

COMMON MISCONCEPTIONS

Children may confuse the single and comparison bar models and may struggle to distinguish which is appropriate for a particular question type. Ask:
• *Does the bar model that you have chosen to draw represent the information presented in the question? Can you identify where on the bar model the answer is found?*

Children may continue to make calculation errors if they do not use the appropriate methods from previous lessons. Ask:
• *Have you used methods that you learned in previous lessons to calculate the answer? Can you explain how you know your answer is correct?*

STRENGTHENING UNDERSTANDING

Encourage children to simulate word problems using real-life objects. This will give them a greater understanding of what they are being asked to calculate.

GOING DEEPER

Challenge children to create their own word problems to match given bar models, or to create a combination of addition and subtraction problems (including difference) using a given set of numbers.

KEY LANGUAGE

In lesson: +, –, =, bar model, altogether, more than, added

Other language to be used by the teacher: part, whole, comparison, addition, subtraction, difference, total, remaining, fewer

STRUCTURES AND REPRESENTATIONS

Bar model, column method

RESOURCES

Optional: resources to represent real-life objects (e.g. Base 10 equipment, counters), bean bags, hoops

 In the eTextbook of this lesson, you will find interactive links to a selection of teaching tools.

Before you teach

• Based on the previous lesson on bar models, what will be the key barriers to overcome during this lesson?
• How can you refine children's representations of the bar model throughout the lesson?

Discover

Unit 3: Addition and subtraction (2), Lesson 9

WAYS OF WORKING Pair work

ASK

• Question ❶ a): *What do you think you need to do to find the solution?*
• Question ❶ b): *How could you represent difference using bar models?*
• *What additional questions could you ask about this picture?*

IN FOCUS Question ❶ b) is the first time that the single bar model taught in the previous lesson cannot be used to represent the question. Establish that the question asks for the difference, not for a part or whole, and agree that therefore a different representation is needed.

ANSWERS

Question ❶ a): There are 61 marbles in the red ⛾ and the yellow ⬭ altogether.

Question ❶ b): There are 25 more marbles in the blue ⛾ than in the green ⛾.

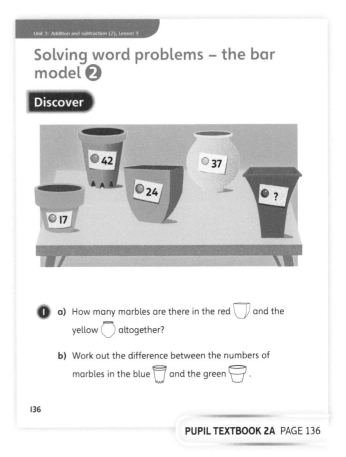

Solving word problems – the bar model ❷

Discover

❶ a) How many marbles are there in the red ⛾ and the yellow ⬭ altogether?

b) Work out the difference between the numbers of marbles in the blue ⛾ and the green ⛾.

136

PUPIL TEXTBOOK 2A PAGE 136

Share

WAYS OF WORKING Whole class teacher led

ASK

• *How are these bar models different from the ones you used in the previous lesson?*
• *Why is the question mark in a different place in the two representations?*

IN FOCUS Draw children's attention to the location of the question mark in the two parts of question ❶ . This shows where the answer is located within the model. It is important that children understand what the question mark and the bar boundaries represent in each case.

STRENGTHEN If children find the concept of difference represented in this way difficult, they could play a game, attempting to throw bean bags into a hoop laid on the ground. They could then compare how many bags landed inside and outside the hoop, and find the difference. They could line the bean bags up in in rows to emulate the bar model.

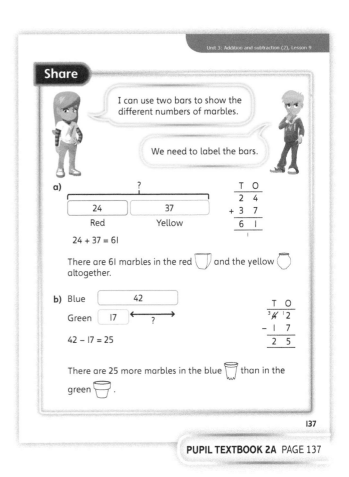

Share

I can use two bars to show the different numbers of marbles.

We need to label the bars.

a)

?	
24	37
Red	Yellow

24 + 37 = 61

```
  T O
  2 4
+ 3 7
  6 1
    1
```

There are 61 marbles in the red ⛾ and the yellow ⬭ altogether.

b) Blue | 42 |
Green | 17 | ←→ ? |

42 − 17 = 25

```
    T O
  ³4̸ ¹2
  - 1 7
    2 5
```

There are 25 more marbles in the blue ⛾ than in the green ⛾.

137

PUPIL TEXTBOOK 2A PAGE 137

Think together

WAYS OF WORKING Whole class teacher led (I do, We do, You do)

ASK

- *Where is the value you need to calculate shown on the bar model?*
- *Which of the representations could you also draw as a single bar model?*

IN FOCUS Question ❷ includes the first instance of a bar model used to find a quantity that is a known amount more than a known quantity. Ensure children understand which part of the bar model they need to calculate.

Question ❸ is a two-step question. Encourage children to show clearly the steps of their working, following Flo's advice, rather than trying to work mentally. Can they explain why they have done what they have?

STRENGTHEN Using concrete manipulatives to represent the numbers within the bars takes children a step back and may enable them to understand what they are calculating more easily.

DEEPEN Challenge children to answer questions such as: What is the smallest total of marbles you could make by combining 2 of the pots? What is the second smallest total you could make? What is the largest number of marbles you could make by combining 2 of the pots?

ASSESSMENT CHECKPOINT Assess whether children can explain the position of the bars in the representation for a specific question, and identify or explain where the answer is found.

ANSWERS

Question ❶ : There are 41 marbles altogether.

Question ❷ : There are 57 marbles in the purple ⏢.

Question ❸ : 17 + 19 = 36
There are 36 marbles in the green ⏢.

36 – 24 = 12
There are now 12 more marbles in the green ⏢ than in the red ⏢ pot.

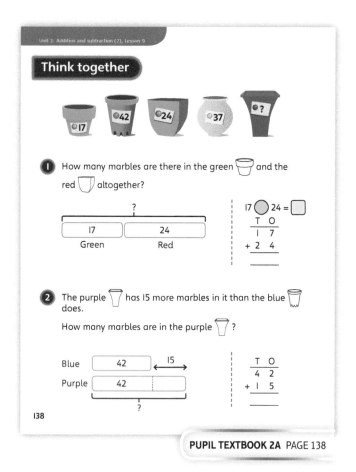

PUPIL TEXTBOOK 2A PAGE 138

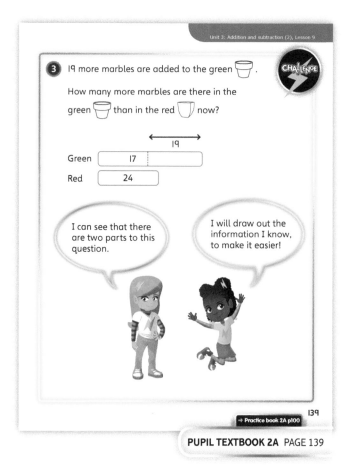

PUPIL TEXTBOOK 2A PAGE 139

Practice

WAYS OF WORKING Independent thinking

IN FOCUS The questions in the **Practice** section have progressively less scaffolding. Questions **3** and **4** both require children to draw their own bar model. If they are reluctant to do so, remind them that this is the focus of this lesson.

STRENGTHEN Giving children the calculations needed for questions **3** (75 – 48 = ?) and **4** (25 + 25 + 16 = ?) will allow children to focus on correctly drawing the bar models.

DEEPEN Challenge children to change one (or more) of the questions so that it uses the other operation (i.e. question **1** becomes an addition question), while keeping the context and numbers used the same.

ASSESSMENT CHECKPOINT Ask children to explain why they have chosen to draw a single or a comparison bar model for each of questions **3** and **4**. A confident explanation indicates a secure understanding of the concept.

ANSWERS Answers for the **Practice** part of the lesson appear in the separate **Practice and Reflect answer guide**.

Reflect

WAYS OF WORKING Independent thinking

IN FOCUS The **Reflect** part of the lesson requires children to make up their own word problem. Encourage them to think carefully about the type of question they are asking their friend to solve; you could ask them to provide a scaffold of the bar model to assist their partner.

ASSESSMENT CHECKPOINT Assess whether the elements within children's word problems link appropriately, and whether the operation needed to answer the question is clear from the language they use. If not, it is likely that the child has not fully understood the concept of addition or subtraction in the context of bar models.

ANSWERS Answers for the **Reflect** part of the lesson appear in the separate **Practice and Reflect answer guide**.

After the lesson ⏸

- Have children demonstrated they have mastered addition and ways to calculate and represent addition problems?
- Have children demonstrated they have mastered subtraction and ways to calculate and represent subtraction problems?
- Are there any common misconceptions that the class are still finding difficult?

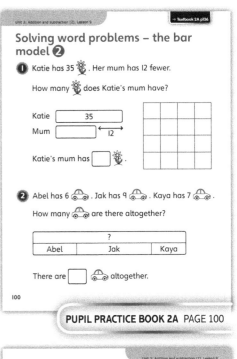

PUPIL PRACTICE BOOK 2A PAGE 100

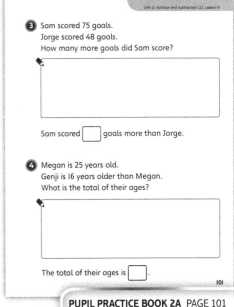

PUPIL PRACTICE BOOK 2A PAGE 101

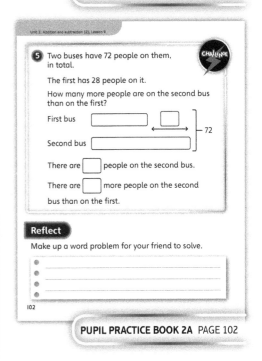

PUPIL PRACTICE BOOK 2A PAGE 102

End of unit check

Don't forget the Power Maths Unit Assessment Grid on p26.

WAYS OF WORKING Group work – adult led

IN FOCUS These questions assess children's understanding of partitioning numbers in different ways and how this supports different mental calculations. The questions also assess children's understanding of the links between addition and subtraction and how to move between the operations.

Think!

WAYS OF WORKING Pairs or small groups

IN FOCUS

- This question requires children to understand that all questions require addition to calculate the unknown whole.
- Children must then be able to understand, as a result of the numbers that they are presented with, that two calculations will require exchange and one calculation will not.
- If children are finding this difficult, ask: *Which is the easiest calculation?*
- Children should be encouraged to use all of the vocabulary given to them to explain their answer.

ANSWERS AND COMMENTARY Children who have mastered this unit will be able to differentiate between addition and subtraction problems, understanding how to represent the numbers provided within the context in different ways, using different resources. Children should be flexible with the methods they can use to calculate different problems as a result of their complexity and should be working efficiently as a result of using known number facts within mental calculations.

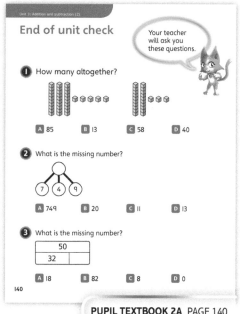

PUPIL TEXTBOOK 2A PAGE 140

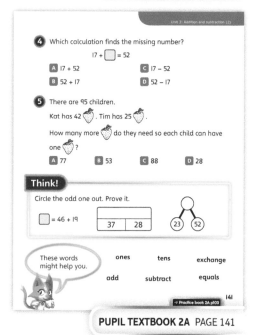

PUPIL TEXTBOOK 2A PAGE 141

Q	A	WRONG ANSWERS AND MISCONCEPTIONS	STRENGTHENING UNDERSTANDING
1	C	B suggests that children have simply added up the total number of blocks without considering the different values of the tens and the ones.	Children should have the opportunity to work with Base 10 equipment as much as possible to correctly understand how to partition the same number in different ways. Numbers should be partitioned into two and more parts.

Children should also practise writing all possible calculations from a complete part-whole diagram, understanding that the equals sign can occur in different places and means 'is the same as'.

Creating number stories that require addition, subtraction or a combination of the two operations will increase children's understanding of the differences between the operations. |
2	B	C suggests children have found the total of the first 2 numbers rather than all 3 numbers. D suggests they have found the total of the final 2 numbers.	
3	A	B suggests that they have not interpreted the bar model correctly and have found the total of the two numbers given rather than the difference.	
4	D	C suggests the child thinks that subtraction is also commutative and the order of the numbers does not matter.	
5	D	B suggests that the child has calculated how many more 95 is than the number of strawberries than Kat has.	

My journal

WAYS OF WORKING Independent thinking

ANSWERS AND COMMENTARY The part-whole model is the odd one out because it does not require exchange to calculate the answer. 3 ones plus 2 ones equals 5 ones. 2 tens and 5 tens equals 7 tens. So the answer is 75. The other questions are also addition as we know both of the parts and not the whole but they require exchange because 6 ones plus 9 ones is 15 ones and 7 ones and 8 ones is 15 ones and 15 ones is greater than 10 ones.

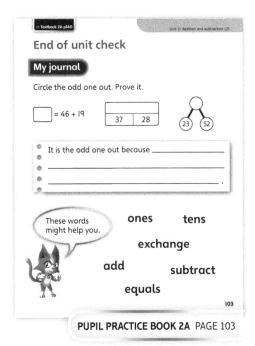

PUPIL PRACTICE BOOK 2A PAGE 103

Power check

WAYS OF WORKING Independent thinking

ASK

- *How confident do you feel about using a number line to show the steps of addition and subtraction?*
- *How confident do you feel about using the column method to calculate additions or subtractions?*
- *Which resource do you find easiest to help you with addition and subtraction?*

Power puzzle

WAYS OF WORKING Pair work or small group

IN FOCUS Use this **Power puzzle** to see if children can work in small groups to find the same totals using different digits. This will assess their fluency of working with numbers within 20 to make different totals. It will also check to see how confident children are at choosing a starting point of their own and working from this point to find different solutions to the problem.

ANSWERS AND COMMENTARY If children can complete the **Power puzzle**, it suggests that they are confident at problem solving and making mistakes in the process of arriving at the correct answer. Children who find the problem difficult may need some help or some hints to start the problem. For example, ask: *What is the total amount of all of the cards? Can you make 15 in 3 different ways using each card once?*

Unequal piles: 9 + 6, 7 + 5 + 3, 8 + 4 + 2 + 1 or 9 + 6, 8 + 5 + 2, 7 + 4 + 3 + 1

Equal piles: 9 + 1 + 5, 8 + 3 + 4, 7 + 6 + 2 or 9 + 2 + 4, 8 + 6 + 1, 7 + 5 + 3

PUPIL PRACTICE BOOK 2A PAGE 104

After the unit ⏸

- Were children more confident at calculating addition or subtraction problems?
- What visual representations did children find most difficult to use accurately?

Strengthen and **Deepen** activities for this unit can be found in the *Power Maths* online subscription.

Unit 4
Money

Mastery Expert tip! "When I taught this unit, I made sure there were lots of practical resources to support the children's understanding. Coins and Base 10 equipment were particularly useful."

Don't forget to watch the Unit 4 video!

WHY THIS UNIT IS IMPORTANT

This unit is important because it builds upon children's learning in year 1. There is a lot of focus within the unit on addition and subtraction of money using part-whole models and bar models, in addition to counting methods – enabling children to find the most efficient strategies, such as counting on from the coin or note of highest value to find the total. Children work with pounds, pence and notes, and towards the end of the unit they will work with pounds and pence together.

WHERE THIS UNIT FITS

→ Unit 3: Addition and subtraction (2)

→ **Unit 4: Money**

→ Unit 5: Multiplication and division (1)

This unit builds upon basic money work children completed in year 1. It also reinforces children's counting skills, as well as addition and subtraction strategies. In this unit, children focus on coins and notes and cover the following topics: calculating total amounts, finding change and word problems. Following this unit, children will move on to learning methods of multiplying and dividing numbers.

Before they start this unit, it is expected that children:

- can count in 2s, 5s and 10s
- have a basic understanding of the value of coins
- can use addition and subtraction strategies in context
- know how to count on a number line and use the part-whole and bar models.

ASSESSING MASTERY

Children who have mastered this unit will know the value of all coins and notes. They will be able to calculate total amounts using efficient strategies, find change, order amounts and solve money word problems. Finally, they will be able to explain their methods confidently, using the appropriate mathematical vocabulary.

COMMON MISCONCEPTIONS	STRENGTHENING UNDERSTANDING	GOING DEEPER
Children may not distinguish between pounds and pence.	Some children will need daily mental counting practice (forwards and backwards, starting from different numbers). Further support could come from a number line.	Ask children to show their methodology on a structure such as the bar model.
Children may count £1 and £2 as pence (because they are coins).	Carry out matching activities, where children represent the value of coins and notes with Base 10 equipment.	Challenge children to create their own money word problems.
Children may make vocabulary errors.	Practise appropriate mathematical vocabulary with children.	Give children amounts such as £2 and 40p. Challenge children to think of a calculation for each amount.

WAYS OF WORKING

Use these pages to introduce the unit focus to children as a whole class. You can use the characters to explore different ways of working too.

STRUCTURES AND REPRESENTATIONS

Part-whole model: This model will help children visualise calculations as a whole made up of two parts. It can help strengthen children's fluency in addition and subtraction. Money is used instead of numbers or counters to develop children's understanding of how to add and subtract coins and notes.

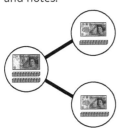

Number line: This model helps children visualise the order of numbers. It can help them demonstrate concepts such as 'one more' and 'one less' in a more efficient way than using concrete resources. It can help children to demonstrate the addition of coins and notes in regular but varying jumps.

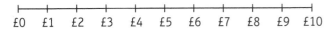

Bar model: This model will help children visualise amounts of money and solve money word problems. It can help children to add amounts of coins and notes by representing them in rectangles.

£20		
£8	£5	£7

KEY LANGUAGE

There is some key language that children will need to know as a part of the learning in this unit:

→ money, coins, notes

→ pounds (£), pence (p)

→ change, left, right, money, buy(s), spend, step

→ how much?, value, amount, total, altogether, parts, between, difference

→ count on, sort, match, compare, add, addition, calculate, subtraction

→ great(er/est), smallest, exact(ly), higher, lower, most, least

→ more than (>), less than (<), equal (=)

→ part-whole model, number line, bar model

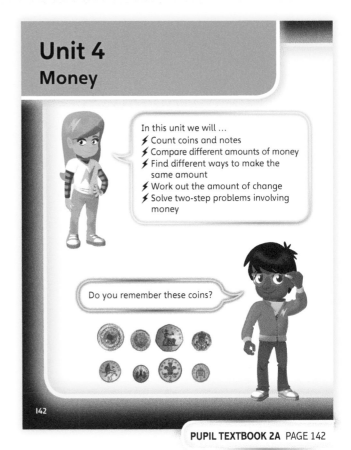

PUPIL TEXTBOOK 2A PAGE 142

PUPIL TEXTBOOK 2A PAGE 143

Counting money – coins

Learning focus

In this lesson, children will learn the value of a range of coins and explore ways to find the total of different amounts.

Small steps

→ Previous step: Solving word problems – the bar model (2)
→ **This step: Counting money – coins**
→ Next step: Counting money – notes

NATIONAL CURRICULUM LINKS

Year 2 Measurement – Money

- Recognise and use signs for pounds (£) and pence (p); combine amounts to make a particular value.
- Recognise and know the value of different denominations of coins and notes (year 1).

ASSESSING MASTERY

Children can identify a coin, know its value, and represent this with a pictorial representation or with apparatus. Children can use a counting on strategy to find the total value of a group of coins.

COMMON MISCONCEPTIONS

Children might confuse the value of the coins (especially the £1 and £2 due to similarities in appearance). Ask:
- *What are the differences between the coins?*

Children may think that a coin is greater in value because it is larger in size. This shows that children do not have a secure understanding of the value each coin represents. Ask:
- *Can you show me the value of each coin using Base 10 equipment?*

STRENGTHENING UNDERSTANDING

Ask children to represent a coin with smaller valued coins to strengthen their understanding of money. For example, if a child is struggling to work out the value of 10p, show it to them as two 5ps, five 2ps or ten 1ps.

Often, when finding the total value of a group of coins, children count each coin individually (5p + 5p + 2p might be counted as 1p + 1p + 1p +1p +1p +1p +1p +1p +1p +1p +1p +1p). Explain that it is more efficient to start with the coin highest in value and then count on.

To strengthen counting skills, regular practice of counting in 2s, 5s and 10s on a number line is necessary.

GOING DEEPER

Children might find several different methods for counting coins. Challenge children to think of strategies that are more efficient, such as pairing 5ps together and then counting in 10ps.

KEY LANGUAGE

In lesson: money, coins, value, much, pence (p), amount, total

Other language to be used by the teacher: count on

STRUCTURES AND REPRESENTATIONS

Base 10 equipment, number lines, currency

RESOURCES

Mandatory: currency (coins 1p–£2), Base 10 equipment

Optional: sorting hoops, trays

 In the eTextbook of this lesson, you will find interactive links to a selection of teaching tools.

Before you teach

- Are children secure counting in 2s, 5s and 10s?
- What resources might support children who are not secure in basic counting?
- What prior knowledge do children have about coins?

Discover

WAYS OF WORKING Pair work

ASK

• *How will you count the coins?*
• *Which was the quickest way to count the coins? Why?*

IN FOCUS This part of the lesson focuses on getting children to begin counting small amounts of money. Question ❶ b) helps children to understand that they can count the coins in different ways and still reach the correct amount. This should help reinforce their understanding of the value of the different coins.

ANSWERS

Question ❶ a): Tray A has 12p, Tray B has 30p, Tray C has 33p.

Question ❶ b): Tray C has 33p. Children could count the amount in a different way, starting by counting the 1ps and then the 10ps in 10s.

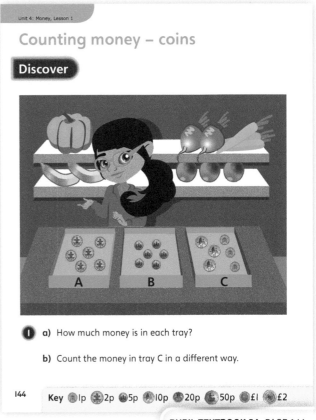

PUPIL TEXTBOOK 2A PAGE 144

Share

WAYS OF WORKING Whole class teacher led

ASK

• *Can you show me the value of 10p using Base 10 equipment?*
• *Why might it be a good idea to count in 10ps first and then 1ps?*

IN FOCUS In this section, children can see coins represented in different ways: firstly by other coins and then Base 10 equipment. Make it clear to children that value can be shown in a variety of ways. When adding the coins, whole class counting aloud is effective. Children should be encouraged to follow the 'hops' on the number line with their fingers on the **Pupil Textbook**.

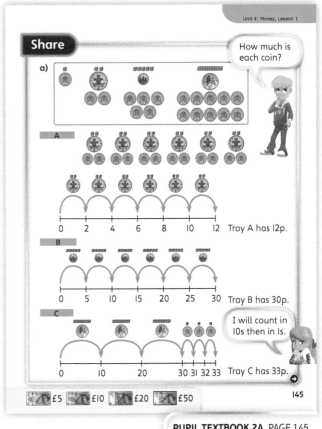

PUPIL TEXTBOOK 2A PAGE 145

Think together

WAYS OF WORKING Whole class teacher led (I do, We do, You do)

ASK

- *How many 2ps make 10p?*
- *20p is the same as 10p, 5p and 2p. Am I right? Can you correct me?*

IN FOCUS Look at question **3** . Encourage children to share different methods of counting. See if children can try counting the higher value coins first. After, ask if children can find any quicker methods of counting. Point out that Sparks says 'Two 10ps are the same as one 20p'. Explore other coins and then show how they could be grouped when counting, for example five 2ps could be grouped and counted as 10p.

STRENGTHEN To strengthen understanding in this section, have coins and Base 10 equipment laid out on a table. Children must match the number of cubes to the value of the coin. Make clear that for 10p, you could use a ten or 10 ones.

To support children with counting skills, practise counting coins. Children could count in 2ps, 5ps, 10ps forwards and backwards. Further to this, see if children can count on from a number (for example start on 13p and count on in 2ps).

DEEPEN To deepen understanding in this section, ask children to focus on question **3** and find all of the combinations of coins that could be grouped to make counting easier, such as five 2ps being counted as 10p.

To deepen counting strategies, have a bowl of coins on the table. The children must take a handful and count them in different ways. They must explain their favourite method to a friend and explain why it was effective.

ASSESSMENT CHECKPOINT Question **2** should help you decide if children are confident at counting coins.

Question **3** will show you which children have a secure understanding of coin values and counting them – children who have a secure understanding will be able to focus on finding more efficient methods and strategies. Children who are not yet secure may make errors with coin value and use long-winded counting methods such as counting in 1ps.

ANSWERS

Question **1** : There is 36p in the tray.

Question **2** : There is 26p in the tray.

Question **3** : There is 70p in the first tray (50p + 10p + 10p) and 43p in the second tray (20p + 5p + 5p + 5p + 5p + 1p + 1p + 1p). Children can count the amounts in different ways. In Tray 1, they could count the two 10ps as one 20p. In Tray 2, children could group the four 5ps into two 10ps or one 20p.

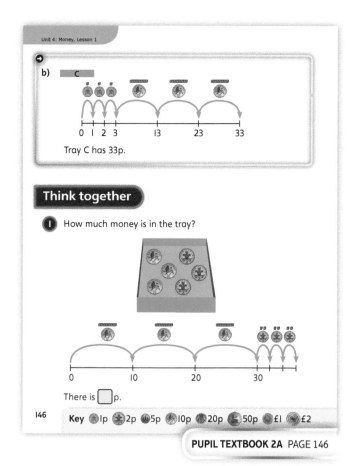

PUPIL TEXTBOOK 2A PAGE 146

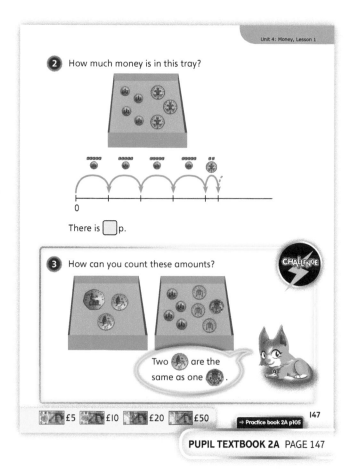

PUPIL TEXTBOOK 2A PAGE 147

Practice

WAYS OF WORKING Independent thinking

IN FOCUS Question **3** puts the greatest jump first on the number line; support children in choosing the 50p (referring to Dexter's comment is good practice).

Question **5** will require children to remember learning from year 1, in which they will have covered odd and even numbers. Remind children of this – an odd and even counting game works well.

STRENGTHEN Some children may need in-lesson support from an adult. Work alongside children using Base 10 equipment to help them count the coins. This will be particularly useful for their understanding in questions such as question **4** b) in which only numbers are shown.

DEEPEN When children are secure in showing the values of 10p and 20p coins with other coins, ask them to apply this knowledge by representing 50p and £1 and £2 in a range of ways, such as showing that £1 is the same as five 20ps. Next, ask children to find all of the ways. Ask: *How do you know you have found them all? Did you use a strategy? Which solution was the most efficient? Why?*

ASSESSMENT CHECKPOINT Question **6** is very effective in assessing children's knowledge of the whole lesson. It requires children to know the value of coins, select different combinations and find totals by counting on. If you want to assess deeper understanding, ask children to include their workings. This will tell you if they have used efficient strategies (such as combining the 5ps and counting them as 10p).

ANSWERS Answers for the **Practice** part of the lesson appear in the separate **Practice and Reflect answer guide**.

Reflect

WAYS OF WORKING Pair work

IN FOCUS Put children in pairs (if possible, put a secure child with one who needs strengthening). Working together on this final task will support all and allow children to teach their partners something, which is an effective mastery method.

ASSESSMENT CHECKPOINT Observe the pairs working together. See which pairs are using effective strategies. Effective strategies may include: grouping the two 5ps as 10p, beginning with the higher value coins and using another method (it may not be more effective, but this shows deep thinking).

ANSWERS Answers for the **Reflect** part of the lesson appear in the separate **Practice and Reflect answer guide**.

After the lesson ⏸

- How many children demonstrated a secure understanding of coin value?
- What challenges did children have when showing coin value? Did any children struggle with counting methods such as counting the higher value coins first?
- What would you do differently (before or during the lesson) to make children's understanding greater?

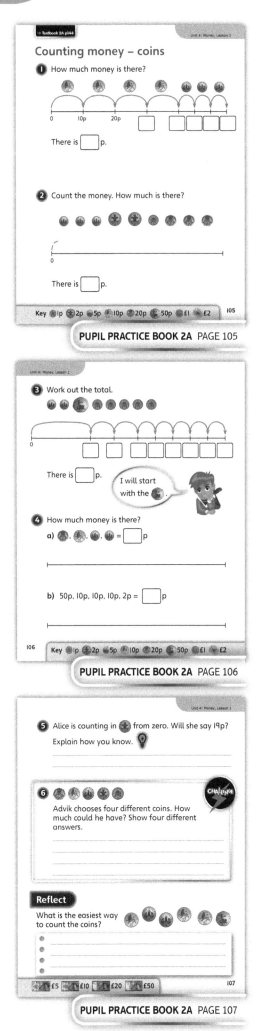

PUPIL PRACTICE BOOK 2A PAGE 105

PUPIL PRACTICE BOOK 2A PAGE 106

PUPIL PRACTICE BOOK 2A PAGE 107

Counting money – notes

Learning focus

In this lesson, children will learn the value of notes and find total amounts of them.

Small steps

→ Previous step: Counting money – coins
→ **This step: Counting money – notes**
→ Next step: Counting money – coins and notes

NATIONAL CURRICULUM LINKS

Year 2 Measurement – Money

- Recognise and use signs for pounds (£) and pence (p); combine amounts to make a particular value.
- Recognise and know the value of different denominations of coins and notes (year 1).

ASSESSING MASTERY

Children can represent the value of notes using coins. Children can confidently find totals of notes, £2 and £1 coins (not yet breaking into pounds and pence).

COMMON MISCONCEPTIONS

Children may think that the Base 10 equipment represents pennies (due to Base 10 representing pennies in the previous lesson). Make it clear that, in this lesson, Base 10 represent pounds. Ask:
- *What other things could Base 10 represent? People? Grams? Cars?*

Children may count the coins before the notes. Ask:
- *Is it easier to count coins before notes? Why not?*

STRENGTHENING UNDERSTANDING

Some children may need to strengthen their counting skills. Practise counting in £2s then £20s and see if children can make the link between them. Also practise counting in £1s and £10s; £5 and £50s. Intervention may be needed before the lesson as this is a required skill for this lesson. Another way to support these children is to provide them with a multiplication grid.

The pound sign (£) is newly introduced in this lesson. Children may find it difficult to scribe. Practise scribing the pound sign (£) with children when there is time over the week (tracing is a good idea).

GOING DEEPER

To deepen understanding in this lesson, give children a total amount, such as £32, and ask them to find all the different combinations of notes and coins that could be used to make that total. Alternatively, see if children can create a multi-step word problem that involves finding totals of notes and coins.

KEY LANGUAGE

In lesson: money, pounds (£), notes, amount, how much, altogether, total

Other language to be used by the teacher: coins, greatest, count on

STRUCTURES AND REPRESENTATIONS

Base 10 equipment, number lines, currency, part-whole model

RESOURCES

Mandatory: notes (£5, £10, £20, £50), coins (£1, £2), Base 10 equipment

Optional: multiplication grid

 In the eTextbook of this lesson, you will find interactive links to a selection of teaching tools.

Before you teach

- How will you introduce notes to children in this lesson?
- Can all the class count in 2s, 5s, 10s, 20s, 50s?
- Have children made the link between counting in 2s and 20s?

Discover

Unit 4: Money, Lesson 2

WAYS OF WORKING Pair work

ASK

- *How many pounds does each note represent?*
- *Why do you use notes? Would it be a good idea to have 50 pound coins in your purse? Why not?*
- *What is the most efficient way to count this amount?*

IN FOCUS Question ❶ introduces children to notes. It will require children to work out the value of each note and then the total. Children will need to be secure in counting in 5s and 10s. Some children will count the £10s and then count the £5s individually such as £10, £20, £30, £40, £41, £42… £55. If this happens, try practising counting in 5s, but starting at different numbers.

ANSWERS

Question ❶ a): The lady on the stall has rasied £55.

Question ❶ b): The lady on the stall now has £58.

Counting money – notes

Discover

❶ **a)** How much money has the lady on the stall raised?

b) She is given three 🪙.

How much does she have now?

148 **Key** 🪙1p ✳️2p 🪙5p 🪙10p 🪙20p 🪙50p 🪙£1 🪙£2

PUPIL TEXTBOOK 2A PAGE 148

Share

WAYS OF WORKING Whole class teacher led

ASK

- *Why does Astrid start with the greatest amount?*
- *Which is correct: £58 or 58£?*
- *How many £5 make £10? How many £5 make £20?*

IN FOCUS Question ❶ b) shows children the order in which to count notes and coins (starting with the greatest amount). If children find this challenging, give them a range of notes and coins and ask them to order them.

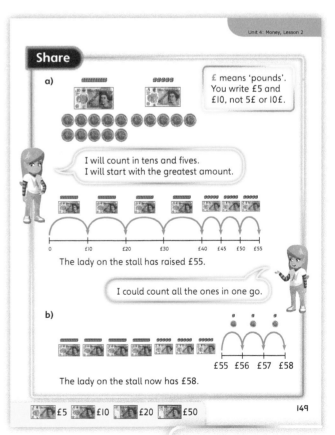

Share

a) £ means 'pounds'. You write £5 and £10, not 5£ or 10£.

I will count in tens and fives. I will start with the greatest amount.

0 £10 £20 £30 £40 £45 £50 £55

The lady on the stall has raised £55.

I could count all the ones in one go.

b)

£55 £56 £57 £58

The lady on the stall now has £58.

🪙 £5 🪙 £10 🪙 £20 🪙 £50 149

PUPIL TEXTBOOK 2A PAGE 149

Think together

Whole class teacher led (I do, We do, You do)

ASK

- *How can we use counting in 2s to help us count in 20s?*
- *£20 is the same amount as how many £2s?*
- *Look at question ③. How do you know you were correct? Can you prove it?*

IN FOCUS In question ③ children will be required to count in 20s. It is very important that links are made between counting in 2s and 20s, however it is vital that children don't just see it as putting a 0 on the end of the 2 times-table. Using Base 10 equipment, show children how, when adding 20 to an amount, only the tens change by 2 – the units remain the same. If children are secure with the concept, they should be able to count in 20s when starting from other numbers such as 13: 33, 53 and so on.

STRENGTHEN Intervention may be needed to support children counting in £2s, £5s, £10s, £20s and £50s. If children are finding counting in £20s difficult, the £20s could be partitioned into £10s (so children could count each one twice in £10s).

DEEPEN To deepen understanding, children could make their own matching exercise – some could include £50 notes.

ASSESSMENT CHECKPOINT Question ② will assess whether children can securely find totals of notes and coins using a number line. Question ③ will determine whether they can do this without a number line to support them.

ANSWERS

Question ① : There is £34.

Question ② : There is £64 altogether.

Question ③ : The first circle has £52, the second circle has £42 and the third circle has £60.

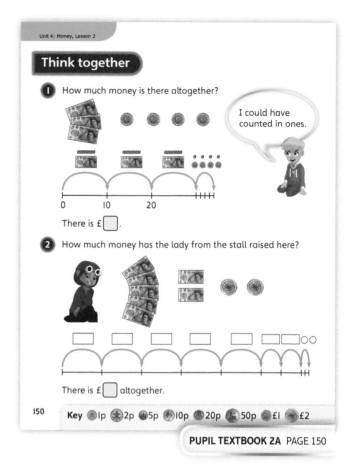

PUPIL TEXTBOOK 2A PAGE 150

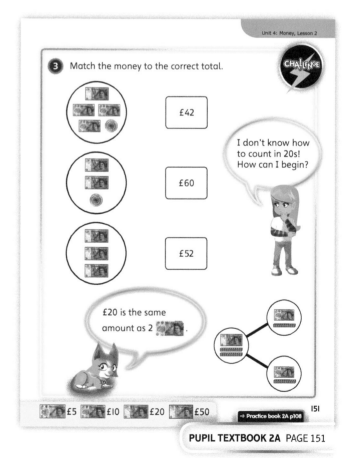

PUPIL TEXTBOOK 2A PAGE 151

Practice

WAYS OF WORKING Independent thinking

IN FOCUS Question ❹ requires children to complete a part-whole model. Children may need to be prompted on how to complete this (especially as notes are new to them).

STRENGTHEN In question ❷, pupils may need support selecting the money. Ask: *Could you start with £50?* Prompt children to partition £43 and then find the notes that make £40 and the coins that make £3.

DEEPEN Ask children to revisit question ❹ and challenge them to make their own part-whole models. Ask: *Can you make a part-whole model with 8 circles?*

ASSESSMENT CHECKPOINT Look at children's answers for question ❸. You will be able to see clearly which children are secure with mentally and independently finding totals. Look out for workings out (probably number lines) for those who still rely on counting support.

ANSWERS Answers for the **Practice** part of the lesson appear in the separate **Practice and Reflect answer guide**.

Reflect

WAYS OF WORKING Independent work

IN FOCUS This **Reflect** activity is open and has a number of different answers. A good way to extend learning here is to see if secure children can find £20 but with a predetermined number of notes and coins. For example, can children explain three different ways to make £20 using 17 coins and notes?

ASSESSMENT CHECKPOINT This question will show if children are secure in knowing the value of notes and if they can find totals. Secure children may show more 'creative' answers such as £10 + £5 + £2 + £1 + £1 + 50p + 50p.

ANSWERS Answers for the **Reflect** part of the lesson appear in the separate **Practice and Reflect answer guide**.

After the lesson ⏸

- Which children need more support with counting in 2s, 5s, 10s, 20s, 50s?
- How can you provide extra support for those who need to strengthen their understanding of the value of notes?
- Which children have mastered counting coins and notes?

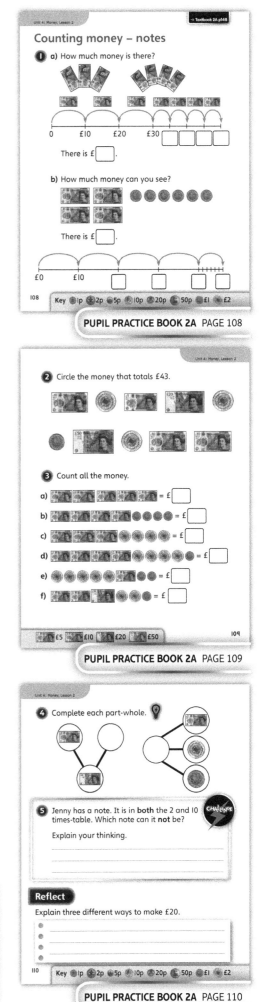

PUPIL PRACTICE BOOK 2A PAGE 108

PUPIL PRACTICE BOOK 2A PAGE 109

PUPIL PRACTICE BOOK 2A PAGE 110

Counting money – coins and notes

Learning focus

In this lesson, children will count different amounts of money and record their answers in pounds and pence (separately).

Small steps

→ Previous step: Counting money – notes
→ **This step: Counting money – coins and notes**
→ Next step: Showing equal amounts of money (1)

NATIONAL CURRICULUM LINKS

Year 2 Measurement – Money

Recognise and use signs for pounds (£) and pence (p); combine amounts to make a particular value.

ASSESSING MASTERY

Children can separate pounds and pence; calculating the pounds first and then the pence. Children can spot their mistakes in calculations and explain their solutions.

COMMON MISCONCEPTIONS

Children may add the notes together and then the coins (mistaking the £1 and £2 for pennies). Ask:
• *Which notes or coins are pounds? Which coins are pence?*

You may find that children calculate the total of the pounds and then continue to count on when totalling the pence. For example, they may say that £10 + £10 + 5p = £25. Ask:
• *What is the difference between 5p and £5?*

STRENGTHENING UNDERSTANDING

To strengthen understanding, continue reinforcing counting skills (2s, 5s, 10s, 20s, 50s). Children can be supported using multiplication grids.

If children are struggling to separate pounds and pence, do some sorting activities with notes and coins (sorting hoops are a good resource to use). It is particularly important to draw out the fact that the £1 and £2 coins are pounds.

GOING DEEPER

To go deeper in this lesson, you could challenge children to create a shopping list consisting of five items. They must find the total amount of the five items and then draw the notes and coins they would use to pay for it.

KEY LANGUAGE

In this lesson: money, coins, notes, how much? sort, pounds, pence, total, amount

Other language to be used by the teacher: count on

STRUCTURES AND REPRESENTATIONS

Number line, this time only supported by images of coins or notes. Counting aloud as a class, and following the number line with fingers, is also a recommended strategy to adopt.

RESOURCES

Mandatory: currency (coins and notes)

Optional: sorting hoops, multiplication grids, trays

 In the eTextbook of this lesson, you will find interactive links to a selection of teaching tools.

Before you teach

• Do children understand the difference between pounds and pence?
• How will you encourage children to explain their methods?

Discover

Unit 4: Money, Lesson 3

WAYS OF WORKING Pair work

ASK

- *Should you count the notes or coins first?*
- *How should you count the pennies?*
- *Is it easier to combine coins that have the same value?*
- *How can you record your answers?*

IN FOCUS Question ① a) introduces children to finding totals of pounds and pence. Watch carefully which strategies are used and how children say or record the answer. Misconceptions are common here and will need to be discussed and resolved (please see the 'common misconceptions' section on the previous page).

Question ① b) challenges children to add £10 to the original calculation. Talk with children about what changes when you add £10. Ask: *Is it the pounds or pence that change?*

ANSWERS

Question ① a): The girl has saved £23 and 21p.

Question ① b): The girl now has £33 and 21p.

Counting money – coins and notes

Discover

① a) How much money has the girl saved?

   b) The girl finds another [image].
       How much money does she have now?

152   **Key** ● 1p ✳ 2p ● 5p ● 10p ● 20p ● 50p ● £1 ● £2

PUPIL TEXTBOOK 2A PAGE 152

Share

WAYS OF WORKING Whole class teacher led

ASK

- *Why do you count the notes and then the coins?*
- *Can you sort all of the coins into pounds and pence?*
- *Do any of the notes represent pence?*

IN FOCUS Question ① b) is important because it is about place value. Children must be aware that if pounds are added to a total, the pence do not change.

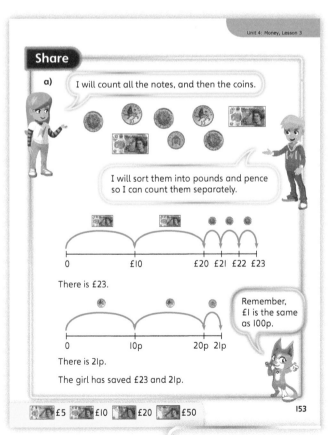

Share

a) I will count all the notes, and then the coins.

I will sort them into pounds and pence so I can count them separately.

0   £10   £20 £21 £22 £23

There is £23.

Remember, £1 is the same as 100p.

0   10p   20p 21p

There is 21p.

The girl has saved £23 and 21p.

[£5] £5 [£10] £10 [£20] £20 [£50] £50   153

PUPIL TEXTBOOK 2A PAGE 153

Think together

WAYS OF WORKING **WAYS OF WORKING** Whole class teacher led (I do, We do, You do)

ASK

- *Look at question ❶. Why are there two separate number lines and not just one?*
- *What is an easy way of counting the notes in question 2?*

IN FOCUS Question ❸ is a good way to draw out misconceptions between pounds and pence. The boy has counted the 2p as 1p and the £1 as £2. If children are secure with spotting the mistake, ask them how they would teach the boy where he went wrong.

STRENGTHEN If children find separating pounds and pence difficult, provide extra intervention in which coins and notes are sorted. Children could draw a table to be kept for future reference.

DEEPEN To deepen children's understanding ask: *When counting money, if you add pounds, do the pennies ever change?* Then ask: *When adding pennies, do the pounds ever change?*

Children will realise that when they reach 99p, any more pennies will increase the pounds.

ASSESSMENT CHECKPOINT Question ❶ will tell you if children can count notes and coins with the support of a number line (which separates the pounds and pence).

Question ❷ will tell you if children can count notes and coins independently, without support.

ANSWERS

Question ❶ : Together there is £15 and 56p.

Question ❷ : Together there is £25 and 26p.

Question ❸ : The boy has made the mistake of counting the 2p as 1p and the £1 as £2.

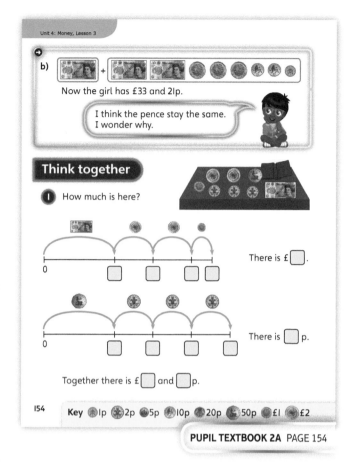

PUPIL TEXTBOOK 2A PAGE 154

PUPIL TEXTBOOK 2A PAGE 155

Practice

IN FOCUS Question **4** gives you some excellent talking points that will really probe children's understanding of this lesson. Ask: *Can you use the one pound coin? Why not? What about the two pence piece? Why not?*

STRENGTHEN In question **3** c) children have no visual prompts for support. Some children may still need visual representations of coins and notes – they could draw the coins themselves.

In question **3** d) children must partition numbers in number sentences. This may be an area that needs practice during or prior to the lesson. Ask children how to partition £27 into £10s and £1s. Next, ask children to partition 33p into 10ps and 1ps. Repeat with different amounts until children are secure.

DEEPEN When children have finished question **5** , look over their answers and ensure they are accurate and well explained. To deepen understanding, ask: *How could you improve your explanation? Have you included what Poppy's errors are and what James's errors are?*

You could also challenge children to see if they can work out how many pennies make the notes such as £5 = 500p. This will show a deep understanding of place value within money.

ASSESSMENT CHECKPOINT Question **4** will allow you to assess whether children can find amounts of money. To find 30 pence, children must use the 20p and two 5ps (there is no 10p available).

ANSWERS Answers for the **Practice** part of the lesson appear in the separate **Practice and Reflect answer guide**.

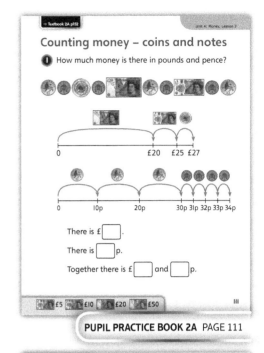

PUPIL PRACTICE BOOK 2A PAGE 111

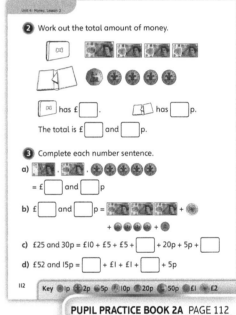

PUPIL PRACTICE BOOK 2A PAGE 112

Reflect

IN FOCUS This **Reflect** question will draw out children's explanatory skills. It is useful for children to provide an example to support their understanding – some children may want to draw their examples.

ASSESSMENT CHECKPOINT Can all children give a satisfactory explanation of counting pounds and pence? Ask children to turn to their partner and teach them their method. This will help you observe any children who you are uncertain about.

ANSWERS Answers for the **Reflect** part of the lesson appear in the separate **Practice and Reflect answer guide**.

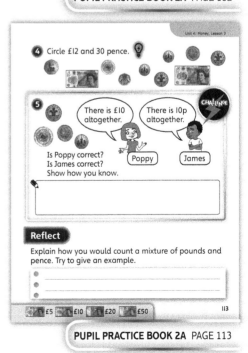

PUPIL PRACTICE BOOK 2A PAGE 113

After the lesson ⏸

- Which children need more support with counting pounds and pence?
- When can children do an intervention activity to prepare them for the next lesson?
- You could set a home learning activity, in which children are encouraged to go shopping with their parents or guardians.

Showing equal amounts of money

Learning focus

In this lesson, children will select the right combination of coins and notes for a given amount. Children will also find how much money is left over.

Small steps

→ Previous step: Counting money – coins and notes
→ **This step: Showing equal amounts of money (1)**
→ Next step: Showing equal amounts of money (2)

NATIONAL CURRICULUM LINKS

Year 2 Measurement – Money

- Find different combinations of coins that equal the same amounts of money.
- Recognise and know the value of different denominations of coins and notes (year 1).

ASSESSING MASTERY

Children can accurately find the coins needed for a given amount (pounds and pence) through calculating number sentences and completing part-whole models. Children can use mental methods and their knowledge of counting on in 2s, 5s and 10s.

COMMON MISCONCEPTIONS

Children may continue to confuse pounds and pence. Ask:
- *If you need to make exactly 52p, would you use a £1 coin?*

STRENGTHENING UNDERSTANDING

Some children may still need support with counting. Provide these children with coins and notes and encourage the use of number lines and multiplication grids to strengthen understanding.

GOING DEEPER

Asking children to think of how they might pay for something will deepen their understanding in this lesson. Get children to find the coins and notes they need in order to pay for an item, but give restrictions. For example, you could tell children that you want to use as many coins as possible. You could also ask children to find the smallest and largest number of coins needed to pay for different amounts. These types of challenges could then be put into word problems.

KEY LANGUAGE

In lesson: coins, notes, money, left, total, parts, match, pounds (£), pence (p), right money, exact(ly), smallest

Other language to be used by the teacher: equal, amount

STRUCTURES AND REPRESENTATIONS

Part-whole model, number line

RESOURCES

Mandatory: currency (coins and notes), part-whole model

Optional: multiplication grid, number lines, Base 10 equipment, coin stencils

 In the eTextbook of this lesson, you will find interactive links to a selection of teaching tools.

Before you teach

- Are children secure with using the part-whole model?
- Do the class, or some children, need a quick recap of finding the total of coins and notes?

Discover

Pair work

ASK

- *What should you do – there is no 20p coin to make 25p?*
- Question **1** b): *What does 'left' mean? What do you have to do?*
- Question **1** b): *What would be a good strategy to make sure you do not count a note or coin that you have already used? (Cross out the notes or coins when used.)*

IN FOCUS In question **1** a) children will look for the 20p coin, in order to make 25p. Children will soon realise there is not one available. Prompt children to look for some other coins that will total 20p.

Question **1** b) will start getting children to see what money is 'left'. Children may need reminding of the meaning of 'left'.

ANSWERS

Question **1** a): Oliver needs 10p + 10p + 2p + 2p + 1p.
Gemma needs £5 + £2 + £1.

Question **1** b): £10 + £1 + 50p + 1p.
They have £11 and 51p left in total.

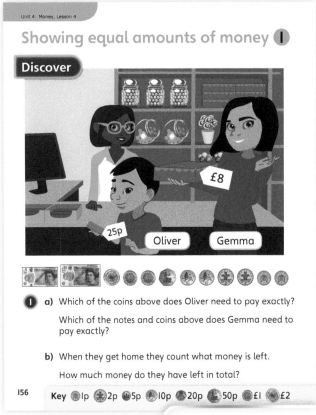

PUPIL TEXTBOOK 2A PAGE 156

Share

Whole class teacher led

ASK

- *How does the part-whole model help you?*
- *Look at question **1** b). Can you point to the pounds? Can you point to the pennies?*

IN FOCUS In question **1** a), it is important to draw out that the part-whole model partitions the number for us. You could ask children why this is not necessary for £8. In question **1** b), be sure to emphasise crossing out used coins. Refer to the example in the **Pupil Textbook**.

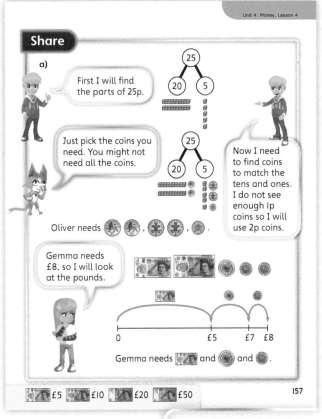

PUPIL TEXTBOOK 2A PAGE 157

Think together

WAYS OF WORKING Whole class teacher led (I do, We do, You do)

ASK

• Question **2** : *What should you do first? How can you partition the pounds and pennies?*

• Question **3** : *Why can you definitely NOT use 1p to make the total amount?*

IN FOCUS Question **3** asks children to choose the coins and notes needed to make the amount. Make children read aloud Ash's question; do they know which ones they can definitely choose (or not choose)? For example, the £20 shouldn't be chosen because it is higher than the total amount, and the 1p will not be chosen either because the total amount is even.

STRENGTHEN In question **1** , you may need to draw out that 64 has been split into 60 and 4. However, there is not a 60p coin or a 4p coin. With your finger, circle five of the rows of Base 10 cubes in the **Pupil Textbook** and ask what coin these represent. Do the same for the leftover row. Then circle two of the single cubes and ask what coin this could be. Children may need extra intervention (similar to what has just been outlined) using the part-whole model with larger amounts of money.

Some children may find it difficult to find a starting point for question **1** . Ask these children which coin is nearest in value to 60p: they should say 50p. Tell children that 50p is an excellent coin to begin with – then they can build upon this.

DEEPEN To deepen understanding, ask children to look at all three questions and see if they can find more than one solution. If children are secure, they should have the confidence to say that there is only one solution for each. Some children will spend a longer period of time trying to find another solution. Explain that there is only one solution and that they need to be confident to say so.

ASSESSMENT CHECKPOINT Questions **1** and **2** will let you assess if children can use the part-whole model or the number line to work out answers (they may have a preference).

Question **3** will test children's reasoning ability. Ask them why they cannot use the £2 coin and listen to their explanation carefully. Some children may need support structuring their explanations.

ANSWERS

Question **1** : 50p + 10p + 2p + 2p

Question **2** : £20 + £10 + £5 + £5 + £1

Question **3** : Children could choose £10 + £1 + 20p + 2p to make £11 and 22p or they could cross out 1p, 5p, 10p, 50p, £2, £5, £20 to leave the exact amount of £11 and 22p.

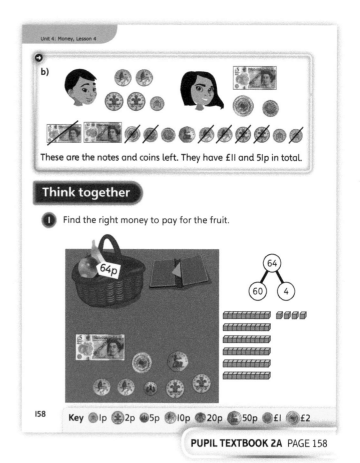

PUPIL TEXTBOOK 2A PAGE 158

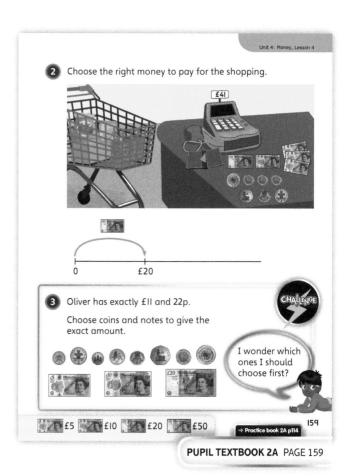

PUPIL TEXTBOOK 2A PAGE 159

Practice

WAYS OF WORKING Independent thinking

IN FOCUS In question **5**, children may draw the size of the coins inaccurately. Encourage children to look at the key at the foot of the **Practice** page for support. Drawing around real coins or using a stencil would work well. Children's drawings do not have to be perfect but they should be accurate.

STRENGTHEN During this independent thinking section, continue to encourage children to use number lines or part-whole models if needed. Children may also want to use physical coins or diagrams to strengthen their understanding.

DEEPEN To deepen understanding, set children a challenge. Ask them to investigate whether all the numbers up to 50 can be made from coins and notes – include the rule that each coin or note can only be used once. This may take longer than the lesson, but would be an excellent home learning activity. As an example, 19p could not be made because it would require a 10p, 5p, 2p and another 2p (or two 1ps) – breaking the 'use only one coin' rule.

ASSESSMENT CHECKPOINT Question **4** will allow you to assess children's competency with adding coins. Some children will have to use a trial and improvement method, whereas some will be able to solve them quickly in their head.

ANSWERS Answers for the **Practice** part of the lesson appear in the separate **Practice and Reflect answer guide**.

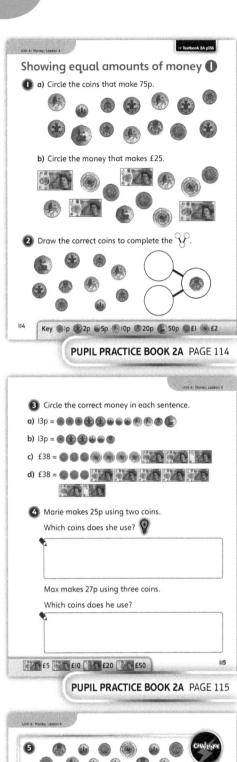

PUPIL PRACTICE BOOK 2A PAGE 114

PUPIL PRACTICE BOOK 2A PAGE 115

Reflect

WAYS OF WORKING Group work

IN FOCUS With children working in small groups, this would be a good activity to have a range of coins for, so children can move them around on their tables. You could make it into a class competition. Keep changing the amount and get children to hold their solutions in the air when they have found them.

ASSESSMENT CHECKPOINT The **Reflect** activity will allow you to see which children can find the total amount, but also allow you to see those who are secure enough to work out if there are any more options (with fewer coins).

ANSWERS Answers for the **Reflect** part of the lesson appear in the separate **Practice and Reflect answer guide**.

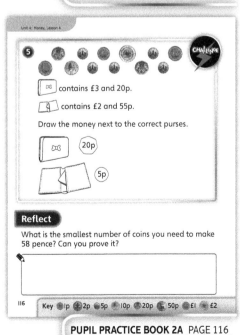

PUPIL PRACTICE BOOK 2A PAGE 116

After the lesson ⏸

- Are children explaining their methods accurately?
- Do any children need further support with money using the part-whole model or number line?

Showing equal amounts of money ②

Learning focus

In this lesson, children will use different combinations of coins and notes to make the same amount of money.

Small steps

→ Previous step: Showing equal amounts of money (1)
→ **This step: Showing equal amounts of money (2)**
→ Next step: Comparing amounts of money

NATIONAL CURRICULUM LINKS

Year 2 Measurement – Money

- Find different combinations of coins that equal the same amounts of money.
- Recognise and know the value of different denominations of coins and notes (year 1).

ASSESSING MASTERY

Children can confidently make the same amount using a combination of different coins and notes. Children can solve money problems and explain their solutions.

COMMON MISCONCEPTIONS

Children may think that there is only one correct answer to an open-ended problem. Ask:
- *Can you look again at that question and see if there is another solution?*

STRENGTHENING UNDERSTANDING

Use the part-whole model to break down larger numbers. This will make a problem more manageable and give children more confidence to approach it.

GOING DEEPER

Children often find an answer, then another, then another. There is no strategy involved. Challenge children to look out for ways to order their workings, so they find all the possible solutions to a problem and do not miss any out.

KEY LANGUAGE

In lesson: money, coins, notes, pence (p), pound (£), parts, right money, ways, equal, amounts, exact(ly)

STRUCTURES AND REPRESENTATIONS

Part-whole model, number line

RESOURCES

Mandatory: currency (coins and notes), part-whole model, number lines

Optional: Base 10 equipment

 In the eTextbook of this lesson, you will find interactive links to a selection of teaching tools.

Before you teach

- Which children may not be confident with solving open-ended problems?
- How can these children be supported in the lesson?
- Are there different amounts that secure children can find out if they finish an activity quickly?

Discover

WAYS OF WORKING Pair work

ASK

• *How many solutions can you find to make 65p?*
• *Which solution uses the greatest number of coins?*

IN FOCUS Children may be used to maths questions with right or wrong answers. Question ❶ b) will be challenging for some, when they realise there are many solutions.

ANSWERS

Question ❶ a): Jenny: 20p + 20p + 10p + 10p + 5p
　　　　　　　　Mark: 50p + 10p + 2p + 1p + 1p + 1p

Question ❶ b): Multiple solutions – some children may say 65 1ps.

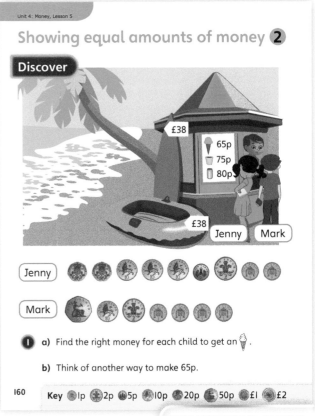

PUPIL TEXTBOOK 2A PAGE 160

Share

WAYS OF WORKING Whole class teacher led

ASK

• *Can you share some of your solutions for question ❶ b)?*
• *How can you tell if you have found all of the solutions?*
• *Which solution uses 11 coins?*

IN FOCUS Question ❶ b) lets the children work in an investigative manner, finding multiple solutions. Encourage secure children to work systematically (maybe using a table to record solutions in order).

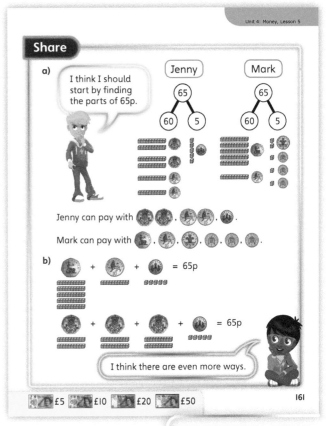

PUPIL TEXTBOOK 2A PAGE 161

Think together

WAYS OF WORKING Whole class teacher led (I do, We do, You do)

ASK

• *Can you find even more ways to make the total amounts in this section?*

• *Can you explain your method of working to the class?*

IN FOCUS Question **2** asks children to find £38 in two different ways – but limiting them to certain notes and coins. Encourage children to make the £30 first and then the £8 (there are two solutions for the man).

STRENGTHEN To strengthen understanding when answering question **3**, ask children to break down 80p in a range of different ways using the part-whole model. For example, 50p and 30p; 70p and 10p; 20p + 20p + 20p + 20p and so on. This will make the challenge easier to solve.

DEEPEN In all questions in this section, challenge children to find all of the answers. Look for children who are using a strategy or system such as starting with the coins of greatest value then working lower.

ASSESSMENT CHECKPOINT If children are secure, they will solve question **3** quickly and confidently, moving on to even more solutions. Those that need strengthening may tend to choose a simple solution such as eight 10ps and then struggle to find other solutions.

ANSWERS

Question **1** : Gemma: 20p + 20p + 20p + 10p + 5p.

Paul: 50p + 5p + 5p + 5p + 5p + 2p + 2p + 1p

Question **2** : The man: £20 + £5 + £5 + £5 + £2 + £1
or £20 + £5 + £5 + £2 + £2 + £2 + £1 + £1

The woman: £20 + £10 + £5 + £1 + £1 + £1

Question **3** : There are multiple solutions for this question.

PUPIL TEXTBOOK 2A PAGE 162

PUPIL TEXTBOOK 2A PAGE 163

Practice

WAYS OF WORKING

IN FOCUS In question **1** children are challenged to match equal amounts. This is a useful exercise as it reinforces prior learning. Children may need to be prompted to calculate the totals of each one first.

STRENGTHEN Children might need strengthening activities when working out how to make certain amounts. For those children who struggle with question **3**, make intervention time for them, so they can practise finding different solutions for different amounts of money. Use the number line method (as in the **Pupil Textbook**) and pair it with coins or notes. Model the method first, and then let the children try. If children are not sure which number to begin with, ask them to look at a coin or note and see which is the nearest to the total value.

DEEPEN Ask children to reflect on question **5** and then challenge them to see if there are any number of coins that cannot make 10p (for instance you could not make 10p using only 3 coins). Then ask children to complete the same challenge to make 50p.

ASSESSMENT CHECKPOINT Question **3** will help you assess whether children can find different ways to make total amounts of money (they must also show their workings on number lines).

To assess mastery of partitioning amounts of money, look at children's answers for question **5**. It will involve a lot of deep thinking to find all the different combinations of coins.

ANSWERS Answers for the **Practice** part of the lesson appear in the separate **Practice and Reflect answer guide**.

Reflect

WAYS OF WORKING Pair work

IN FOCUS This is a word problem, so vocabulary might need to be explained to the class. Children could highlight key vocabulary. When children complete the task, ask them to find more answers. Then, as an end of lesson question, you could ask children to prove that Sarah could have 58 coins.

ASSESSMENT CHECKPOINT This **Reflect** question puts the learning throughout the lesson into context. You will be able to assess the children who understand the challenge and those who can find multiple solutions. It will also allow you to see which children are working through the problem systematically – therefore showing mastery of the topic.

ANSWERS Answers for the **Reflect** part of the lesson appear in the separate **Practice and Reflect answer guide**.

After the lesson ⏸

- Which children need more support partitioning amounts?
- Who struggled with the word problem in the **Reflect** section? Could these children be given time to practise similar problems?

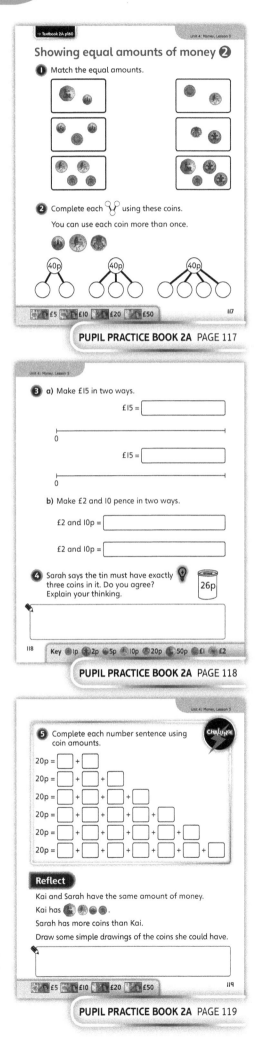

PUPIL PRACTICE BOOK 2A PAGE 117

PUPIL PRACTICE BOOK 2A PAGE 118

PUPIL PRACTICE BOOK 2A PAGE 119

Comparing amounts of money

Learning focus

In this lesson, children will compare amounts of money using the correct vocabulary and the signs <, > and =.

Small steps

→ Previous step: Showing equal amounts of money (2)
→ **This step: Comparing amounts of money**
→ Next step: Calculating the total amount

NATIONAL CURRICULUM LINKS

Year 2 Measurement – Money

- Solve simple problems in a practical context involving addition and subtraction of money of the same unit, including giving change.
- Recognise and know the value of different denominations of coins and notes (year 1).

ASSESSING MASTERY

Children can correctly compare different amounts and use the <, > and = signs to represent the relationship between them. Children can use the correct vocabulary when giving an answer, such as £5 > 89p 'Five pounds is more than 89p.'

COMMON MISCONCEPTIONS

Children may confuse < and >. Ask:

- *What do the signs < and > mean? Can we show what they mean using a diagram?*

STRENGTHENING UNDERSTANDING

Children will need reinforcement of the signs <, > and = so they remember them. Daily intervention in which children order numbers is a good idea. Another idea is to create a classroom display.

GOING DEEPER

Children who are secure in the lesson could order more than two amounts, for example: order £2, 99p and 210p. Children could then go on to find more than one representation by re-ordering the numbers, such as £2 > 99p < 210p or 210p > £2 > 99p or 99p < 210p > £2.

KEY LANGUAGE

In lesson: more than (>), less than (<), equal (=), total, amount, higher, lower, compare, between, pound (£), pence (p), most, least, great(er/est)

STRUCTURES AND REPRESENTATIONS

Base 10 equipment, pictorial representations

RESOURCES

Mandatory: currency (coins and notes)

Optional: Base 10 equipment, pictorial representations

 In the eTextbook of this lesson, you will find interactive links to a selection of teaching tools.

Before you teach

- Have you created a classroom display or prompt card to support children with remembering the signs <, > and =?
- Do children remember the vocabulary for the signs that they covered in year 1?
- You could start the lesson with a quick recap of children's learning in year 1 (ordering objects).

Discover

Pair work

ASK

- How should you work out question ① a)?
- Which stall raised the most money? Which stall raised the least?

IN FOCUS Question ① b) is open-ended. You will probably find that most children give £7 or £8 as answers. It might be interesting to see if children can find other options. Ask: *Can anyone find halfway between £6 and £9?*

ANSWERS

Question ① a): The boy on stall A raised more money.

Question ① b): The girl on stall C could have raised any value between £6 and £9.

PUPIL TEXTBOOK 2A PAGE 164

Share

WAYS OF WORKING Whole class teacher led

ASK

- Why is it useful to work out the totals first?
- Look at question ① b) – using the vocabulary 'less than', can you read aloud your answer?

IN FOCUS Question ① b) brings in comparing three amounts of money. This may be challenging for children so remind them to look at what each sign means and try to find a solution. Reading the answers aloud is a useful strategy that promotes mastery of this lesson.

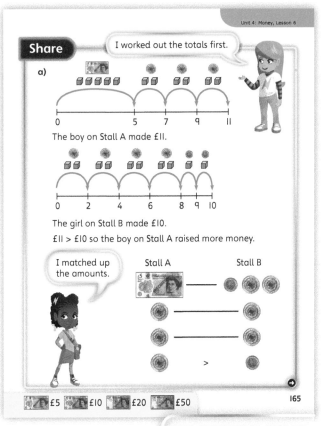

PUPIL TEXTBOOK 2A PAGE 165

Think together

WAYS OF WORKING Whole class teacher led (I do, We do, You do)

ASK

- *Can you remind your partner of what the signs mean?*
- *Can you find more solutions for the problems in question* ❷ *?*
- *Why should you compare the pounds first?*

IN FOCUS In question ❷, there are a number of solutions. Children will need to realise that in the first part, the ten pound note must be used on the right side of the <. For the second part, children should find the total of each amount and then realise that the 10p and 20p will be the coins required respectively.

STRENGTHEN When completing question ❸, some children may not have understood that the value of the £1 coin is the same as 100 pennies. Some intervention may be needed here, in which amounts such as 134p are partitioned using the part-whole model (partitioning the 100p and the 34p). Next, remind children of how many pennies there are in a pound. Children should realise that 134p can be recorded as £1 and 34p.

DEEPEN To deepen understanding, ask children to investigate whether you only need to count the pounds when ordering amounts. Ask: *Can the pennies ever affect the result? What if one group has £2 and 3p and the other group has £1 and 110p?*

ASSESSMENT CHECKPOINT Questions ❶, ❷ and ❸ should help you decide if children are using <, > and = correctly and whether they understand that they are referring to the amount of money. Assess if children are able to read the number sentences aloud.

ANSWERS

Question ❶ a): £47 > £37

Question ❶ b): 118p < 123p

Question ❷ : £20 + £5 + £1 < £10 + £5 + £10 + £2

50p + 20p + 5p + 10p = 20p + 20p + 10p + 5p + 5p + 5p + 20p

Question ❸ : £11 and 15p > £5 and 15p.

£1 = £1

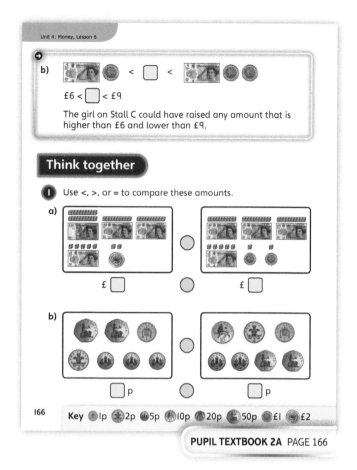

PUPIL TEXTBOOK 2A PAGE 166

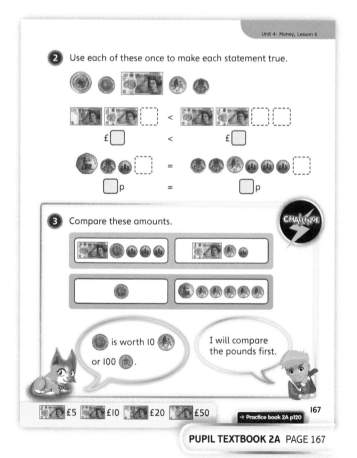

PUPIL TEXTBOOK 2A PAGE 167

Practice

WAYS OF WORKING Independent thinking

IN FOCUS Question ❹ will challenge some children. Stop the class and ask them for strategies they used to work out the answer. Encourage children to start with a low number for the first box and then work out the total of that side of the = sign. Then look at the other side of the = sign and solve the problem. It is worth asking children to try and find more than one solution.

STRENGTHEN In some of the questions in the **Practice** section, some children may quickly jump to the conclusion that if someone has a higher quantity of coins, they have a higher value of money. Strengthen their understanding by finding the totals of each first.

DEEPEN Ask children to look at question ❹ again. Challenge them to find the range of numbers that could go in each box (both the first and second box could hold any answer between £15 and £0).

ASSESSMENT CHECKPOINT Question ❷ will allow you to assess whether children can compare amounts with a pictorial representation and without.

Question ❺ will draw out whether children can compare amounts in real-life problems.

ANSWERS Answers for the **Practice** part of the lesson appear in the separate **Practice and Reflect answer guide**.

Reflect

WAYS OF WORKING Independent thinking

IN FOCUS Children will be required to prove a statement in the **Reflect** question. Children must be concise with their answers and not write long-winded explanations. An exemplary answer could be: 'Bag 1 has a total of £15 in it. Bag 2 has a total of £10 in it. £15 is greater than £10. Therefore the statement is correct.'

ASSESSMENT CHECKPOINT This exercise will show you if children have grasped the key vocabulary of this lesson and can use it in context.

ANSWERS Answers for the **Reflect** part of the lesson appear in the separate **Practice and Reflect answer guide**.

After the lesson ⏸

- Will you need to recap the signs again? More than once?
- Are children using the correct vocabulary when referring to <, > and = ?
- Should you arrange some intervention exercises for those who are not secure with comparing amounts of money?

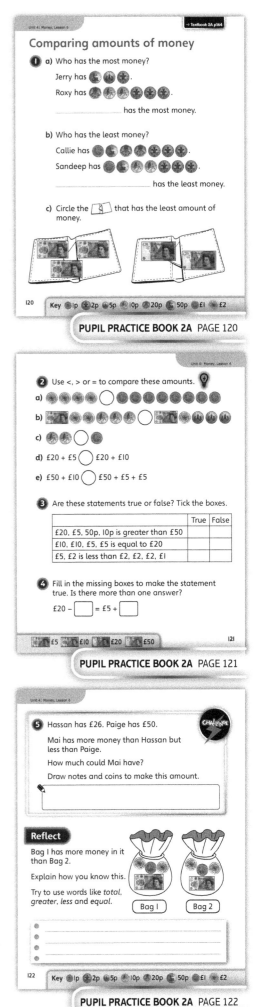

195

Calculating the total amount

Learning focus

In this lesson, children will find the total cost of given items. Children will add pounds and pence, but not cross the 100 boundary.

Small steps

→ Previous step: Comparing amounts of money
→ **This step: Calculating the total amount**
→ Next step: Finding change

NATIONAL CURRICULUM LINKS

Year 2 Measurement – Money

Solve simple problems in a practical context involving addition and subtraction of money of the same unit, including giving change.

ASSESSING MASTERY

Children can securely calculate total amounts by adding the pounds together and then the pence. Children can use the bar model effectively to support their understanding of a problem.

COMMON MISCONCEPTIONS

Children may make errors when adding pounds and pence by not adding them separately. Ask:
• *What should your first step be when calculating the total amount?*

Another misconception children have is starting with the lower amount and then adding on the higher amount. Ask:
• *Which is easier to solve: 5 + 89 or 89 + 5?*

When children have to add more than two amounts, they can become confused. Ask:
• *How can you add three amounts? Could you start with adding two amounts first and then add the final amount after?*

STRENGTHENING UNDERSTANDING

Partitioning the amounts into pounds and pence will be key in this lesson. Using number lines to add the partitioned values will make the calculations more manageable and strengthen children's understanding.

Continue practising counting aloud with children in 2s, 5s, 10s, 20s and 50s. This must include beginning at different numbers such as 11, 21, 31, 41 and so on.

The bar model may not be fully understood by some of the pupils. Explain it to children and make it clear that the amounts we are adding appear in the bottom bars and the total amount appears in the top bar.

Some children may need counting support – a 100 square may be useful for them.

GOING DEEPER

In this lesson, children who are secure with calculating totals could add more than two amounts of money.

KEY LANGUAGE

In lesson: buy(s), spend, money, add, addition, total, notes, coins, amount, pound (£), pence (p), altogether

Other language to be used by the teacher: calculate

STRUCTURES AND REPRESENTATIONS

Bar model, number lines

Column addition should be used by some children.

RESOURCES

Mandatory: currency (coins and notes), bar model

Optional: 100 square

 In the eTextbook of this lesson, you will find interactive links to a selection of teaching tools.

Before you teach

• Will some children struggle to count on?
• Do they need extra practice adding 10 to a number?
• Do children remember the bar model, or is a quick recap useful?

Discover

WAYS OF WORKING Pair work

ASK

• Question ❶ a): Should you start with the football boots and then count on? Or should you start with the jacket and then count on?

• Question ❶ b): What counting on strategy could you use?

IN FOCUS In question ❶ b), children will have to look carefully at the amounts to see which items total £26. Tell children that they can definitely cross out the tennis racket, as it costs far too much. Remind children that they could use their estimation skills. Ask: *What ten is £26 nearest to?* Then ask children to round the amounts each item costs to the nearest ten. This will make the answer very clear.

ANSWERS

Question ❶ a): The girl spends £33 in total.

Question ❶ b): The boy buys ⁄ and 🏠 (£18 + £8 = £26).

Share

WAYS OF WORKING Whole class teacher led

ASK

• What do the bar models show you?

• Why is the bar model useful?

• How did you work out question ❶ b)?

IN FOCUS In question ❶ b) some children will have added amounts together at random. Children who are more secure will be able to choose appropriate amounts to add, by using their estimation skills.

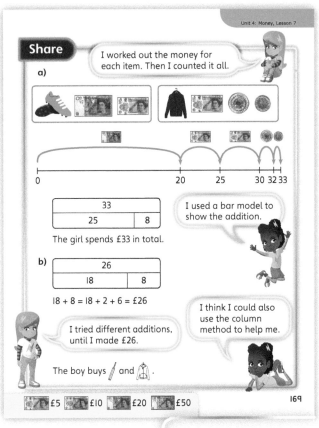

197

Think together

Think together

WAYS OF WORKING Whole class teacher led (I do, We do, You do)

ASK

- *Which addition strategies would be useful to carry out in this section?*
- *Does anyone need a 100 square to help them count?*
- *In question **3**, why does Dexter think it is a good idea to separate the pounds and pence?*

IN FOCUS Question **3** introduces children to adding pounds and pence together. It is very important to talk to children about partitioning the pounds and pence and then adding together separately. Some children could use notes and coins to support their counting.

STRENGTHEN Provide children with coins and notes for counting support. Using 100 squares may be helpful when counting on from larger numbers.

If children are still mixing the pounds and pence, draw a line and tell children to keep the pounds on the left and the pence on the right.

DEEPEN Deepen understanding by reversing question **3**: giving children total amounts and then asking them to think of amounts that they would add together to make it. Tell children the amounts they add must be a mixture of pounds and pence. For example, you could ask: *What amounts of pounds and pence could be added to make £5 and 40p?*

ASSESSMENT CHECKPOINT When children complete question **3**, it will be clear to see who can keep the pounds and pence separate when calculating total amounts.

Throughout the section, assess children's calculation strategies.

ANSWERS

Question **1**: £40 + £18 = £58.

He spends £58 in total.

Question **2**: £12 + £45 = £57.

Marie spends £57 in total.

Question **3**: £3 and 50p + £5 = £8 and 50p

£2 and 30p + £2 and 50p = £4 and 80p

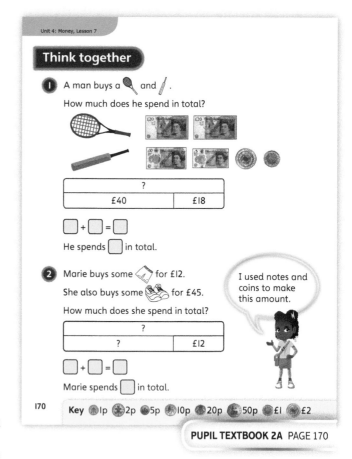

PUPIL TEXTBOOK 2A PAGE 170

PUPIL TEXTBOOK 2A PAGE 171

Practice

WAYS OF WORKING Pair work

IN FOCUS Children are introduced to adding three amounts of money in question ❹. Explain that children must add two amounts first and then count on the final amount. In addition, children must represent the calculation on a bar model. Do an example of this on the board and be clear that the amounts should represent the length of the bars (although children will struggle with this). Ask children if the bar representing £9 should be longer or shorter than the bar representing £5.

STRENGTHEN Some children may not be confident with column addition as used in question ❸ – especially in the context of money. Some extra intervention may be needed in which the method is explained; add the pence, then add the pounds.

DEEPEN Question ❹ introduces children to finding the total of three amounts of money and then representing this on a bar model. Challenge children to think of three or more amounts of money and ask them to calculate the total and then construct a bar model to represent their calculation.

ASSESSMENT CHECKPOINT Question ❸ will allow you to assess whether children can add 2-digit numbers and represent the calculation in a bar model. Furthermore, you will be able to check whether children can use the column addition method (although you will probably see other strategies too: partitioning, using notes and coins, number lines).

ANSWERS Answers for the **Practice** part of the lesson appear in the separate **Practice and Reflect answer guide**.

Reflect

WAYS OF WORKING Independent thinking

IN FOCUS Children are required to write a word problem for this **Reflect** section. Provide a word bank of the key words in this lesson to support children. Some children may provide simple answers such as 'Mrs Bat has 27p and finds 14p. How much has she got altogether?' Secure children may provide answers such as 'Mrs Bat buys a book for 27p. She realises she has paid 14p too much for the book! How much did she pay for the book?'

ASSESSMENT CHECKPOINT You will be able to assess children's use of mathematical vocabulary and if children can put a number sentence involving money into context.

ANSWERS Answers for the **Reflect** part of the lesson appear in the separate **Practice and Reflect answer guide**.

After the lesson

- How many children are secure or insecure with:
  1) adding 2-digit amounts of money
  2) adding the pounds and pence separately
  3) column addition
  4) putting calculations into context
  5) key vocabulary?

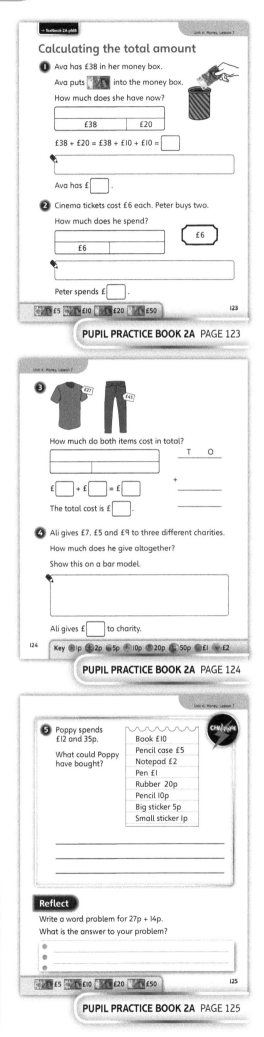

PUPIL PRACTICE BOOK 2A PAGE 123

PUPIL PRACTICE BOOK 2A PAGE 124

PUPIL PRACTICE BOOK 2A PAGE 125

Finding change

Learning focus

In this lesson, children will work out how much change should be received after paying for something. There will be a focus on finding the difference between the cost and the amount paid.

Small steps

→ Previous step: Calculating the total amount
→ **This step: Finding change**
→ Next step: Solving two-step word problems

NATIONAL CURRICULUM LINKS

Year 2 Measurement – Money

Solve simple problems in a practical context involving addition and subtraction of money of the same unit, including giving change.

ASSESSING MASTERY

Children can find the change needed by choosing an efficient strategy, for example subtracting or counting on to find the difference. Children can work out the change from £1 by converting it to 100p, and solve problems involving change effectively.

COMMON MISCONCEPTIONS

Children may not have remembered that £1 = 100p (this may need to be recapped, or displayed in the classroom). Ask:
• *How many pennies in £1? £2? £3? What about £10?*

STRENGTHENING UNDERSTANDING

To strengthen understanding in this lesson, practise using the number line to subtract and count on to find the difference.

Children may subtract when it is much more efficient to use the counting on method. For instance, for the question 67 – 65, children may hop back 65 instead of simply counting on 2. Model the two methods and then ask: *Which method was easier? Which was quicker?*

GOING DEEPER

To deepen learning, ask children to create some of their own real-life word problems in which change must be calculated.

KEY LANGUAGE

In lesson: change, subtraction, count on, difference, pound (£), pence (p), left, more than, coins

STRUCTURES AND REPRESENTATIONS

Number lines, bar models

RESOURCES

Mandatory: currency (coins and notes)

Optional: Base 10 equipment, 100 squares

 In the eTextbook of this lesson, you will find interactive links to a selection of teaching tools.

Before you teach

• Are children secure with subtracting and finding the difference on the number line?
• Who needs extra support or practice counting forwards and backwards in 2s, 5s and 10s (starting on a range of numbers)?

Discover

WAYS OF WORKING Pair work

ASK

- *Do you remember how many pennies make one pound?*
- *What does 'change' mean?*
- *What strategies could be used to work these questions out?*

IN FOCUS Question ① b) will require children to remember that £1 = 100p. Some children may not remember this. Remind them of previous work with money and see if they can recall it.

ANSWERS

Question ① a): 50p – 45p = 5p.

Eshan gets 5p change.

Question ① b): 100p – 30p = 70p.

Lucy would get 70p change.

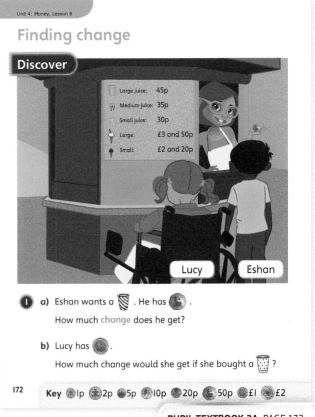

Share

WAYS OF WORKING Whole class teacher led

ASK

- *Look at question ① a). Which is the best method to use? Subtraction or counting on to find the difference?*
- *Look at question ① b). How can your number bonds to 10 help you with this question?*

IN FOCUS Question ① b) is a good opportunity to link to prior learning. Talk to children about their number bonds to 10 which they covered in year 1. Ask children if they can think of a number fact that would help them with this question. Children who are secure will make the connection between 30p + 70p = 100p and 3p + 7p = 10p. Be careful here – it is important that children do not think they can simply put a 0 on the end of the numbers.

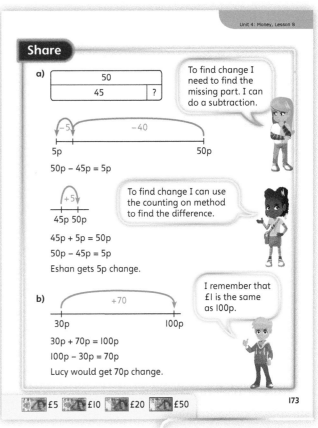

Think together

WAYS OF WORKING Whole class teacher led (I do, We do, You do)

ASK

- *Look at question ① . Can you show me this subtraction using Base 10 equipment?*
- *Look at question ③ . Is it best to subtract? Why? Why not?*

IN FOCUS Question ② asks children to find out how much MORE Sarah has than Ian. Children often associate the word 'more' with addition and may well add the two amounts. Talk children through the problem and draw out that it is comparing Ian's and Sarah's amount ('than' being a key word to point out here).

STRENGTHEN Number line practice to calculate change will be needed for some children. Pairing resources such as Base 10 equipment or coins with the number line will strengthen understanding.

Children may be more confident counting on than back. Strengthen the counting on to find the difference method first.

DEEPEN Ask children to look at question ① again and think about if it would be easier to subtract the 5p first and then the 30p.

If secure in this section, children could move on to think about change from a £2 coin, a £5 note or a £10 note.

ASSESSMENT CHECKPOINT Question ③ is a good way to assess which strategy has been used. You will be able to see which children can calculate mentally, which need to use a structure or representation, and which need to use coins or Base 10 equipment.

ANSWERS

Question ① : 75p − 35p = 40p.

He has 40p left.

Question ② : £51 − £35 = £16.

Sarah has £16 more than Ian.

Question ③ : £3 and 50p − £2 and 20p = £1 and 30p.
Lesley spent £1 and 30p more than her brother.

Think together

① Jamal has 75p. He buys a 🥤.

How much money does he have left?

75	
35	

−5   −30

| | | 75 |

Tens	Ones
|||||||||||	🪙
|||||||||||	🪙
|||||||||||	🪙
|||||||||||	🪙

☐p − ☐p = ☐p

He has ☐p left.

I will check how much 🥤 costs first.

174   **Key** 🪙1p 🪙2p 🪙5p 🪙10p 🪙20p 🪙50p 🪙£1 🪙£2

PUPIL TEXTBOOK 2A PAGE 174

---

② Ian was given £35 for his birthday.

Sarah has saved £51.

How much more did Sarah have than Ian?

£51

| Sarah |

| Ian | |

£35   ?

£☐ − £☐ = £☐

Sarah has £☐ more than Ian.

③ Lesley bought a large ice cream.
Her brother bought a small ice cream.   **CHALLENGE**

How much more did Lesley spend than her brother?

Large juice:	45p
Medium juice:	35p
Small juice:	30p
Large:	£3 and 50p
Small:	£2 and 20p

I will think about the coins to help answer this question.

💷£5 💷£10 💷£20 💷£50   → Practice book 2A p126   175

PUPIL TEXTBOOK 2A PAGE 175

Practice

WAYS OF WORKING Pair work or independent thinking

IN FOCUS Question ❸ will require some deep thinking. Children will have to firstly find the change and then work out which coins are needed. Having coins ready on children's tables will help them work out which four make 14p.

STRENGTHEN When children are completing question ❶, they may become confused that, although they are finding the difference, an addition number sentence is used (£32 + ? = £50). This is a good opportunity to strengthen understanding of how number sentences work. Explain that when there is a missing number in an addition sentence, children must in fact, subtract. Try giving children a number sentence and ask them to move the numbers around to form related sentences, for example, 3 + 4 = 7, 4 + 3 = 7, 7 − 3 = 4, 7 − 4 = 3.

DEEPEN Revisit question ❸. Ask children to make up similar problems that they can swap with a friend and find each other's solutions.

ASSESSMENT CHECKPOINT All of the questions in this section will let you observe which strategies children are using and how confident they are with them.

Question ❹ is a chance to assess whether children can find change from £1 independently.

ANSWERS Answers for the **Practice** part of the lesson appear in the separate **Practice and Reflect answer guide**.

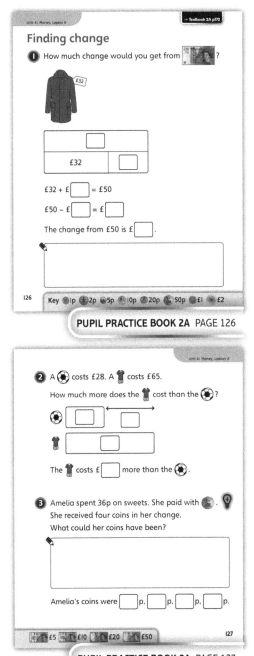

PUPIL PRACTICE BOOK 2A PAGE 126

PUPIL PRACTICE BOOK 2A PAGE 127

Reflect

WAYS OF WORKING Independent thinking

IN FOCUS Children will be required to use their explanatory skills in this **Reflect** activity. They must focus on what vocabulary they should use and the number sentence involved.

ASSESSMENT CHECKPOINT You will be able to assess which strategy is used. Some children may go into detail of how to work out 50p − 25p.

ANSWERS Answers for the **Reflect** part of the lesson appear in the separate **Practice and Reflect answer guide**.

After the lesson ⏸

- How can you do more intervention with children who need more practice with finding the difference using a number line?
- After marking the **Practice** section, could you work with some children who made errors, to strengthen their understanding?

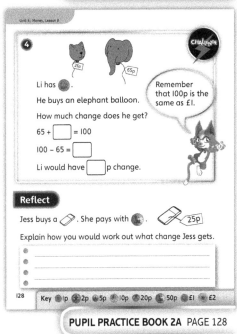

PUPIL PRACTICE BOOK 2A PAGE 128

Solving two-step word problems

Learning focus

In this lesson, children will use prior knowledge to solve two-step word problems.

Small steps

→ Previous step: Finding change
→ **This step: Solving two-step word problems**
→ Next step: Making equal groups

NATIONAL CURRICULUM LINKS

Year 2 Measurement – Money

Solve simple problems in a practical context involving addition and subtraction of money of the same unit, including giving change.

ASSESSING MASTERY

Children can quickly call upon all previous knowledge of money, and apply it to solve word problems. Children can display mastery through comprehension of the questions, understanding of the vocabulary and the use of efficient methods.

COMMON MISCONCEPTIONS

Children often do not comprehend what the question is asking them. Ask:
• *Read the question carefully. What operations will you use? What will the number sentences be?*

STRENGTHENING UNDERSTANDING

Children may need practice reading the questions aloud and discussing the vocabulary used. This is a good opportunity for intervention groups – working through problems as a team.

GOING DEEPER

To deepen understanding, ask children to represent a word problem using structures and representations. Using bar models and number lines will deepen understanding in this lesson.

KEY LANGUAGE

In lesson: buy, change, spend, total, step, cost, altogether, how much?

STRUCTURES AND REPRESENTATIONS

Bar models, number lines

RESOURCES

Mandatory: currency (coins and notes)

Optional: Base 10 equipment

 In the eTextbook of this lesson, you will find interactive links to a selection of teaching tools.

Before you teach

• Have you displayed the key vocabulary somewhere in the classroom?
• Which children will need support with calculating?
• How can you provide this support?

Discover

WAYS OF WORKING Pair work

ASK

- *Which calculation do you need to do first?*
- *Which calculation do you need to do second?*

IN FOCUS For both question ① a) and question ① b), draw children's attention to the two steps in the questions; it may not be immediately obvious to children that they will need to do two separate calculations to find the answer.

ANSWERS

Question ① a): £8 + £5 = £13, £20 − £13 = £7.

Cora will get £7 change.

Question ① b): £3 + £3 = £6, £13 + £6 = £19.

Cora spends £19 in total.

PUPIL TEXTBOOK 2A PAGE 176

Share

WAYS OF WORKING Whole class teacher led

ASK

- *What items should you be adding up in question ① b)?*
- *Read the question again. Do you understand what the question is asking you?*

IN FOCUS Question ① b) asks children to build on the knowledge gained from question ① a). Many children will add the price of the two large popcorns to the answer from question ① a) (£7). This is incorrect. The question asks how much has been SPENT in total. It is important to highlight this to children when explaining.

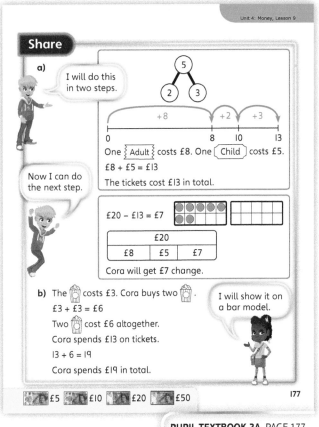

PUPIL TEXTBOOK 2A PAGE 177

Think together

WAYS OF WORKING Whole class teacher led (I do, We do, You do)

ASK

- *Look at question* **1** *. Is Astrid correct when she says she will put the total Alfie spent into a part in the bottom bar?*
- *How can the bar model help us solve question* **3** *?*

IN FOCUS Question **3** is a great chance to show how effective the bar model is at modelling a word problem. Talk the question through with children and ask them to find out the missing bar. They can draw another bar model to solve the rest of the problem.

STRENGTHEN To strengthen understanding, revise the questions in this section and ask children to talk you through the bar models. Ask: *What part of the word problem does each bar represent?*

DEEPEN Secure children may rush through this section. Ensure they go back and look carefully at the bar models – they may have missed some key learning points. To deepen understanding, why not ask the children to construct a bar model for question **2** as well?

ASSESSMENT CHECKPOINT All questions in this section provide insight into whether children can interpret a two-step word problem with support from a bar model.

ANSWERS

Question **1** : £8 + £3 = £11; He spent £11 in total.
£15 – £11 = £4; Alfie gets £4 change.

Question **2** : £8 + £5 + £5 = £18.
She has spent £18 in total. £20 - £18 = £2.
Jane has £2 left so she cannot buy a £3 popcorn too.

Question **3** : 50p – 20p = 30p; A small drink costs 30p.
50p + 30p = 80p; James spends 80p in total.

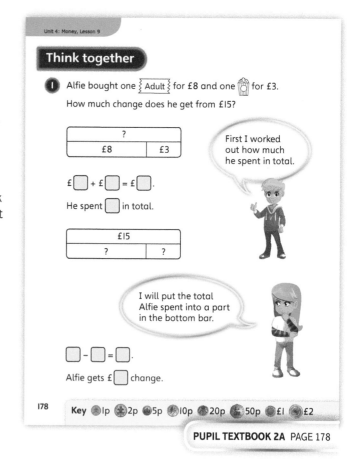

PUPIL TEXTBOOK 2A PAGE 178

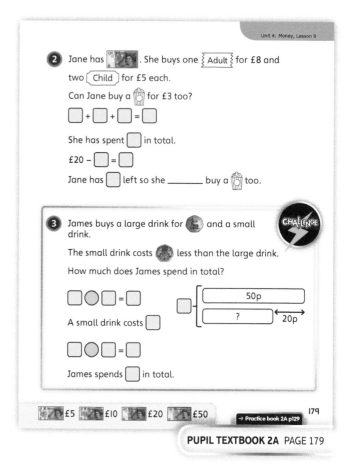

PUPIL TEXTBOOK 2A PAGE 179

Practice

WAYS OF WORKING Independent thinking or pair work

IN FOCUS For this section, depending on your class, you may want to do independent thinking or pair work. If children have been struggling with vocabulary during the unit, pair work may be best for them (or adult support) because this section is fairly word heavy.

In question **3**, children are likely to calculate the answer as 25p (minus the). To focus their learning, ask them to write down what the costs and what the costs. Then repeat the question to them – find the TOTAL cost. They will then see that they have to add 65p and 25p together to find the final answer. Breaking questions down into simple steps is important for children of this age.

STRENGTHEN Provide key vocabulary banks for children who need this support. Ask these children to highlight the key words before they begin a problem to help strengthen their understanding.

DEEPEN To deepen understanding, challenge children to create their own two-step money problems.

ASSESSMENT CHECKPOINT All questions in this section will allow you to assess whether children are able to comprehend and interrogate word problems.

ANSWERS Answers for the **Practice** part of the lesson appear in the separate **Practice and Reflect answer guide**.

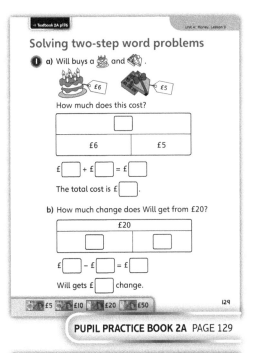

PUPIL PRACTICE BOOK 2A PAGE 129

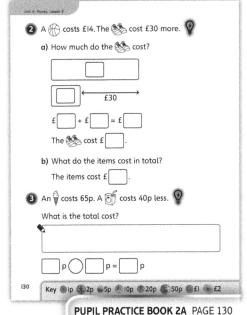

PUPIL PRACTICE BOOK 2A PAGE 130

Reflect

WAYS OF WORKING Pair work

IN FOCUS When writing a second step for a problem, children must have a good grasp of what the first part of the question is asking. Once children are secure with it, they can think what will fit as an appropriate second part.

ASSESSMENT CHECKPOINT Children will have to use the correct mathematical vocabulary in this section. Assess if they are using the words correctly. This will also allow you to assess their explanatory skills. Can children use structures and representations to support their explanations?

ANSWERS Answers for the **Reflect** part of the lesson appear in the separate **Practice and Reflect answer guide**.

After the lesson ⏸

- How many children mastered the lesson?
- How many children need extra support with word problems?
- Could children explain their answers clearly and concisely?

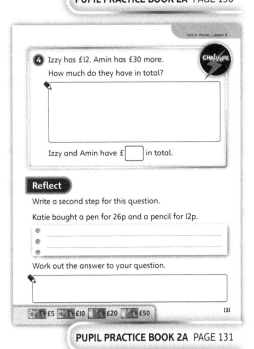

PUPIL PRACTICE BOOK 2A PAGE 131

End of unit check

> **Don't forget the Power Maths Unit Assessment Grid on p26.**

IN FOCUS

- It is good practice to encourage children to work out the values of all of the amounts in the **End of unit check** – even if secure children can spot the correct answer immediately.
- Questions **1** and **2** focus on children's understanding of the value of all coins and notes.
- Question **3** will assess children's ability to calculate total amounts using efficient strategies.
- Question **4** will assess children's ability to compare two amounts and describe their relationship to each other.

Think!

WAYS OF WORKING Pair work or small groups

IN FOCUS

- This question has been chosen to deepen thinking. Children have to recognise the coins, find the total amount of 2ps and then compare the two amounts and assess whether their relationship to each other is described correctly by the given sign.
- Some children may argue that the answer is 'true' because the question does not specify value – it would actually be true if the question was about the quantity of coins. This is an excellent talking point with the class.
- The vocabulary you should expect to hear from the children: pence, greater than, less than, equal to.
- Encourage children to think through or discuss the meaning of the signs <, >, = before writing their answer in **My journal**.

ANSWERS AND COMMENTARY Children will demonstrate mastery in this unit by being able to count using all different values of coins and notes. They will be able to compare different amounts of money and find different ways to make the same amount. Children will be able to work out the amount of change needed and solve two-step problems involving money. They will use appropriate mathematical vocabulary and be able to explain their methods confidently.

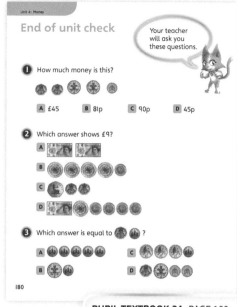

PUPIL TEXTBOOK 2A PAGE 180

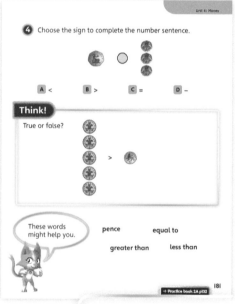

PUPIL TEXTBOOK 2A PAGE 181

Q	A	WRONG ANSWERS AND MISCONCEPTIONS	STRENGTHENING UNDERSTANDING
1	D	Choosing A suggests that the child may not have looked carefully at the units and picked £45. Choosing B suggests that the child may have started counting 20p, 40p… then continued in 20ps, instead of 2ps (ending up on 81p).	Children should practise representing coins with Base 10 equipment. Daily group counting practice is important. Coins and notes could be counted. Children could have intervention sessions in which they check their answers for mistakes. Ordering numbers using <, >, = would make for a useful exercise.
2	B	Choosing C suggests that they have counted the 50p as £5 and the 20ps as £2s (ending up on (90p).	
3	A	This question is a good chance to spot miscounting.	
4	A	Children may not be confident with what the signs <, >, = mean and need reinforcement.	

My journal

WAYS OF WORKING Independent thinking

ANSWERS AND COMMENTARY

The answer is 'false' because five 2ps are equal (=) to 10p.

Talk through children's answers and look at the language used.

Have children miscounted the value? Ask:
• *What are the values of these coins?*

Have they forgotten what the sign > means? Ask:
• *What do >, < and = mean?*

To go deeper and challenge children, ask:
• *What would you change to make the answer 'true'?*

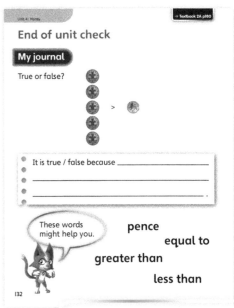

PUPIL PRACTICE BOOK 2A PAGE 132

Power check

WAYS OF WORKING Independent thinking

ASK

• *How confident do you feel about calculating money?*
• *Do you think you could go to the shops, buy three things and pay for them all by yourself?*
• *Would you know if you got the correct change?*
• *What did you find easiest in this unit?*
• *What do you feel you could improve upon in this unit?*

Power play

WAYS OF WORKING Pair work or small groups

IN FOCUS This game is an excellent way to end the unit. Children work out how many different amounts they can make with three of the coins supplied. Children take it in turns to choose three coins and write down the amounts they make. The children will realise that they now have a good understanding of money. Look out for those who might need a little support, as it is important that they feel that they have progressed over the unit.

ANSWERS AND COMMENTARY This game will allow you to observe which children understand how to add coins together to make different amounts. Keep children's written recordings to look at after the session.

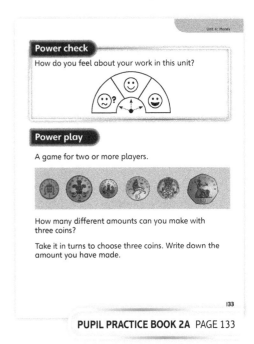

PUPIL PRACTICE BOOK 2A PAGE 133

After the unit ⏸

• How did the unit go?
• What would you change?
• How could the children now apply their knowledge?
• How many children do you think have mastered this unit?

Strengthen and **Deepen** activities for this unit can be found in the *Power Maths* online subscription.

Unit 5
Multiplication and division ①

Don't forget to watch the Unit 5 video!

WHY THIS UNIT IS IMPORTANT

This unit focuses on multiplication in the context of skip counting, equal groups, times-tables, multiplication sentences and scaling problems. It is an essential basis for children understanding the times-tables and what × means.

Within this unit, children will gain a solid grounding in equal groups and what this means, as well as how to recognise any groups that are not equal. This is the first big idea relating to multiplication and it is essential knowledge before moving through the rest of the lessons. Children will be introduced to arrays as a representation of multiplication, which will help highlight the commutative properties of multiplication. Throughout this unit, repeated addition sentences will appear alongside multiplication sentences so that children have a reference to help them understand what × means in context.

As well as calculating different multiplication sentences using equal groups, number lines and arrays, this unit introduces an equal parts bar model. This may be more challenging for children to understand as they have to count the number of equal parts. There is also a lesson on word problems and language such as 'times bigger' or 'twice as many' is used.

WHERE THIS UNIT FITS

→ Unit 4: Money
→ **Unit 5: Multiplication and division (1)**
→ Unit 6: Multiplication and division (2)

This unit follows Unit 4 in which children have been building their experience of money. In Unit 5, children will look at a number of important multiplication and division methods and skills, and will gain a more solid understanding of equal groups. Children will continue to expand their knowledge of multiplication and division in Unit 6.

Before they start this unit, it is expected that children:
- know how to jump forward on a number line
- understand how to skip count using a resource, such as a number line or 100 square
- know what odd and even numbers are.

ASSESSING MASTERY

Children who have mastered this unit will understand that the different parts of a multiplication sentence represent the number in a group and the number of groups and they will be able to apply this in different contexts. Children will know that no matter which way round the numbers go in a multiplication sentence, the total will still be the same. They will be able to skip count the rows or the columns in an array rather than counting individual objects. Children will understand that 'twice as many' and '2 times bigger' are the same as multiplying by two.

COMMON MISCONCEPTIONS	STRENGTHENING UNDERSTANDING	GOING DEEPER
Children may not make an array accurately and have an uneven number in rows or columns.	Skip count a range of everyday objects that have a different value, such as pairs of socks or 5p coins.	Ask children to make as many arrays as they can using 5 or 7 counters. What do they notice? [Only one-row arrays are possible because these are prime numbers.]
When thinking about multiplication in context, children may add together the number in a group of objects and the number of groups instead of multiplying them.	When drawing bar models, encourage children to make the groups of objects first and then draw around them to promote understanding of what the bar represents.	Give children a set amount of counters, such as 12, and ask them to make as many arrays as they can using those counters.

WAYS OF WORKING

Use these pages to introduce the unit focus to children. Ask them if they recognise any of the structures on this page, such as the number line. Ask them what is special about the group of counters (the array).

STRUCTURES AND REPRESENTATIONS

Number line: Number lines help children see the equal jumps being made. The number of jumps is also the other number in a multiplication sentence.

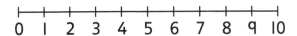

Array: The array is organised into rows and columns, which helps children to distinguish between each number in a multiplication calculation. Each counter represents one object.

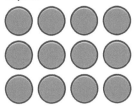

Bar model:

A comparison bar model that compares two amounts.

5	5	5

5

An equal parts bar model that displays a whole as a certain amount bigger than one part.

?

5	5	5	5

KEY LANGUAGE

There is some key language that children will need to know as part of the learning in this unit:

- → equal groups
- → repeated addition
- → skip counting
- → number in a group
- → number of groups
- → times
- → times-table
- → multiply/multiplication (×)
- → more than, less than (< and >)
- → array
- → rows/columns
- → bar model
- → equal parts
- → number of equal parts
- → times bigger/times taller/ times greater
- → twice as big

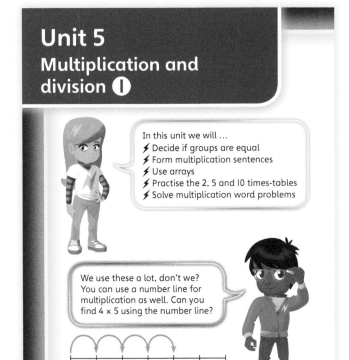

PUPIL TEXTBOOK 2A PAGE 182

PUPIL TEXTBOOK 2A PAGE 183

Making equal groups

Learning focus

In this lesson, children will understand that objects can be grouped together and that groups containing the same number of objects are equal groups. Children will make written sentences from these equal groups.

Small steps

→ Previous step: Solving two-step word problems
→ **This step: Making equal groups**
→ Next step: Multiplication as equal groups

NATIONAL CURRICULUM LINKS

Year 2 Number – Multiplication and Division

Solve one-step problems involving multiplication and division, by calculating the answer using concrete objects, pictorial representations and arrays with the support of the teacher.

ASSESSING MASTERY

Children can recognise equal and unequal groups of physical resources and pictorial representations and explain why the groups are equal or unequal. Children can simultaneously count the number of objects in a group and the number of groups, and can write correct repeated addition sentences repeating the number of equal groups and the number of objects in each group.

COMMON MISCONCEPTIONS

When filling in sentences about the number of objects in a group and the number of equal groups, children may confuse these numbers. While this does not change the total, each number has a separate and distinct meaning. Ask:
• *What does each number represent? Is what you have written what the picture shows?*

STRENGTHENING UNDERSTANDING

Refer to examples of equal groups in the classroom, especially where objects are grouped physically into a bag, box or pack, such as pens in a pack or pencils in a pot. This provides a physical distinction between the number in a group and the number of groups while allowing children to count individual objects within groups.

GOING DEEPER

Ask children to rearrange unequal groups of multilink cubes into equal groups. Show two stacks of cubes where one is five cubes long and one is three cubes long. Ask: *How can these stacks be rearranged so that there are two equal groups?*

KEY LANGUAGE

In lesson: equal groups, same, different

Other language to be used by the teacher: multiply, multiplication, repeated addition, add, unequal groups, how many?, number in a group, number of objects

STRUCTURES AND REPRESENTATIONS

Array, counters

RESOURCES

Mandatory: counters and multilink cubes

Optional: classroom objects in equal groups that make a clear distinction between the objects being put into groups and what the groups are, such as pens in packs, eggs in egg boxes

 In the eTextbook of this lesson, you will find interactive links to a selection of teaching tools.

Before you teach

• Have children seen addition sentences in which more than two numbers are added together?
• Do children fully understand the meaning of the word 'equal'?
• What objects and contexts in your classroom can be used to model equal groups?

Discover

WAYS OF WORKING Pair work

ASK

- *How do you know whether the groups are equal or unequal?*
- *Do you have to count all the objects in all the groups to check?*
- *How could you show that the cakes are in equal groups?*

IN FOCUS Questions ❶ a) and ❶ b) introduce the notion of equal groups. The cakes and muffins are all arranged in the same formation for easy comparison. The cookies are in unequal groups and the groups containing the same number of cookies are arranged in a different formation on the tray. Children may believe that groups have to look the same to contain the same number.

ANSWERS

Question ❶ a) There are 2 equal groups of 🧁 .

There are 5 equal groups of 🧁 .

Question ❶ b) The 🍪 are not in equal groups.

There are 5 🍪 in 2 of the groups and 3 🍪 in another group.

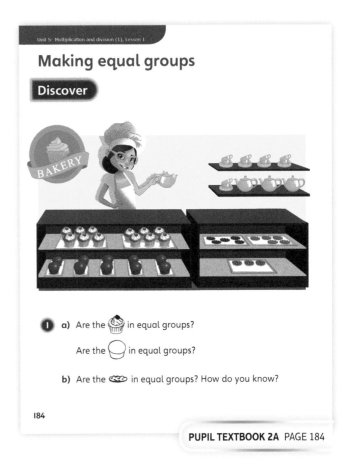

PUPIL TEXTBOOK 2A PAGE 184

Share

WAYS OF WORKING Whole class teacher led

ASK

- *Does the formation of the counters match the formation of the cakes and muffins?*
- *Why do the formation of the cakes and muffins look different?*
- *What does the 6 mean in each group of cakes? What does the 2 mean in each group of muffins?*
- *Why do both groups of cakes or muffins have the same total?*

IN FOCUS Once they have counted the cakes, children might notice that both groups of cakes contain the same total. Encourage children to circle each group with their finger so that they can see six groups of 2 cakes and two groups of 6 cakes. Repeat the circling exercise with the 5 equal groups of muffins.

Refer to what Sparks says about the meaning of equal groups and ask children to repeat this definition to a partner.

STRENGTHEN Can children see the existence of alternative groups within the cakes and muffins and circle them? Show that the rows of cakes can be grouped into equal groups of 2 cakes and the columns of muffins can be grouped into groups of 5 muffins.

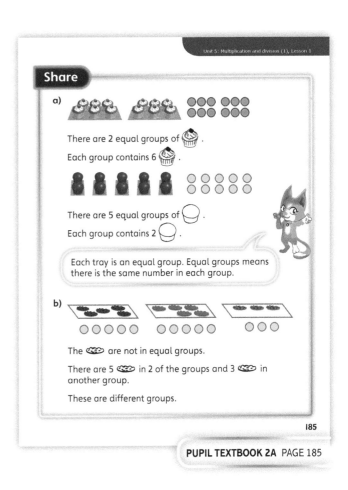

PUPIL TEXTBOOK 2A PAGE 185

Think together

WAYS OF WORKING Whole class teacher led (I do, We do, You do)

ASK

- *How many groups are there?*
- *How many objects are there in each group?*

IN FOCUS Question ❶ shows that the same number of equal groups can contain different numbers of objects.

Question ❷ asks children to identify the number of equal groups. The donuts are in three equal groups of 3, so ask children to make the distinction between what each 3 means.

In question ❸, James has equal groups of donuts apart from the last pack, which is much smaller. Hannah has different formations of muffins on each plate and in the box of four muffins, but each group still contains an equal number of muffins.

What do children think about what Ash says? Do they think that appearances matter when judging whether there are equal groups?

STRENGTHEN Children can represent the different groups using physical resources. Counters can be placed on whiteboards or paper and drawn around to form equal groups. Multilink cubes can be joined together to form equal groups.

DEEPEN Can children change the number of equal groups and the number of objects in each group and compare what this looks like, using physical resources such as multilink cubes and counters? This is a precursor to understanding the commutative law of multiplication.

ASSESSMENT CHECKPOINT In questions ❶ and ❷, do children put the correct numbers in each sentence? Can they differentiate between the different components? In question ❸, do children automatically say that Hannah does not have equal groups or do they know that they have to count the groups to check? Do children understand that there are four muffins in the closed box because of the numeral 4 on the front? Do they recognise that this is equal to the number of muffins in the groups they can see?

ANSWERS

Question ❶ : There are 4 groups of 3 .

There are 4 groups of 5 .

Question ❷ : There are 2 equal groups of 3 .

There are 3 equal groups of 3 .

There are 5 equal groups of 3 .

Question ❸ : Hannah has equal groups.

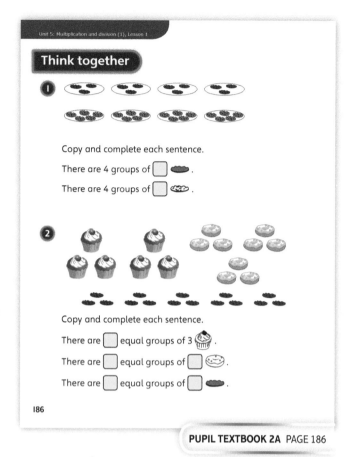

PUPIL TEXTBOOK 2A PAGE 186

PUPIL TEXTBOOK 2A PAGE 187

214

Practice

WAYS OF WORKING Independent thinking

IN FOCUS Each sentence in question ❶ follows the same structure but the missing value changes (for example, the number of equal groups, the number in each group and both numbers together). Children need to use the picture and accurately count each component to fill in the sentences correctly.

Question ❷ requires children to match pictures to sentences. Children need to interpret the sentences correctly and identify which picture represents each sentence.

Question ❹ requires that children refer to what Dexter says and count every group in order to determine which group contains a different number of objects.

STRENGTHEN Ask children to represent the drawing in question ❺ using different physical resources to represent the children, the clouds and the birds. Check that the number of each resource matches the picture and ask what each resource represents.

DEEPEN Ask children to draw their own pictures containing multiple equal groups and to talk about their picture. You could give them a context, such as 'the classroom' or 'the beach', and choose the sets of objects that they should include or they could choose for themselves. Is there a structure to how children group the objects in their picture? Do they align them in rows or columns or place them randomly on the page?

ASSESSMENT CHECKPOINT Can children apply what they have practised in the previous questions and complete the three sentences in question ❺? Do they use the correct numbers without mixing them up? Can they explain what each number represents.

ANSWERS Answers for the **Practice** part of the lesson appear in the separate **Practice and Reflect answer guide**.

Reflect

WAYS OF WORKING Pair work

IN FOCUS Both groups of counters contain four counters. However, they are in two different formations: a row and a square. Children should count the counters in each group and identify that there are the same number of counters in each group but a different number of groups in each set of groups.

ASSESSMENT CHECKPOINT Can children articulate that the number 4 is the number of counters in each group, which is the same in each set of groups even though the groups of counters look different? The difference is the number of fours: do children explain it as the number of groups or the number of fours?

ANSWERS Answers for the **Reflect** part of the lesson appear in the separate **Practice and Reflect answer guide**.

After the lesson ⏸

- Are children confident when identifying equal and unequal groups?
- Can children relate this to real life and identify equal groups in the world around them when asked?
- How did children differentiate between the number of groups and number in each group when talking with their peers? What language or phrases did they use?

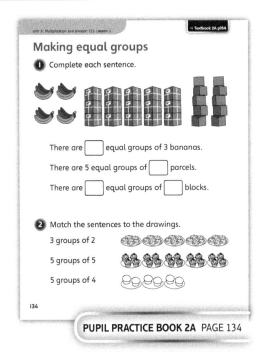

PUPIL PRACTICE BOOK 2A PAGE 134

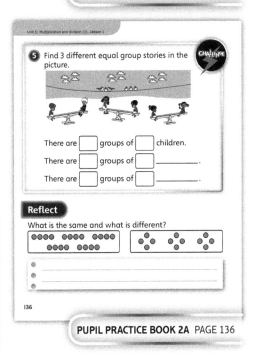

PUPIL PRACTICE BOOK 2A PAGE 135

PUPIL PRACTICE BOOK 2A PAGE 136

215

Multiplication as equal groups

Learning focus

In this lesson, children will write repeated addition and multiplication sentences to match a picture. Children will match sentences describing the number of equal groups with the correct multiplication and repeated addition sentences.

Small steps

→ Previous step: Making equal groups
→ **This step: Multiplication as equal groups**
→ Next step: Adding equal groups

NATIONAL CURRICULUM LINKS

Year 2 Number – Multiplication and Division

- Calculate mathematical statements for multiplication and division within the multiplication tables and write them using the multiplication (×), division (÷) and equals (=) signs.
- Solve problems involving multiplication and division, using materials, arrays, repeated addition, mental methods, and multiplication and division facts, including problems in contexts.

ASSESSING MASTERY

Children can correctly write a repeated addition sentence and a multiplication sentence to match a picture showing groups of objects. Children can derive a multiplication sentence from a repeated addition sentence and vice versa.

COMMON MISCONCEPTIONS

Children may incorrectly add the wrong number, repeatedly, in repeated addition sentences. For example, 'three groups of 4 chairs' may be written with three 3s or four 4s, especially as those numbers are so close together. Ask:
- *What are you repeatedly adding? How many do you have?*

STRENGTHENING UNDERSTANDING

When writing repeated addition sentences, children can keep track of how many they are adding by lining up physical resources such as multilink cubes or counters on a piece of paper and labelling each part of the line of physical resources. This helps children avoid having too many or too few of the number and helps when translating this into a multiplication sentence. Use the sentence structure, 'There are ___ equal groups of ___' alongside this to make it clear what × means.

GOING DEEPER

The two ways of interpreting multiplications look different. Ask children who have grasped the concept of multiplication as equal groups to show 4 × 3 in two different ways: as 3 + 3 + 3 + 3 and 4 + 4 + 4. Can they explain what is different each time?

KEY LANGUAGE

In lesson: total number, add, groups, same, addition, **multiplication**, +, ×, =

Other language to be used by the teacher: multiply, repeated, equal groups, add, number in a group, number of objects, skip count

STRUCTURES AND REPRESENTATIONS

Array, counters

RESOURCES

Mandatory: counters and multilink cubes

Optional: classroom objects in equal groups that make a clear distinction between the objects being put into groups and what the groups are, such as pens in packs, eggs in egg boxes

 In the eTextbook of this lesson, you will find interactive links to a selection of teaching tools.

Before you teach

- In the previous lesson, were children confident when identifying equal groups?
- Did children confuse the number of objects in a group and the number of equal groups when filling out sentences in the previous lesson?
- How will you provide scaffolding for the introduction of ×?

Discover

Pair work

ASK

• *How do you know when to stop adding?*
• *How do you know which number to keep adding?*

IN FOCUS The picture and questions provide a practical context for repeatedly adding a number. Using the picture as a guide, discuss with children which number will be repeatedly added and why.

ANSWERS

Question ❶ a): There are 3 groups of 5 chairs. The total is worked out using 5 + 5 + 5 or 5 × 3.

Question ❶ b): There are 6 groups of 2 chairs. The total is worked out using 2 + 2 + 2 + 2 + 2 + 2 or 2 × 6.

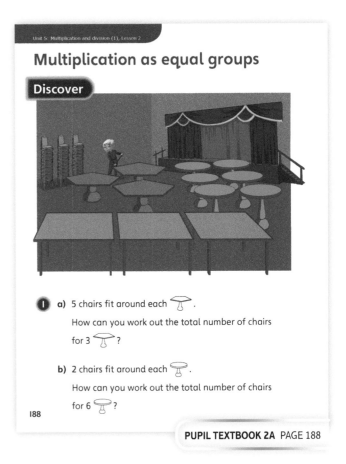

PUPIL TEXTBOOK 2A PAGE 188

Share

Whole class teacher led

ASK

• *What does each number represent, tables or chairs?*

IN FOCUS The practical context enables children to distinguish between the number of groups (tables) and the number of objects in each group (chairs). The counters underneath each table represent the number of chairs and have been separated out into groups.

Refer to what Astrid is saying about adding three groups to find the total number of chairs. Ask children to show you where the three groups are on the page.

DEEPEN Flo shows the multiplication sentence 3 × 5. Ask children to translate this into a sentence identifying the group. Children should understand that 3 × 5 is three groups of 5 chairs while 5 × 3 would be five groups of 3 chairs.

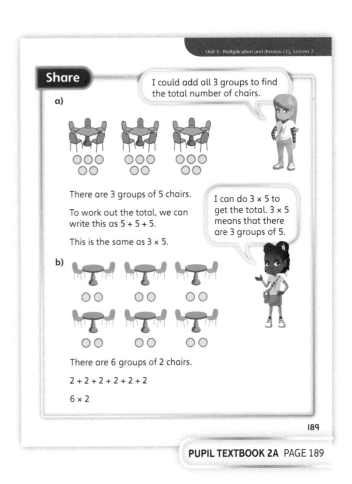

PUPIL TEXTBOOK 2A PAGE 189

Think together

WAYS OF WORKING Whole class teacher led (I do, We do, You do)

ASK

- Questions ❶ and ❷ : *How many tables are there? How many chairs are there?*
- Questions ❶ and ❷ : *What number do you need to keep adding?*
- Questions ❶ and ❷ : *What does × mean in these multiplication sentences?*

IN FOCUS Questions ❶ and ❷ provide pictorial representations, enabling children to count the number of chairs and repeatedly add them until they run out of tables. Children can then translate this into a multiplication sentence and use × to represent the number of times the number of chairs is added.

In question ❸ , Henry's multiplication sentence is not correct because one of the four groups does not contain three birds. Refer to what Ash says and ask children whether they agree with this. Why do they agree or disagree?

STRENGTHEN Ask children to draw counters in sorting hoops to represent the number of tables and chairs in question ❷ , as provided for question ❶ . Children can write the number of chairs underneath each set of counters to help them to repeatedly add the number of chairs.

In question ❸ , can children add one bird to the correct group in order to make 4 × 3 correct?

DEEPEN Ask children to put question ❷ into a sentence that contains the words 'equal groups'. For example, they could say, 'there are four groups of 3 chairs,' or, 'there are three chairs around each table and there are four tables'.

Some children may realise that the same numbers are used in questions ❶ and ❷ , but switched around so that they have different roles. Ask children to compare the sentences and explain what they find.

ASSESSMENT CHECKPOINT In question ❶ , check that children understand that one counter represents one chair and one sorting hoop represents one table.

In question ❷ , children might start to repeatedly add 4 because there are four tables. However, this means they will have completed 4 × 4. Ask children to look closely at the number of addition boxes (four) and what this number represents in the picture (tables). This means that the number of chairs is repeatedly added because the number of tables has already been defined.

ANSWERS

Question ❶ : 4 + 4 + 4 = 12

            3 × 4 = 12

Question ❷ : 3 + 3 + 3 + 3 = 12

            4 × 3 = 12

Question ❸ : Henry is not correct. One of the three groups does not contain three birds

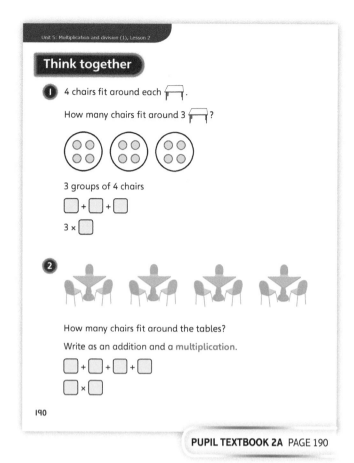

PUPIL TEXTBOOK 2A PAGE 190

PUPIL TEXTBOOK 2A PAGE 191

Practice

WAYS OF WORKING Independent thinking

IN FOCUS Question ❶ asks children to fill in the gaps in repeated addition sentences and multiplication sentences. The missing number in the multiplication sentences keeps changing so children need to refer to the pictures and understand what each number represents.

Question ❸ requires children to apply their knowledge of repeated addition and multiplication to the number of groups. Point out '2 groups of 2' because the number of groups and the number of objects in each group is the same, so only the operation changes. Ask children why that is and whether it would be the same for other numbers.

STRENGTHEN Ask children to represent the pictures in questions ❶ and ❷ using physical resources. This will help them to fill in the blanks and will show you how children are working.

DEEPEN Question ❹ asks children to fill in multiplication and addition sentences in one way, but there are two ways to write each sentence. For example, when answering question ❹ a), can children spot that 4 × 3 can also be written as 3 × 4? Can they also write the corresponding addition sentence, 4 + 4 + 4?

The sheep in question ❺ are not in physically constrained groups, unlike the frogs on the lily pads. Can children come up with a context for the sheep, such as being in pens or in fields?

ASSESSMENT CHECKPOINT In questions ❶ and ❷, check that children can articulate what each number represents in each multiplication sentence. Can children articulate what is being repeatedly added (for example, the number of sheep, cows or cats)?

When children write their own multiplication sentences for question ❺, which number do they start with? Do they realise that this does not matter as long as the other number matches what is happening in the story? Can children explain what they are adding or multiplying each time?

ANSWERS Answers for the **Practice** part of the lesson appear in the separate **Practice and Reflect answer guide**.

Reflect

WAYS OF WORKING Pair work

IN FOCUS The **Reflect** section highlights the important fact that additions and multiplications need to match and that the number that is repeatedly added must be correctly represented in the multiplication sentence. Incorrect pairings can be corrected by changing the addition so that there are six 3s or changing the multiplication so that it is 5 × 3.

ASSESSMENT CHECKPOINT Do children count the number of 3s to work out the answer? Do they understand the role of both 3s in the first example? Do they want to correct the addition sentence or the multiplication sentence?

ANSWERS Answers for the **Reflect** part of the lesson appear in the separate **Practice and Reflect answer guide**.

After the lesson ⏸

- Did children understand what × means?
- Could children relate repeated addition to the number of equal groups?
- Did any children make mistakes when counting up the number of groups and putting this into a multiplication?

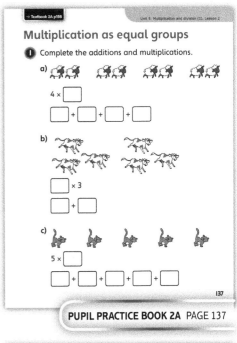

PUPIL PRACTICE BOOK 2A PAGE 137

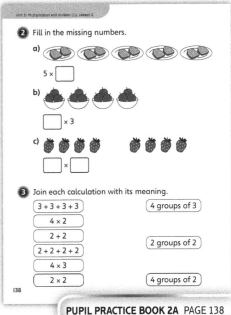

PUPIL PRACTICE BOOK 2A PAGE 138

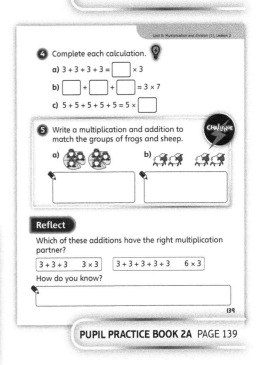

PUPIL PRACTICE BOOK 2A PAGE 139

Adding equal groups

Learning focus

In this lesson, children will use a number line alongside repeated addition and multiplication sentences to work out a total.

Small steps

→ Previous step: Multiplication as equal groups
→ **This step: Adding equal groups**
→ Next step: Multiplication sentences

NATIONAL CURRICULUM LINKS

Year 2 Number – Multiplication and Division

- Solve problems involving multiplication and division, using materials, arrays, repeated addition, mental methods, and multiplication and division facts, including problems in contexts.
- Solve one-step problems involving multiplication and division, by calculating the answer using concrete objects, pictorial representations and arrays with the support of the teacher.

ASSESSING MASTERY

Children can attribute repeated addition to how many jumps are shown on a number line. Children can make the link between the number of jumps on the number line and the number in the multiplication sentence.

COMMON MISCONCEPTIONS

Children may find it confusing to switch between repeated addition and multiplication and they may use the wrong operation. For example, when writing 4 + 4 as a multiplication, they may put 4 + 2 as they have correctly identified that there are two 4s, but neglected to change the operation. Ask:

- *Does 4 + 2 match the picture? Work out the total and compare it with the picture.*

STRENGTHENING UNDERSTANDING

In this lesson, an array is used alongside the number line to represent the number of objects. Ask children to circle the repeated additions in the array and to count the numbers as they go. This will reinforce their understanding that there must be equal groups because each row will be the same.

GOING DEEPER

If children are confident when counting rows and circling them as they go, ask them to do the same for columns. Do they make the link between the number of columns and the other number in the multiplication sentence?

KEY LANGUAGE

In lesson: how many?, groups, multiplication, in total, represent, addition

Other language to be used by the teacher: array, multiply, repeated addition, equal groups, add, number in a group, number of objects, skip counting

STRUCTURES AND REPRESENTATIONS

Number line, array, counters

RESOURCES

Mandatory: counters, arrays, number lines

Optional: multilink cubes, counters

 In the eTextbook of this lesson, you will find interactive links to a selection of teaching tools.

Before you teach

- Were children confident when drawing pictures of equal groups in previous lessons?
- In previous lessons, were children confident when using a number line for repeated addition?

Discover

WAYS OF WORKING Pair work

ASK

- *How did you work out the total?*
- *What numbers can you see in the chocolate bars?*
- *Is each row of chocolate equal?*

IN FOCUS The picture shows equal groups, but not with distinct categories as seen in previous lessons. Children may have a variety of ways of working out the number of pieces of chocolate, such as counting one by one, skip counting the rows, skip counting the columns or skip counting in a smaller number easier to manage, such as 2.

ANSWERS

Question **1** a): There are 8 pieces of white chocolate.

Question **1** b): There are 18 pieces of dark chocolate.

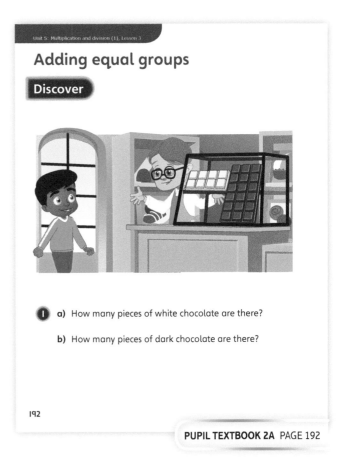

Adding equal groups

Discover

1 a) How many pieces of white chocolate are there?

b) How many pieces of dark chocolate are there?

192

PUPIL TEXTBOOK 2A PAGE 192

Share

WAYS OF WORKING Whole class teacher led

ASK

- *What jumps have been made on each number line?*
- *Can you see the size of the jumps on the chocolate bars? Can you see that one row of squares of chocolate is one jump?*

IN FOCUS Point out the links between the different pictorial representations used to help children visualise each problem. For example, refer to what Dexter says and ask children to make the link between the counters and the picture of the chocolate bar. Once children are satisfied that there are 4 in each row, refer to what Astrid says about using a number line. Ask children to explain what jumps have been made on the number line and how they link to the picture of the chocolate bar.

Refer to what Sparks says to see whether children can link the number of jumps on the number line with the number that they need to multiply by.

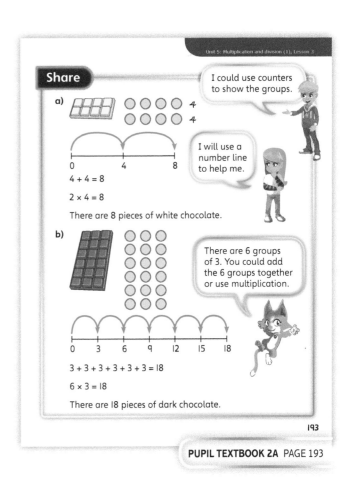

Share

I could use counters to show the groups.

a)
4
4

$4 + 4 = 8$

$2 \times 4 = 8$

There are 8 pieces of white chocolate.

I will use a number line to help me.

b)
There are 6 groups of 3. You could add the 6 groups together or use multiplication.

$3 + 3 + 3 + 3 + 3 + 3 = 18$

$6 \times 3 = 18$

There are 18 pieces of dark chocolate.

193

PUPIL TEXTBOOK 2A PAGE 193

Think together

Whole class teacher led (I do, We do, You do)

ASK

- Question ❶ : *What is the size of each jump on the number line?*
- Question ❷ : *How many jumps are made on the number line?*

IN FOCUS Talk through and model question ❶ using physical resources.

Question ❷ provides less scaffolding and requires children to use previous learning about what size of jump they are making on the number line. Ask: *What number are you jumping up by each time? How many jumps should you make? When should you stop jumping up?*

Question ❸ builds on question ❷ by adding another basket. One of the 5s in the multiplication sentence will change to 6 to represent the additional basket of apples.

STRENGTHEN Ask children to represent the baskets of apples in question ❷ using multilink cubes. They should produce five stacks of five multilink cubes. When answering question ❸ , ask them to add another stack of multilink cubes. Ask: *What has changed? The number of apples in a basket or the number of baskets?*

DEEPEN Can children articulate what would happen if a basket was taken away? Encourage them to experiment with the multilink cubes to work out that one of the 5s in the multiplication sentence will change to a 4 to represent the missing basket of apples.

ASSESSMENT CHECKPOINT When answering question ❷ , do children say that they are jumping up by the number of apples or the number of bowls of apples? The numbers are the same but it is important that children can relate what they are doing to the picture.

ANSWERS

Question ❶ : 2 + 2 + 2 + 2 + 2 + 2 + 2 + 2 + 2 = 20

$\quad\quad$ 10 × 2 = 20

Question ❷ : 5 + 5 + 5 + 5 + 5 = 25

$\quad\quad$ 5 × 5 = 25

$\quad\quad$ Each 5 represents the number of apples in a basket and the number of baskets.

Question ❸ : 5 + 5 + 5 + 5 + 5 + 5 = 30

$\quad\quad$ 6 × 5 = 30

PUPIL TEXTBOOK 2A PAGE 194

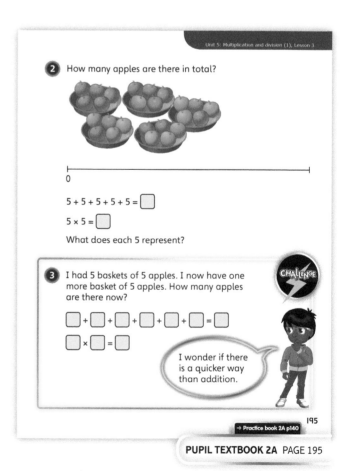

PUPIL TEXTBOOK 2A PAGE 195

Practice

WAYS OF WORKING Independent thinking

IN FOCUS Children repeatedly add 10 to the number line in question ③ then use this number line to help them complete multiplication sentences related to the 10 times-table. Question ⑤ asks children to compare number sentences using <, > or =, which requires them to work out the answer to each number sentence first.

STRENGTHEN In questions ①, ② and ③, point out to children that the repeated addition sentence for each number line can be seen in the jumps. This is because each jump tells you what has been added. Show them that taking away the jumps and the line leaves the repeated addition sentence, with the repeated number being added the correct number of times.

DEEPEN Using the number line in question ③, can children generate more multiplication sentences based on the 10 times-table? Can they identify a pattern in these sentences?

ASSESSMENT CHECKPOINT Question ⑤ does not provide a number line or picture to help children work out the multiplication sentences. What strategies do children use when working them out? Listen for skip counting or look for drawings of equal groups or number lines.

ANSWERS Answers for the **Practice** part of the lesson appear in the separate **Practice and Reflect answer guide**.

Reflect

WAYS OF WORKING Pair work

IN FOCUS The **Reflect** part of the lesson asks children for different factor pairs for 20. Children may come up with completely unrelated pairs, such as 2 × 10 and 4 × 5, or they may keep the same pair and switch the numbers around, such as 2 × 10 and 10 × 2.

ASSESSMENT CHECKPOINT Do children's chosen numbers multiply to make 20? Can they switch the numbers around and know that the answer will be the same? When drawing on the number line, do children label each jump correctly?

ANSWERS Answers for the **Reflect** part of the lesson appear in the separate **Practice and Reflect answer guide**.

After the lesson

- Were children confident that the number line represented both repeated addition and multiplication sentences?
- Did children struggle with any parts of the lesson or concepts or mix them up, such as relating the number line to the multiplication sentence?
- How did you encourage confident children to think more deeply about multiplication?

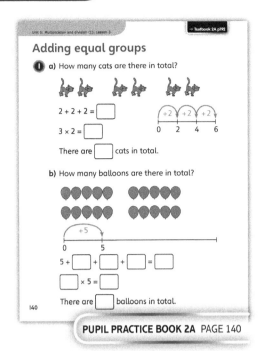

PUPIL PRACTICE BOOK 2A PAGE 140

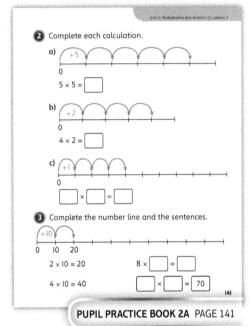

PUPIL PRACTICE BOOK 2A PAGE 141

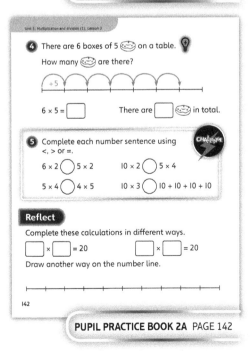

PUPIL PRACTICE BOOK 2A PAGE 142

223

Multiplication sentences

Learning focus

In this lesson, children will be introduced to two multiplication calculations and two repeated addition calculations.

Small steps

→ Previous step: Adding equal groups
→ **This step: Multiplication sentences**
→ Next step: Using arrays

NATIONAL CURRICULUM LINKS

Year 2 Number – Multiplication and Division

Solve problems involving multiplication and division, using materials, arrays, repeated addition, mental methods, and multiplication and division facts, including problems in contexts.

ASSESSING MASTERY

Children can work out multiplication sentences within different contexts, such as money and sides of a shape, and can work out the cost of several items and relate this back to a multiplication sentence. Children can create their own stories from multiplication sentences and draw equal groups to represent these sentences.

COMMON MISCONCEPTIONS

When working with money, children will have to work out the cost of a number of items. The addition of the £ sign may confuse them and some children may start writing £ in front of the number of items needed rather than in front of the cost of the item. Ask:

• *What do the two £ signs mean in this calculation? ? × £? = £?*

STRENGTHENING UNDERSTANDING

Provide real coins for children to handle and manipulate. Explain that a 2p coin is not two distinct objects put into a group but is one object that represents the number 2. When counting with coins, children will unitise how much each coin is worth in order to skip count with them.

GOING DEEPER

There are different tables in this lesson explaining the cost of different items. Can children create their own table of the cost of some items of their choice? Can they ask their own questions about how many of each item were bought and how much the items cost?

KEY LANGUAGE

In lesson: how much, calculation, adding, spend/spent, multiplication

Other language to be used by the teacher: multiply, repeated addition, cost of

STRUCTURES AND REPRESENTATIONS

Number line, counters

RESOURCES

Mandatory: number lines, counters

Optional: real or plastic coins, paper banknotes, plastic 2D and 3D shapes

 In the eTextbook of this lesson, you will find interactive links to a selection of teaching tools.

Before you teach

• In previous lessons, were children confident when using number lines to represent repeated addition?
• When have children discussed money before?
• What curriculum links could you make?
• How will you provide prompts and scaffolding to help children to create their own multiplication stories?

Discover

WAYS OF WORKING Pair work

ASK

- *Where is 5p in the table?*
- *Where does the table show how many of each coin have been collected?*
- *In the row of the table that contains the numbers 3 and 2, which number represents the money? How do you know?*

IN FOCUS Children will extract information from the table to answer the questions. They will read the table and see each row as showing a separate piece of information. Point out to children that replacing the coins with × would write out the multiplication sentences within the table.

ANSWERS

Question ① a): 30p has been collected.

Question ① b): The first row of the table represents 3 × 2. The 3 represents the number of coins. The 2 represents the 🪙 .

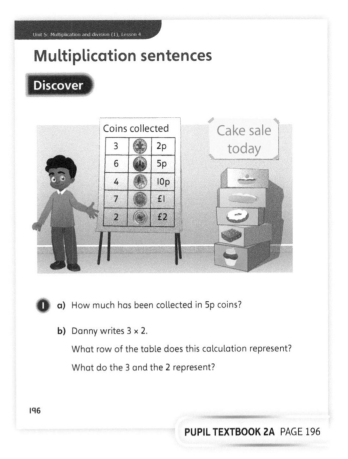

Multiplication sentences

Discover

① a) How much has been collected in 5p coins?

b) Danny writes 3 × 2.

What row of the table does this calculation represent?

What do the 3 and the 2 represent?

196

PUPIL TEXTBOOK 2A PAGE 196

Share

WAYS OF WORKING Whole class teacher led

ASK

- *What do you think Dexter means by 'the right number of 5s'?*
- *What information does Astrid need to get from the table?*

IN FOCUS Question ① a) requires children to extract the number of 5s from the correct row of the table and link the number of 5s in the table to the number of 5s that need to be added on the number line.

Question ① b) points out that there are two types of coin that represent the number 2, but you should make it clear that only one row in the table shows that there are three of those coins.

STRENGTHEN Have a set of 5p coins available for children to recreate the repeated addition number line. Each coin can be placed inside each jump to represent + 5.

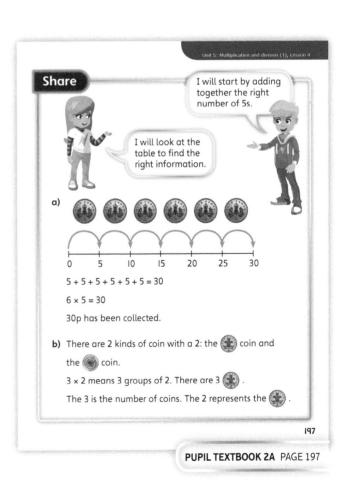

Share

I will start by adding together the right number of 5s.

I will look at the table to find the right information.

a)

5 + 5 + 5 + 5 + 5 + 5 = 30

6 × 5 = 30

30p has been collected.

b) There are 2 kinds of coin with a 2: the 🪙 coin and the 🪙 coin.

3 × 2 means 3 groups of 2. There are 3 🪙 .

The 3 is the number of coins. The 2 represents the 🪙 .

197

PUPIL TEXTBOOK 2A PAGE 197

Think together

WAYS OF WORKING Whole class teacher led (I do, We do, You do)

ASK

- Question **1** : *What does the word 'spend' mean? How will you work out what has been spent?*
- Question **2** : *Which number needs the £ sign? Why?*

IN FOCUS Children will extract information from the table to complete the multiplication sentences in question **1** . They need to work out the cost of each item and then multiply the cost by the number of items that were bought.

Refer to what Flo says in question **3** about identifying what is in 2s in the picture. This is a good prompt for children who struggle to see the multiplication sentence. Some children may identify the 4 first because there are four see-saws.

STRENGTHEN To make the context of 'cost' and 'spending' more real, ask children to recreate each scenario using a set of coins and notes. Have children compare a group of five £2 coins with a group of five £5 notes. Ask: *What is the same about each group of money? How is this shown in the multiplication sentences?*

DEEPEN In question **3** , the 4 × 2 story is represented by two children on each of the four see-saws. Ask children to describe or draw what the picture would look like if the numbers were switched around.

ASSESSMENT CHECKPOINT In question **1** , check whether children have correctly interpreted what the 5 and the 2 represent by checking whether they write 2 × £5 = £10 instead of 5 × £2 = 10.

Question **2** asks children to arrange the correct number of counters to match each multiplication sentence. Do children draw circles around each group of counters? Do they lay out the correct number of counters without distinguishing any groups?

ANSWERS

Question **1** : They spent £10 on 🍦.

5 × £2 = £10

They spent £15 on 🍰.

3 × £5 = £15

Question **2** : The 4 × 3 row requires 3 more groups of 3 counters.

The 5 × 5 row requires 5 groups of 5 counters.

Question **3** : Children should identify that each see-saw has two children on it and that there are four see-saws in total.

4 see-saws × 2 children on each see-saw = 8 children in total.

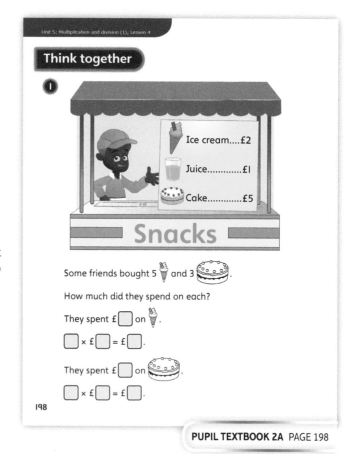

PUPIL TEXTBOOK 2A PAGE 198

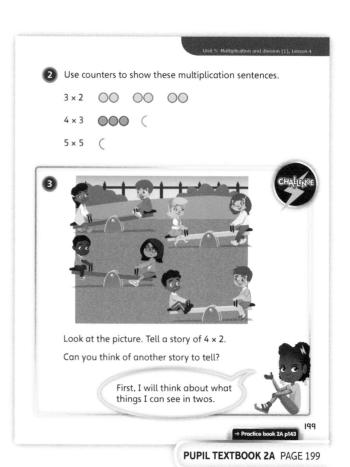

PUPIL TEXTBOOK 2A PAGE 199

Practice

WAYS OF WORKING Independent thinking

IN FOCUS Question ❶ requires children to derive multiplication sentences from the picture, providing less scaffolding as the questions progress until they write their own sentence without any prompting pictures or blank spaces to fill in.

Question ❷ requires children to work out each multiplication sentence for the total cost of the items before they can match the sentence to the correct cost. It also challenges children by including a repeated addition sentence that matches the cost of three cakes, because children cannot simply match the numbers in the sentences as there is no 3 in the repeated addition sentence.

STRENGTHEN Question ❷ requires children to remember a lot of information. Ask children to work out each multiplication sentence using the information in the table. They will then be able to match up the sentences.

In question ❺, children can redraw the number of cherries and the number of apples into rows for comparison.

DEEPEN In question ❸, ask children how the multiplication sentence and answers would change if the 2 represented £2 or 2p (£2 × 4 = £8 and 2p × 4 = 8p). Can they show this using a set of coins?

ASSESSMENT CHECKPOINT When drawing their own picture story for question ❸, note which contexts children use. Do children use a context they have seen before, which they can repeatedly add with ease, or have they come up with their own context? Do they draw their objects in equal groups spread across the page or in an array formation in separate rows?

ANSWERS Answers for the **Practice** part of the lesson appear in the separate **Practice and Reflect answer guide**.

Reflect

WAYS OF WORKING Pair work

IN FOCUS Asking children to tell different stories for 2 × 5 and 5 × 2 requires them to think about the different things represented by 5: either the number in a group or the number of groups.

ASSESSMENT CHECKPOINT Can children think of their own contexts where the 5 and 2 are interchangeable or do they have to be given a context from a previous lesson? If children are struggling to think of a context, suggest frogs on lily pads so that the 5 can represent the number of frogs on one lily pad in one story, and the number of lily pads in another.

ANSWERS Answers for the **Reflect** part of the lesson appear in the separate **Practice and Reflect answer guide**.

After the lesson ⏸

- Were children confident using their knowledge of multiplication within the context of money?
- How easy was it for children to think of their own contexts where equal groups were required?
- In the **Reflect** part of the lesson, did children learn from each other and understand their partner's interpretation of the same number sentence?

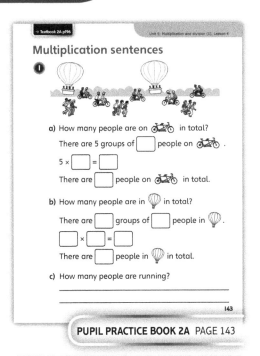

PUPIL PRACTICE BOOK 2A PAGE 143

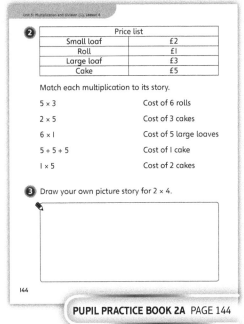

PUPIL PRACTICE BOOK 2A PAGE 144

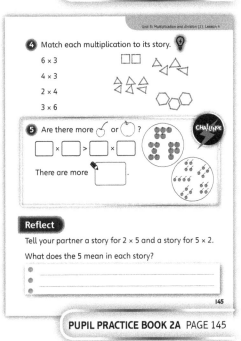

PUPIL PRACTICE BOOK 2A PAGE 145

Using arrays

Learning focus

In this lesson, children will learn how to relate arrays to a repeated addition sentence and multiplication sentence. Children will use arrays to fill in sentence scaffolds and make their own arrays.

Small steps

→ Previous step: Multiplication sentences
→ **This step: Using arrays**
→ Next step: 2 times-table

NATIONAL CURRICULUM LINKS

Year 2 Number – Multiplication and Division

- Calculate mathematical statements for multiplication and division within the multiplication tables and write them using the multiplication (×), division (÷) and equals (=) signs.
- Solve problems involving multiplication and division, using materials, arrays, repeated addition, mental methods, and multiplication and division facts, including problems in contexts.

ASSESSING MASTERY

Children can understand the basic properties of an array (having an equal number in each row and column) and the commutative law of multiplication by looking at the array in different ways and grouping it into rows and columns. They can write different repeated addition sentences and multiplication sentences from one array as well as making their own array based on a multiplication sentence.

COMMON MISCONCEPTIONS

When using counters to make their own array for the first time, children may not line up the counters correctly, creating an unequal number in rows or columns. Squared paper or a squared background guides children to line up the counters correctly.

STRENGTHENING UNDERSTANDING

When looking at two arrays that use the same numbers and have the same total, such as in the **Discover** part of the lesson, show children that they can make one array and rotate it 90° horizontally. Encourage children to do this as many times as necessary until they can appreciate that only the orientation has changed, not the total.

GOING DEEPER

The counters in an array can be rearranged to create alternative arrays. For example, counters can be stacked on top of each other and even though the array looks different the number in each row or total remains the same.

KEY LANGUAGE

In lesson: how many?, in total, more than, array, row, column, amount, number sentence, multiplication, addition, calculation

Other language to be used by the teacher: equal, unequal, number in a group, multiply

STRUCTURES AND REPRESENTATIONS

Array, number line, counters

RESOURCES

Mandatory: multilink cubes or counters to make arrays

Optional: squared paper or a squared background

 In the eTextbook of this lesson, you will find interactive links to a selection of teaching tools.

Before you teach

- Children have seen counters organised into an array in Unit 5, Lesson 1. How will you make the link to this previous introduction to arrays?
- Are children familiar with the words 'row' and 'column' from other contexts? How will you make these words more memorable, such as using actions or making a classroom display?

Discover

ASK

• *Is there a way to count the muffins other than counting one by one?*

• *How can Ali and Ed have baked the same number if the trays of muffins look so different?*

IN FOCUS Both bakers have made the same number of muffins but they are displayed in different orientations. Children may not recognise this initially and may only realise after they have counted them. Discuss any patterns in the muffins to explain why they are the same amount.

ANSWERS

Question **1** a): Ali baked 15 🥤 in total.

Question **1** b): Ed baked 15 🥤 in total.

Ed and Ali baked the same number of 🥤.

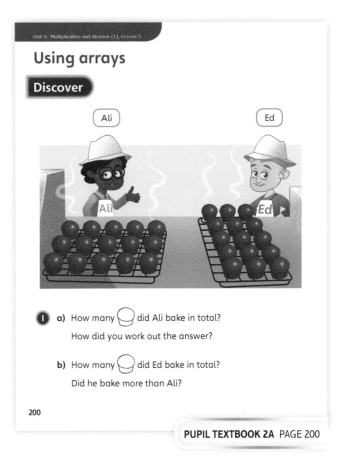

PUPIL TEXTBOOK 2A PAGE 200

Share

ASK

• *How many rows are there in each array?*

• *How many muffins are in each row?*

IN FOCUS   Refer to what Astrid says and link it to the picture by focusing on the word 'row'. This **Share** part of the lesson only focuses on rows, but the orientation of the array changes so that there is a different amount in each row in questions **1** a) and **1** b).

Children are supported by familiar representations for multiplication: number lines showing repeated jumps alongside repeated addition and multiplication sentences. This means that each row in the array can be represented as a jump on the number line.

STRENGTHEN Using a labelled number line, children can mark jumps of 5 and 3 in different colours to show that five jumps of 3 and three jumps of 5 both end at 15. The numbers are used as both the size of the jump and the number of jumps.

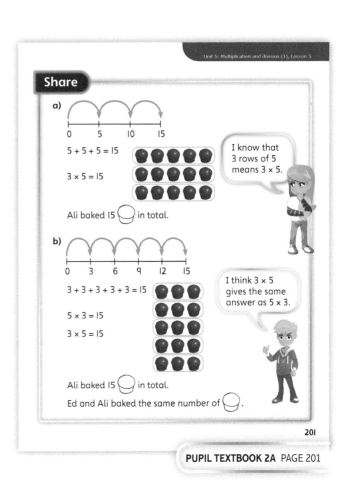

PUPIL TEXTBOOK 2A PAGE 201

Think together

Whole class teacher led (I do, We do, You do)

ASK

- Question **1** : *How has the array been grouped differently? Has the total changed?*

IN FOCUS In question **1** b), the array has been grouped into rows so children will need to group it into columns. The sentence scaffolds indicate how many numbers need to be added if children are unsure.

Question **2** only requires children to fill out the multiplication sentence, but they will group both rows and columns onto the same array. The array is more abstract than the pictorial representations in questions **1** a) and **1** b).

Question **3** asks children to draw their own array, which they then split into columns and rows, and to write all of the corresponding sentences.

STRENGTHEN To support children, draw the outline of a 5 × 2 array on squared paper so that children can draw in the dots or fill it with counters.

DEEPEN Can children draw or make two arrays showing both 5 × 2 and 2 × 5 (as they did in the **Discover** part of the lesson)? If children are unsure what this will look like, rotate their array 90° horizontally.

ASSESSMENT CHECKPOINT In question **2** , do children trust that there is an equal number of objects in each row or column or do they have to count to check?

Refer to what Sparks says. Are children aware of how many number sentences they can make from one array? Do they know that these sentences will be addition and multiplication sentences?

ANSWERS

Question **1** a): 6 + 6 = 12

        2 × 6 = 12

        2 + 2 + 2 + 2 + 2 + 2 = 12

        6 × 2 = 12

Question **1** b): 5 × 10 = 50

        10 × 5 = 50

Question **2** : 5 × 4 = 20

        5 + 5 + 5 + 5 = 20

        4 × 5 = 20

Question **3** : Children should make accurate arrays for 5 × 2 showing the groups in both rows and in columns.

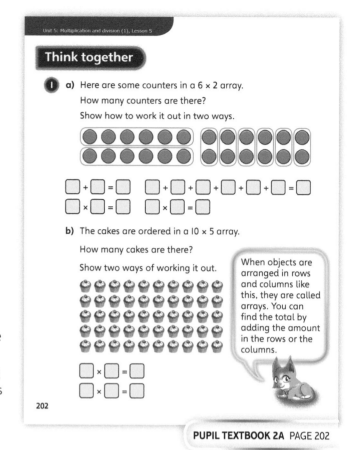

PUPIL TEXTBOOK 2A PAGE 202

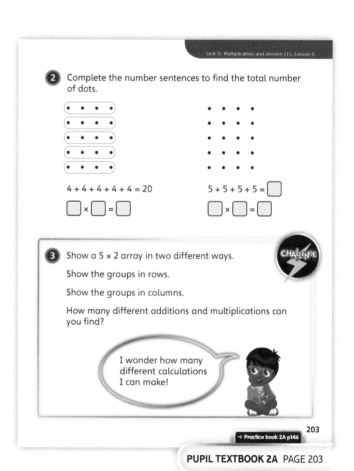

PUPIL TEXTBOOK 2A PAGE 203

Practice

WAYS OF WORKING Independent thinking

IN FOCUS Question ③ asks children to think about the orientation and placement of their arrays and how to fit their arrays onto the group of counters.

STRENGTHEN In question ④, ask children to make each array using physical resources to assess whether each sentence is true or false. Ask: *If you compare 10 × 3 and 10 × 2, what is different?*

DEEPEN Question ⑤ asks children to draw arrays where the number of rows and columns are the same, forming a square. If children grasp this quickly, tell them that the total of these arrays are called square numbers. Do children recognise any square numbers from times-tables that they have learned?

ASSESSMENT CHECKPOINT In question ③, are children aware that each number in the multiplication sentence represents first the number of rows and then the number of columns? This tests whether children understand the commutativity of arrays.

In question ④, can children instantly identify that 10 × 3 = 2 × 10 is false? Explain that switching the position of the 10 does not mean that the other number can change.

ANSWERS Answers for the **Practice** part of the lesson appear in the separate **Practice and Reflect answer guide**.

Reflect

WAYS OF WORKING Pair work and whole class

IN FOCUS Children discuss in pairs whether arrays for 2 × 7 can look different. Ask: *Does it matter whether you have used big dots, small dots, red dots, squares, counters or cubes?* Ask each child to make the array for 2 × 7, then choose some examples that look very different and show them to the class. Ask the class what really matters when making an array, guiding the discussion to conclude that there should be an equal number in each row and column and that the rows and columns should match the number in the multiplication sentence.

ASSESSMENT CHECKPOINT Show children examples of arrays that are completely different in size, shape and colour but that still show 2 × 7. Can children articulate the similarities as well as the obvious differences?

ANSWERS Answers for the **Reflect** part of the lesson appear in the separate **Practice and Reflect answer guide**.

After the lesson

- Were children confident filling in different sentence scaffolds based on one array or did they need the array to be split up or grouped to help them fill in the sentence scaffolds?
- Could children make arrays using a variety of resources or draw them on squared and plain paper?
- Did children recognise any of the arrays as times-table facts?

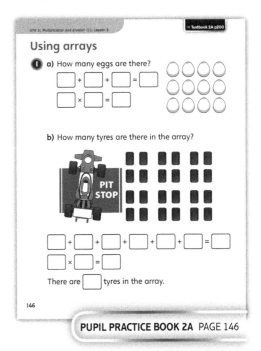

PUPIL PRACTICE BOOK 2A PAGE 146

PUPIL PRACTICE BOOK 2A PAGE 147

PUPIL PRACTICE BOOK 2A PAGE 148

2 times-table

Learning focus

In this lesson, children will learn the 2 times-table in a number of contexts. They will work out 2 times-table multiplication sentences and compare them using < and >.

Small steps

→ Previous step: Using arrays
→ **This step: 2 times-table**
→ Next step: 5 times-table

NATIONAL CURRICULUM LINKS

Year 2 Number – Multiplication and Division

Recall and use multiplication and division facts for the 2, 5 and 10 multiplication tables, including recognising odd and even numbers.

ASSESSING MASTERY

Children can work out multiplication sentences involving multiplying by 2 and can link this to an array, a number line and a repeated addition sentence. Children know that the 2 times-table involves only even numbers and that to multiply a number by 2 is the same as doubling it.

COMMON MISCONCEPTIONS

Counting up in 2s can be tricky when going over 10 as children may count '…6, 8, 10, 11…'. Use a visual prompt such as a number line or a 100 square to demonstrate skipping one before going to the next number. Unfortunately, the English language does not state 12 as 'ten-two', so it may take children longer to become familiar with this idea. Ask:
• *If you have counted 10 when jumping up in 2s, can you say the number after 10 or do you skip it? Show me on a number line.*

STRENGTHENING UNDERSTANDING

Use this opportunity to skip count with different objects while teaching the 2 times-table. Children can skip count objects that pair up in 2s, such as socks, shoes or wheels on a bicycle. They can also skip count with money with the 2p coin or the £2 coin, which is one object that has the value of two.

GOING DEEPER

The numbers in the 2 times-table are all even numbers: they can only end in the digits 0, 2, 4, 6 and 8. If children have not identified this for themselves in this lesson, guide them by highlighting all of the numbers in the 2 times-table on a 100 square. Children should see that they have five highlighted columns of numbers and that all the numbers in each column end with the same digit.

KEY LANGUAGE

In lesson: times-table, how many?, represent, count, number line

Other language to be used by the teacher: double, skip count, even, multiply

STRUCTURES AND REPRESENTATIONS

Number line, array

RESOURCES

Mandatory: counters, number lines, arrays

Optional: objects that come in pairs, such as socks, shoes and wheels on a bicycle, or that represent 2, such as 2p coins and £2 coins

 In the eTextbook of this lesson, you will find interactive links to a selection of teaching tools.

Before you teach

• Do children already know what even numbers are? Do they know what doubling is? Are you going to be able build on this knowledge or will you have to start from the beginning?
• How can you ensure that children become fluent in skip counting in 2s by the end of this lesson?
• What classroom resources come in pairs that you could use to make this times-table seem more concrete?

Discover

WAYS OF WORKING Pair work

WAYS OF WORKING Pair work

ASK

• *How many ice cubes are needed for each glass?*
• *If you are skip counting, how many numbers do you need to jump up by? How do you know when to stop?*
• *If you are multiplying, what does each number represent?*

IN FOCUS Children have to read the sentence about ice cubes to know how many are needed for each glass. They may work out how many are needed for 3 glasses and 8 glasses by drawing or counting on a number line or they may just know it as a fact.

ANSWERS

Question ❶ a): $2 + 2 + 2 = 6$

$3 \times 2 = 6$

6 ice cubes are needed for 3 🥤.

Question ❶ b): $2 + 2 + 2 + 2 + 2 + 2 + 2 + 2 = 16$

$8 \times 2 = 16$

16 ice cubes are needed for 8 🥤.

PUPIL TEXTBOOK 2A PAGE 204

Share

WAYS OF WORKING Whole class teacher led

ASK

• *How have the two ice cubes been represented?*
• *How many 2s need to be counted in each picture?*
• *How does the number line help you keep track of how many twos you have added?*

IN FOCUS Dexter says he used counters to represent the ice cubes and counted them one by one. The counters have been put in 2s next to each glass. Explore with children whether there is a quicker way to count the ice cubes. Point out what Flo says about counting in 2s if children are unsure.

In question ❶ b), one glass and two counters have been placed above each jump on the number line. It is important that children see the two counters that they are counting up in while simultaneously seeing the object that is worth 2 when counting up, as when using coins.

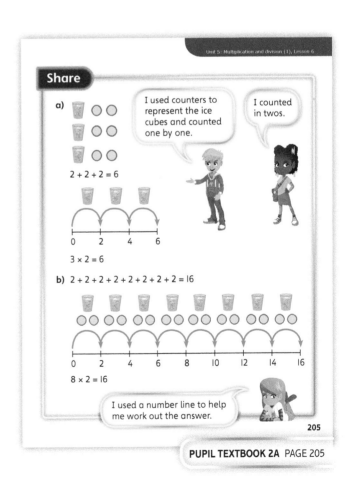

PUPIL TEXTBOOK 2A PAGE 205

Think together

WAYS OF WORKING Whole class teacher led (I do, We do, You do)

ASK

- Question **1** : *What number are you jumping up by on the number line?*
- Question **1** : *Where are the 2s in the array? Can you circle them with your finger?*

IN FOCUS Question **1** gives multiple ways of working out 9 × 2. Children can count up in 2s on the number line as seen in the **Share** part of the lesson and they can also group the array of counters into 2s as seen in Lesson 5.

Questions **2** and **3** allow children to use the answer to the previous question to add on two ice cubes as one more glass is repeatedly added.

STRENGTHEN Encourage children to recreate or draw the array of 9 × 2 counters in question **1** and use this to help them with questions **2** and **3** . Demonstrate that every time one new glass is added two counters are added to the array.

DEEPEN Are children able to make the link between the 10th glass and the 11th and 12th glass? If they are confident that two more ice cubes need to be added for one more glass, can they use this knowledge to work out how many ice cubes need to be added for two, three and four more glasses?

ASSESSMENT CHECKPOINT Do children need to work out each multiplication sentence from 0 or can they use the previous fact to help them? Do they show an awareness of the ratio 1:2 (though you will not use the language of ratios with children) and understand that, for every one glass added, two ice cubes are added?

ANSWERS

Question **1** : $2 + 2 + 2 + 2 + 2 + 2 + 2 + 2 + 2 = 18$

$9 × 2 = 18$

18 ice cubes are needed for 9 🥤.

Question **2** : $2 + 2 + 2 + 2 + 2 + 2 + 2 + 2 + 2 + 2 = 20$

$10 × 2 = 20$

20 ice cubes are needed for 10 🥤.

Question **3** a): $11 × 2 = 22$

22 ice cubes are needed for 11 🥤.

Question **3** b): $12 × 2 = 24$

24 ice cubes are needed for 12 🥤.

PUPIL TEXTBOOK 2A PAGE 206

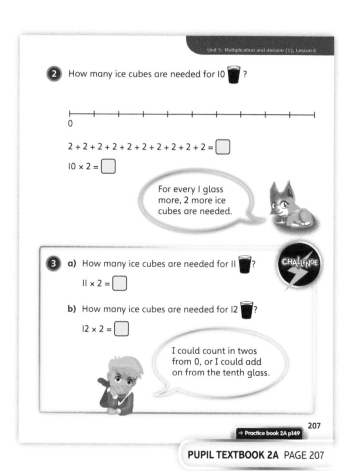

PUPIL TEXTBOOK 2A PAGE 207

Practice

WAYS OF WORKING Independent thinking

IN FOCUS Question **1** provides a pictorial representation of counting objects in 2s. In question **1** a) the multiplication sentence scaffold has been given to children. In question **1** b), children need to fill it in for themselves.

Question **5** requires taking the total of a multiplication sentence and grouping that into 2s in order to complete the second multiplication sentence.

STRENGTHEN Encourage children to take the multiplication sentences from question **3** and sort them into their own categories. For example, they could choose <7 and >7 or <5 and >5.

DEEPEN Ask children what other numbers can be put into the machine in question **4** . Give children some constraints by asking: *What numbers can you put into the machine where the answer will be …, for example, …less than 10? …less than 20? …have an 8 in it? …have a 4 in it?*

ASSESSMENT CHECKPOINT In question **2** b), children may write 5 × 2 instead of 4 × 2 because they add two people to the 3 rather than realising that the arrival of two more people means that there is only one more group of two people.

Do children rely on a strategy to work out multiplying a 1-digit number by 2 or are they starting to rely on their memory for these number facts when answering question **4** ?

ANSWERS Answers for the **Practice** part of the lesson appear in the separate **Practice and Reflect answer guide**.

Reflect

WAYS OF WORKING Pair work

IN FOCUS This part of the lesson allows children to draw their own way of proving a multiplication sentence. Encourage them to use objects from around the classroom to demonstrate if they wish. Once children have had a go, they should compare their method with their partner's and discuss the similarities and differences.

ASSESSMENT CHECKPOINT Look at the representations that children draw. Is it a group of dots, a number line, an array or something else? How do children show their method? Do they circle an equal number of 2s? Are the jumps evenly spaced? Do they circle columns or rows in their array?

ANSWERS Answers for the **Reflect** part of the lesson appear in the separate **Practice and Reflect answer guide**.

After the lesson ⏸

- How fluent did children become in the use of the 2 times-table?
- Could children work out 2 times-table facts from other facts or did they have to count from 0?
- Were children able to double numbers in their heads or were they reliant on a visual strategy?

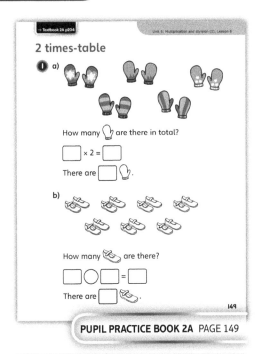

PUPIL PRACTICE BOOK 2A PAGE 149

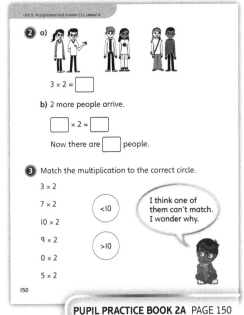

PUPIL PRACTICE BOOK 2A PAGE 150

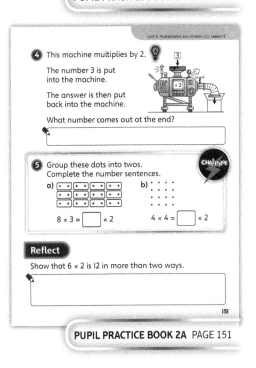

PUPIL PRACTICE BOOK 2A PAGE 151

235

5 times-table

Learning focus

In this lesson, children will learn the 5 times-table in a number of contexts. They will work out 5 times-table multiplication sentences using arrays, number lines and pictorial representations.

Small steps

→ Previous step: 2 times-table
→ **This step: 5 times-table**
→ Next step: 10 times-table

NATIONAL CURRICULUM LINKS

Year 2 Number – Multiplication and Division

Recall and use multiplication and division facts for the 2, 5 and 10 multiplication tables, including recognising odd and even numbers.

ASSESSING MASTERY

Children can work out multiplication sentences involving multiplying by 5 and can link this to an array, a number line and a repeated addition sentence. Children can explain how to use one multiplication fact to work out another multiplication fact without starting from 0.

COMMON MISCONCEPTIONS

When counting up in 5s, children may be unsure which ten comes next, especially higher numbers with which they are less familiar. They may be able to count '…15, 20, 25, 30, 35….' and then become uncertain. Sometimes they may revert to the previous ten or skip to the next one. This is because they are trying to keep track of what the next ten will be as well as remembering the pattern of ending in 5 and then 0. Ask:
• *Listen to the number you just said. How many tens are in it? What would one more ten be?*

STRENGTHENING UNDERSTANDING

Encourage children to use their fingers as base 5 resources when skip counting in 5s, such as repeatedly adding five by raising their hand or putting their hand onto the table. Children could make 5 times-table hand paintings for display in the classroom. Give them the opportunity to skip count in 5s using physical resources that naturally have 5 parts, such as gloves, 5p coins and pentagons.

GOING DEEPER

The 5 times-table is a mixture of odd and even numbers that only ever end in 5 or 0. Encourage children to highlight multiples of 5 on a 100 square so that they can see the pattern that this makes, resulting in a highlighted column of 5s and a highlighted column of 10s. Discuss why the pattern alternates odd and even, using resources to show 'one being left over' every other time.

KEY LANGUAGE

In lesson: times-table, how many?, count, multiplication, diagram, number sentences

Other language to be used by the teacher: skip count, multiply, odd, even, bar model, additive, multiplicative

STRUCTURES AND REPRESENTATIONS

Number line, array, bar model

RESOURCES

Mandatory: counters, number lines, arrays

Optional: objects with 5 parts, such as gloves, 5p coins, £5 notes and pentagons

 In the eTextbook of this lesson, you will find interactive links to a selection of teaching tools.

Before you teach

• How confident were children in the previous lesson when learning the 2 times-table? What links could you make to the previous lesson?
• How will you expose the patterns of odd and even in the 5 times-table?
• What classroom resources come in 5s that you could use to make this times-table seem more concrete?

Discover

Unit 5: Multiplication and division (1), Lesson 7

WAYS OF WORKING Pair work

ASK

- *How will the coach work out how many water bottles are needed?*
- *When a new team arrives, do you have to start counting the total from 0 or can you count on from your previous answer?*

IN FOCUS The picture shows three groups of 5 children. Each group wears a different coloured kit so that children can differentiate the groups. The players are not lined up in rows or columns so children may count individually to work out the total. When one more team arrives, children could represent this on the picture by adding five counters onto the page.

ANSWERS

Question ❶ a) 15 bottles of water are needed.

Question ❶ b) 20 bottles of water are needed.

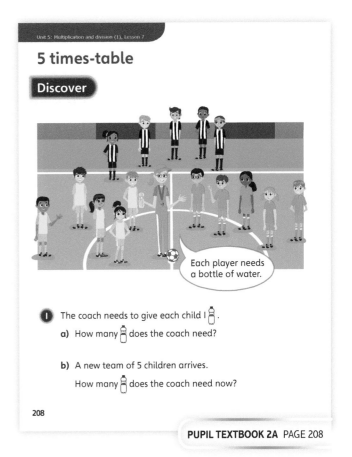

5 times-table

Discover

Each player needs a bottle of water.

❶ The coach needs to give each child 1 🍼.

a) How many 🍼 does the coach need?

b) A new team of 5 children arrives.
How many 🍼 does the coach need now?

208

PUPIL TEXTBOOK 2A PAGE 208

Share

WAYS OF WORKING Whole class teacher led

ASK

- *Is there an easier way than counting in 1s? What do you think Flo is suggesting?*
- *Where are the 5s in the array of shirts or counters? Can you circle them?*
- *When one more team arrives, what do you need to add on?*

IN FOCUS The shirts have been rearranged into rows, which makes it easier to see that each team contains an equal number of players. An array of counters alongside the shirts provides a pictorial representation. Dexter says he will count in 1s, but encourage children to think about what Flo says about counting in 5s.

When another team arrives in question ❶ b), encourage children to compare the two arrays and talk about what is different. The new row of different shirts should act as a clue if children struggle to see it in the array.

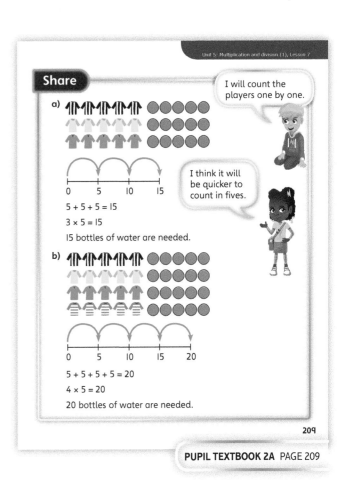

Share

I will count the players one by one.

a)

$5 + 5 + 5 = 15$

$3 \times 5 = 15$

15 bottles of water are needed.

I think it will be quicker to count in fives.

b)

$5 + 5 + 5 + 5 = 20$

$4 \times 5 = 20$

20 bottles of water are needed.

209

PUPIL TEXTBOOK 2A PAGE 209

Think together

WAYS OF WORKING Whole class teacher led (I do, We do, You do)

ASK

- *Where are the 5s in the array?*
- *How much is each jump worth?*
- *Question ❸ : Why does this 5 times-table look like a staircase? What keeps getting added?*

IN FOCUS Questions ❶ and ❷ provide arrays and number lines as scaffolding to help children complete the multiplication sentences. Question ❶ includes intervals of 5 on the number line but question ❷ requires children to fill this in themselves.

Question ❸ shows a pictorial representation of repeatedly adding 5 but asks children to complete each of the corresponding multiplication sentences. Encourage children to notice the pattern of the first number going up by 1 each time while 5 is added.

STRENGTHEN Children could draw their own 5 times-table staircase on a large piece of paper using 5ps, drawing the staircase pattern around the coins and writing the corresponding multiplication sentences next to each row.

DEEPEN Ask children to draw an array based on a number line jumping up in 5s. For example, if you were to show children a number line with two jumps of 5, which land on 10, could they use this to draw a 2 × 5 array?

ASSESSMENT CHECKPOINT When working on the number line, do children fill out each interval underneath or do they simply fill in the answer at the end of the number line? Do they relate their work on the number line to the array or do they see them as two separate calculations?

Question ❷ b) requires more jumps than 6 × 5 in question ❷ a). Do children know where to stop or do they keep going irrespective of what the array shows?

ANSWERS

Question ❶ : 5 × 5 = 25

Question ❷ a): 6 × 5 = 30

Question ❷ b): 8 × 5 = 40

Question ❸ : 1 × 5 = 5
2 × 5 = 10
3 × 5 = 15
4 × 5 = 20
5 × 5 = 25
6 × 5 = 30
7 × 5 = 35
8 × 5 = 40
9 × 5 = 45
10 × 5 = 50
11 × 5 = 55
12 × 5 = 60

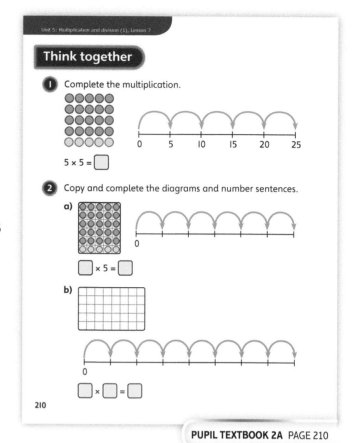

PUPIL TEXTBOOK 2A PAGE 210

PUPIL TEXTBOOK 2A PAGE 211

Practice

WAYS OF WORKING Independent thinking

IN FOCUS Question ③ introduces the 5 times-table as a bar model. Children have seen additive bar models with two unequal parts added together to make the whole. This is a multiplicative bar model where the parts are all equal and are multiplied by the number of equal parts to make the total.

Question ⑥ requires children to use the given number fact to work out 20 × 5 efficiently. It builds on the concept that one more 5 is added to a previous total so the difference between 19 × 5 and 20 × 5 is one more 5.

STRENGTHEN Provide 5p and 10p coins for children to use when completing question ⑦. Children could choose eight coins and add up the total value. Ask: *What if you started with eight 5p coins and repeatedly switched one 5p coin for one 10p coin?* This activity could be represented by drawing a table with eight spaces for coins in each row with the total value of the coins written beside each row.

DEEPEN Do children recognise that a 10p coin is the same as two 5p coins? Can they write the multiplication sentence for a mixture of 5p and 10p coins? For example, 5 + 5 + 10 or 4 × 5 for two 5ps and one 10p.

ASSESSMENT CHECKPOINT In question ③, can children work out from the bar model that one of the missing numbers is 9? The number 9 is not written anywhere so children have to count the number of equal 5s in the bar model.

In question ④, the number 5 is used twice: to represent the number of flowers in a vase and the number of vases. Can children articulate that distinction?

Question ⑤ e) concerns a multiplication sentence involving 0. Does this confuse children or are they confident that the answer will be 0?

ANSWERS Answers for the **Practice** part of the lesson appear in the separate **Practice and Reflect answer guide**.

Reflect

WAYS OF WORKING Pair work and whole class

IN FOCUS Children could add one more 6 to work out 6 × 6 = 36 or one more 5 for 7 × 5 = 35. Children could also take away a 6 to work out 6 × 4 = 24 or a 5 for 5 × 5 = 25. Doubling and halving could also be used. Encourage children to draw arrays to demonstrate their calculations, using different colours to indicate which number they are changing.

ASSESSMENT CHECKPOINT Are children confident that they know what each number in the multiplication sentence represents and confident in manipulating them? Are they able to draw the 6 × 5 array and then take off and add columns and rows? Are these actions accurately reflected in the new multiplication sentence that they write or do they add or take away the wrong number? Are children aware that if they do something to one of the factors the same must happen to the answer?

ANSWERS Answers for the **Reflect** part of the lesson appear in the separate **Practice and Reflect answer guide**.

After the lesson ⏸

- Were children confident colouring in the 5 times-table on a 100 square and explaining the pattern?
- Did children make links between this lesson and Lesson 6 on the 2 times-table?
- Did children notice the pattern of odd and even in the 5 times-table? Could they explain why this is?

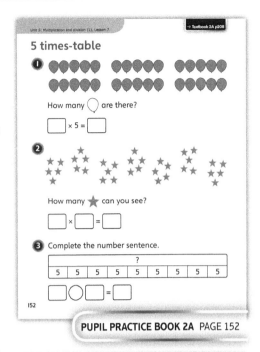

PUPIL PRACTICE BOOK 2A PAGE 152

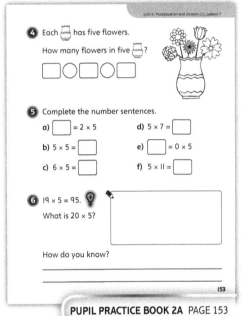

PUPIL PRACTICE BOOK 2A PAGE 153

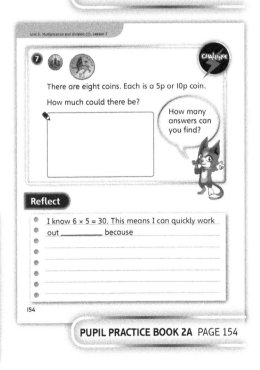

PUPIL PRACTICE BOOK 2A PAGE 154

10 times-table

Learning focus

In this lesson, children will learn the 10 times-table in a number of contexts and make explicit links to place value. They will order, compare and reason about sentences involving × 10.

Small steps

→ Previous step: 5 times-table
→ **This step: 10 times-table**
→ Next step: Solving word problems – multiplication

NATIONAL CURRICULUM LINKS

Year 2 Number – Multiplication and Division

Recall and use multiplication and division facts for the 2, 5 and 10 multiplication tables, including recognising odd and even numbers.

ASSESSING MASTERY

Children can work out multiplication sentences involving multiplying by 10, going beyond the 100 barrier. They can recognise and understand that multiples of 10 always end in 0, and they can also compare these multiplication sentences to numbers being multiplied by 5 using < and >.

COMMON MISCONCEPTIONS

Children can struggle to make the link between 90 and 100 when counting up in 10s. Often, children might say, '80, 90…20,' because they are aware there is a break in the pattern but do not know what the next number should be. They may have difficulty understanding and interpreting 10 × 10 = 100 as there are a lot of 1s and 0s which have little meaning unless children have a good understanding of place value. Show them multiples of 10 up to 100 and ask them: *What pattern do you notice about the start of each multiplication table? If you were counting on from 9, what number would you reach next?* Explain that the same pattern happens with 90 and 100.

STRENGTHENING UNDERSTANDING

Show children that there are lots of patterns to spot in the 10 times-table. Ask children to look at 10 times-table multiplication sentences and explain the pattern they spot when the number 10 is multiplied and what happens to the answer as a result. Be careful not to encourage children to think of it as simply adding a 0. Instead, explain that the number gets ten times bigger: all the digits move up the place value columns and 0 is there as a place value holder.

GOING DEEPER

Encourage children to cut out different × 10 arrays from a 100 square. For example, cutting out 7 × 10 will mean cutting out 1–70. Give children a blank 100 square and ask them to cut out the same array using columns of 10 instead of rows of 10. This highlights the commutative properties of the array and of multiplication.

KEY LANGUAGE

In lesson: times-table, how many?, in total, count, multiplication, groups, more than

Other language to be used by the teacher: skip count, multiply, bar model, place value

STRUCTURES AND REPRESENTATIONS

Number line, array, bar model, Base 10 equipment

RESOURCES

Mandatory: number lines, arrays, bar models, Base 10 equipment, number cards displaying digits 0, 2, 3 and 4

Optional: objects that represent 10 or come in groups of 10, such as 10p coins or ten-packs of pens

 In the eTextbook of this lesson, you will find interactive links to a selection of teaching tools.

Before you teach

- How will you make links between the 10 times-table and place value in this lesson?
- How will you link learning the 10 times-table to learning the 5 times-table in the previous lesson?
- Are children familiar enough with the 100 square to spot 10 arrays in it and the pattern of the multiples that always end in 0?

Discover

WAYS OF WORKING Pair work

ASK

- *To find out how many stickers are on three sheets, could you count one by one or is there a quicker way?*
- *Question* **1** *b): What numbers do you need in a multiplication sentence to work out the total?*

IN FOCUS This question requires children to count the number of stickers on each sheet to work out how many are on three sheets. The stickers are not arranged in obvious groups of 10 in equal rows so children are likely to count each sticker individually.

In question **1** b), 6 sheets of stickers are not shown so children cannot count individual stickers and will have to find another way to find out the total.

ANSWERS

Question **1** a): $3 \times 10 = 30$

There are 30 stickers on 3 sheets.

Question **1** b): $6 \times 10 = 60$

Jamal has 60 stickers in total.

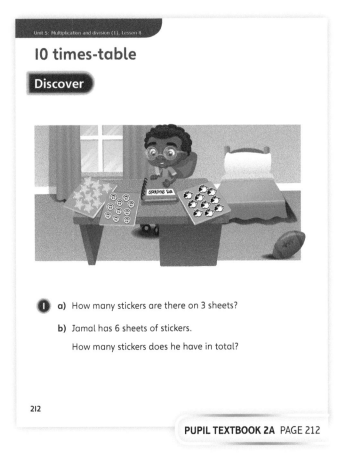

PUPIL TEXTBOOK 2A PAGE 212

Share

WAYS OF WORKING Whole class teacher led

ASK

- *Question* **1** *a): Flo wonders whether multiplication would help answer this question. How could you use multiplication to help?*
- *Question* **1** *b): How much is each cube worth? How many cubes are there? Are the groups equal?*

IN FOCUS The number of stickers on a sheet has been rearranged as a row of ten counters in an array. Astrid says she can count in 10s, which is shown on the number line and as a repeated addition sentence in questions **1** a) and **1** b).

Refer to what Sparks says. The pictorial representation of multilink cubes shows six cubes stacked on top of each other, with each cube representing 10. The numbers are shown next to each cube to help children count up.

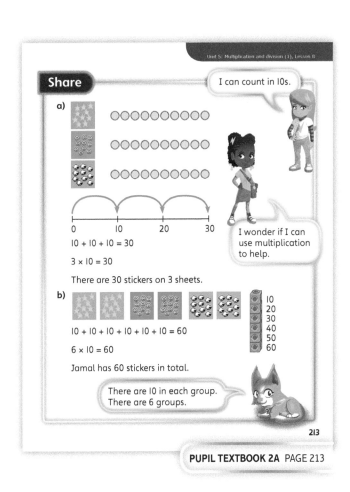

PUPIL TEXTBOOK 2A PAGE 213

Think together

Whole class teacher led (I do, We do, You do)

ASK

- Question **1** : *How will you work out the missing numbers on the number line?*
- Question **2** : *How do you know how many jumps you need to make? What is each jump worth?*

IN FOCUS In question **1** , some intervals on the number line have been filled in but children need to work out and fill in the remaining intervals.

Blank number lines have been given in question **2** , requiring children to fill in all the intervals and keep track of how many jumps are required.

In question **3** , refer to what Ash says about each row being ten more than the previous row. Ask children to make a link between this and the number of tens in the multiplication sentence.

STRENGTHEN To help children understand question **2** c), show them a 100 square to reinforce that ten groups of 10 is 100. Demonstrate that the rows in the 100 square represent the jumps of 10 on the number line that they have just created.

DEEPEN Ask children to draw an array based on a number line jumping up in 10s. For example, if you showed them a number line with two jumps of 10 finishing on 20, could they use this to draw a 2 × 10 array?

ASSESSMENT CHECKPOINT When filling in the missing intervals on the number line in question **1** , do children count on 10 from the last number or do they have another strategy?

In question **2** , children need to fill in their own number lines as they add each jump of 10. Do they show any awareness that they are going to need more jumps as they keep adding tens and reflect this in how big they make their jumps on the number line? Do they make each jump smaller or do they start by making them all equal and then have to squash the rest of the jumps for 9 × 10 and 10 × 10?

ANSWERS

Question **1** : The missing numbers on the number line are:
40, 50, 60, 70

7 × 10 = 70

Question **2** a): 8 × 10 = 80

Question **2** b): 9 × 10 = 90

Question **2** c): 10 × 10 = 100

Question **3** :
1 × 10 = 10	9 × 10 = 90
2 × 10 = 20	10 × 10 = 100
3 × 10 = 30	11 × 10 = 110
4 × 10 = 40	12 × 10 = 120
5 × 10 = 50	
6 × 10 = 60	
7 × 10 = 70	
8 × 10 = 80	

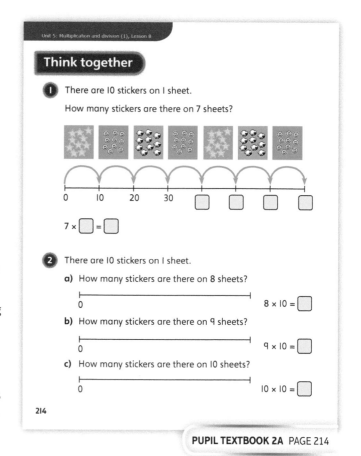

PUPIL TEXTBOOK 2A PAGE 214

PUPIL TEXTBOOK 2A PAGE 215

Practice

WAYS OF WORKING Independent thinking

IN FOCUS In question **2** a), Base 10 equipment is used to represent an equal group of 10. Children have come across Base 10 equipment in place value units and should be familiar with them. Question **2** b) uses a bar model with equal parts, in which each part is worth 10, and requires children to write a multiplication sentence based on this bar model to work out the total.

Question **3** requires children to use their knowledge of the 5 times-table alongside their knowledge of the 10 times-table to compare each calculation and order them using <, > or =.

In question **5** there are a lot of unknown variables in the multiplication sentences and children may need to use trial and error if they are struggling.

STRENGTHEN Use Base 10 equipment to model the situation in question **2** . Ask children to count out the pieces using the language 'one ten, two tens, three tens…'.

Print out number cards used in question **5** so that children can move them around to try out different number sentences. This will help them to reason about each number sentence before attempting to insert the numbers. For example, in question **5** b) children need to work out that they are looking for a number more than 3×5 (15) and use this information to help choose the correct numbers to complete the sentence.

DEEPEN Continuing question **5** , can children create comparisons of multiplication sentences using the given numbers? Provide the sentence scaffolds '__ × __ > ___ × ___' and '___ × ____ < ___ × ____'. Children could create two separate multiplication sentences from the given numbers, work out which total is greater and put the numbers into the sentence scaffold.

ASSESSMENT CHECKPOINT When working with the bar model, are children aware that the other number in the number sentence is the number of equal parts in the bar model, rather than simply what each equal part represents?

ANSWERS Answers for the **Practice** part of the lesson appear in the separate **Practice and Reflect answer guide**.

Reflect

WAYS OF WORKING Pair work and whole class

IN FOCUS This question will ascertain whether children understand the pattern of digits in the 10 times-table.

ASSESSMENT CHECKPOINT Are children immediately able to discredit the idea that 99 is in the 10 times-table? Do children understand that some but not all numbers in the 5 times-table are in the 10 times-table? Use a 100 square with multiples of 5 and multiples of 10 highlighted to visually reinforce this distinction.

ANSWERS Answers for the **Reflect** part of the lesson appear in the separate **Practice and Reflect answer guide**.

After the lesson

- Were children confident counting up in 10s using Base 10 equipment, 10p coins or any other object representing 10?
- Did children make a link between multiplying by 10 and the place value columns?
- Did children make links between the 10 times-table and the 5 times-table while still being able to distinguish between them?

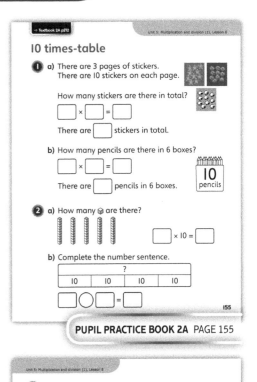

PUPIL PRACTICE BOOK 2A PAGE 155

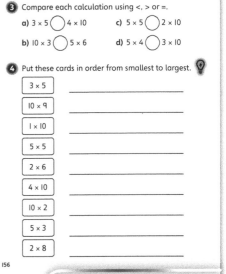

PUPIL PRACTICE BOOK 2A PAGE 156

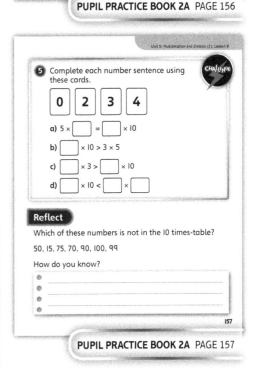

PUPIL PRACTICE BOOK 2A PAGE 157

Solving word problems – multiplication

Learning focus

In this lesson, children will apply their knowledge of multiplication to answer scaling questions where the concept 'times as big' is introduced. Children will use sentence scaffolds to compare quantities by saying how many 'times bigger' something is.

Small steps

→ Previous step: 10 times-table
→ **This step: Solving word problems – multiplication**
→ Next step: Making equal groups

NATIONAL CURRICULUM LINKS

Year 2 Number – Multiplication and Division

Solve problems involving multiplication and division, using materials, arrays, repeated addition, mental methods, and multiplication and division facts, including problems in contexts.

ASSESSING MASTERY

Children can work out how many times greater one number is than another number, using physical resources to help. They can work out multiplication problems that use phrases such as 'times bigger', 'times taller', 'times as many' or 'twice as high' and know which multiplication sentence to use.

COMMON MISCONCEPTIONS

When comparing two amounts where both are greater than one, children may take the value of the bigger amount and say that it is that amount times bigger than the smaller number. For example, children comparing 4 and 2 may say that 4 is 4 times bigger than 2. Ask:
- *What does 4 times 2 look like? Does that match the amount you have?*

STRENGTHENING UNDERSTANDING

Model the questions in this lesson using physical resources, especially when both numbers are greater than one.

GOING DEEPER

Ask children to draw bar models to represent each problem.

When comparing two amounts, the smaller amount can be represented by one box and the larger amount can be represented above by a number of the same boxes, which will show how many times greater it is. Each box can then be labelled with its value. For example: There are 5 kittens and 15 puppies. There are 3 times as many puppies as there are kittens.

5	5	5

5

When working out a total using multiplication, the unknown total can be represented by one box containing a question mark, with the equal constituent parts shown underneath it. For example: Tim has 5 pencils. Jess has 4 times as many pencils as Tim. How many pencils does Jess have?

?

5	5	5	5

KEY LANGUAGE

In lesson: multiplication, **times**, times as tall, times as many?, how many, represent, chart, calculation

Other language to be used by the teacher: times bigger, times-table facts, multiplicative, additive

STRUCTURES AND REPRESENTATIONS

Bar model

RESOURCES

Mandatory: multilink cubes, counters

Optional: blank bar model scaffolds

 In the eTextbook of this lesson, you will find interactive links to a selection of teaching tools.

Before you teach

- Have children come across the language 'times bigger' or 'times greater' before? In what context?
- Are children confident enough with the concept of equal groups to be able to make accurate comparisons in this lesson?

Discover

WAYS OF WORKING Pair work

ASK

- *What does '2 times as tall' mean?*
- *What does '5 times as tall' mean?*

IN FOCUS Children should work in pairs and use multilink cubes or another stackable physical resource to model the problem. Ask them to hold up one cube to represent the height of the prince. Read aloud the line about the height of the princess and ask how many cubes they will need to represent her height. If children are unsure, re-read '2 times as tall as the prince', substituting the name of the physical resource they are holding for 'the prince'. Repeat this process for the king's height.

ANSWERS

Question ❶ a): 2 🎲 represent the princess.

Question ❶ b): I need 5 🎲 to represent the king.

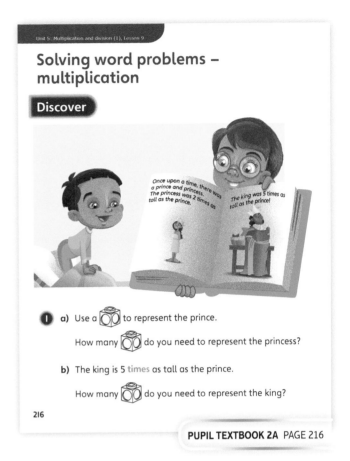

Solving word problems – multiplication

Discover

❶ a) Use a 🎲 to represent the prince.

How many 🎲 do you need to represent the princess?

b) The king is 5 **times** as tall as the prince.

How many 🎲 do you need to represent the king?

216

PUPIL TEXTBOOK 2A PAGE 216

Share

WAYS OF WORKING Whole class teacher led

ASK

- *What does one cube represent?*
- *What does '2 times' and '5 times' one cube mean? Can you show me?*

IN FOCUS Make clear the link between the words in the story, the number of multilink cubes and the numbers in each multiplication sentence. Refer to what Dexter is saying about what '2 times' means. Rewrite the multiplication sentences as '2 × 1 cube = 2 cubes' to make this clearer.

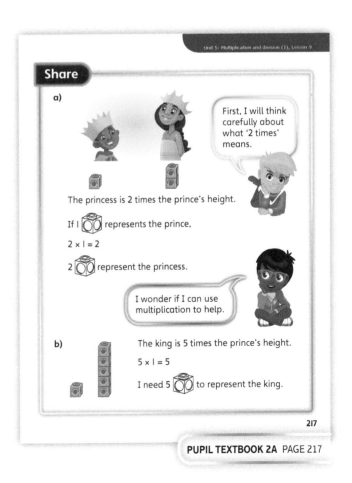

Share

a)

First, I will think carefully about what '2 times' means.

The princess is 2 times the prince's height.

If I 🎲 represents the prince,

$2 \times 1 = 2$

2 🎲 represent the princess.

I wonder if I can use multiplication to help.

b) The king is 5 times the prince's height.

$5 \times 1 = 5$

I need 5 🎲 to represent the king.

217

PUPIL TEXTBOOK 2A PAGE 217

Think together

WAYS OF WORKING Whole class teacher led (I do, We do, You do)

ASK

- *What does 'times as many' mean?*
- *Is '2 times as many' the same as '× 2'?*
- *Is this linked to any times-tables you have been learning?*

IN FOCUS Question ❶ requires children to count the number of weather symbols before making comparisons using the 'times as many' sentence scaffold. The labelled bar model demonstrates the different multiplicative relationships between the symbols. Encourage children to make the link between '× 2' and '2 times as many'.

Question ❸ uses a different starting unit of 5. Refer to what Flo says about using blocks to help with the calculations and ask children to build the king's height as a starting point.

STRENGTHEN Children are likely to be able to articulate the difference between the different weather symbols in question ❶, but this is an additive relationship. Point out circles around the equal groups in the bar model to take the focus away from how many are in one group and to demonstrate that, no matter what the starting unit is, both relationships are 2 times greater. Use multilink cubes to show that 2 times greater than one cube is two cubes and that 2 times greater than two cubes is four cubes. The 'times as many' relationship does not change.

DEEPEN Children can arrange counters in the arrangement shown in question ❷ and then draw around them to create their own bar model. Alternatively they could use squared paper and have one square represent one counter, and then colour the bars the same colour as the counters for ease of comparison.

ASSESSMENT CHECKPOINT In question ❷, do children circle the equal groups of two or do they treat each counter as an individual item? Do children say that there are 6 times as many rather than 3 times as many because they have not treated the two yellow counters as one unit?

ANSWERS

Question ❶ a): 2 days ☁🌧
4 days ☁

Question ❶ b): There are 2 times as many days of ☁🌧 as ☀.
There are 2 times as many days of ☁ as ☁🌧.

Question ❷: There are 3 times as many ⬤ as ◯.

Question ❸: The dragon is 10 ⬛ tall.

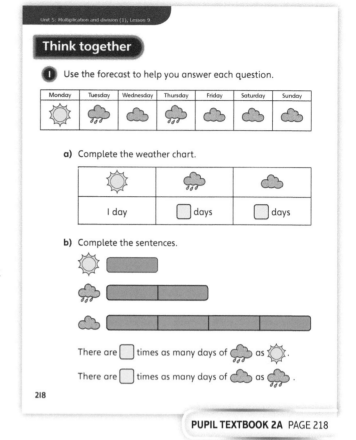

PUPIL TEXTBOOK 2A PAGE 218

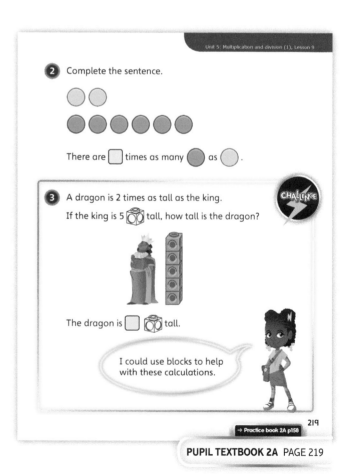

PUPIL TEXTBOOK 2A PAGE 219

Practice

WAYS OF WORKING Independent thinking

IN FOCUS Children should use multilink cubes to model questions ❶ and ❷. In question ❶ a), the multiplication sentence scaffold is partially filled in. Question ❶ b) reduces the amount of scaffolding provided and requires children to fill in a blank multiplication sentence scaffold.

Question ❸ asks children to work out each individual multiplication calculation in order to compare them. They can shade in the bar model to help them count up each 5 or 10 and compare.

STRENGTHEN Provide sentence scaffolds to prompt children to write their own number story, such as '3 times as many', '3 times as tall' and '3 times bigger'. Ask children to draw their problem and model it using physical resources. Children can compare the problems they have made, checking that they can all link back to the original bar model.

DEEPEN Using the number story that they have created, children can write their own comparison number sentences, such as '___ is / has 3 times bigger / taller / more than ___ which is / who has 4'. Can they apply their context back to the mathematical language of scaling and 'times bigger'?

ASSESSMENT CHECKPOINT When making the tower for question ❶, do children make one tower of 6 to represent the house and then place another tower of 6 on top to represent the tower? Or do children keep the cubes for the house and tower separate and make three stacks of 6, one of which represents the house and two of which represent the tower?

In question ❷, do children circle the counters in groups of 3 because that is how many dark counters there are?

In question ❹, are children able to work out that the total will be 3 times bigger because there are three equal parts of 4 or do they need help to understand this?

ANSWERS Answers for the **Practice** part of the lesson appear in the separate **Practice and Reflect answer guide**.

Reflect

WAYS OF WORKING Pair work

IN FOCUS This part of the lesson provides an opportunity for children to refine their earlier work on multiplication and repeated addition sentences, reinforce their understanding of 'twice as high' and explain their methods.

ASSESSMENT CHECKPOINT Do children draw the birds' legs or do they use more abstract methods such as a bar model or a number line?

Are children able to articulate how many cubes Prisha's tower contains without using cubes? Do they link this problem back to the multiplication sentence 2 × 5 = 10? Listen to their explanation of how many cubes are needed. Do they use the language 'twice as many' or '2 times bigger'?

ANSWERS Answers for the **Reflect** part of the lesson appear in the separate **Practice and Reflect answer guide**.

After the lesson ⏸

- Would children be able to use 'twice as big' in other contexts?
- Were children aware of the link between what they were doing and times-table facts they already knew?
- Were children able to represent the problems both physically with multilink cubes and abstractly with bar models?

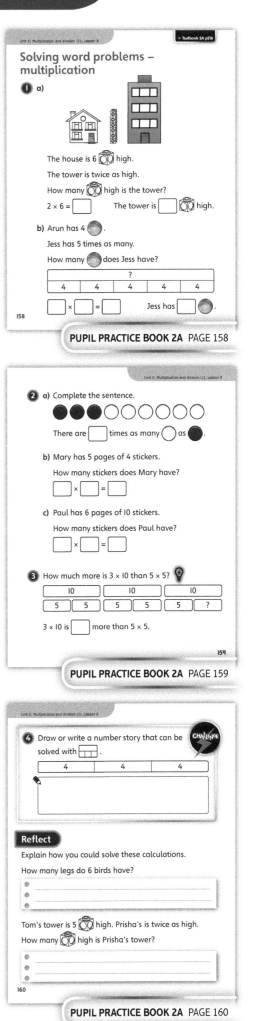

End of unit check

Don't forget the Power Maths Unit Assessment Grid on p26.

WAYS OF WORKING Group work – adult led

IN FOCUS Question ❶ requires children to count the objects in the groups to see whether the groups are equal. The groups in diagram A have the same amount but each looks different.

In question ❷, children relate their understanding of multiplication sentences to a repeated addition sentence. Children should spot that there are five 5s being added in A, which does not match the multiplication sentence.

Question ❸ ascertains whether children understand how an array relates to repeated addition and multiplication sentences.

Question ❹ uses children's knowledge of < and >.

Question ❺ shows six 5s and three 10s and asks which is longer.

Think!

WAYS OF WORKING Pair work

IN FOCUS This question draws out children's knowledge of different times-tables and common multiples. It highlights whether children have an understanding of different times-tables.

Ask children to recite the 2 times-table and 5 times-table. What do they notice about the numbers they are saying?

Encourage children to discuss the word 'digit' before writing their answer in **My journal**, and ask why the digit 0 is so important here.

ANSWERS AND COMMENTARY To show mastery, children can come up with other numbers that would be in the 2 times-table and 5 times-table. They will have an understanding that these numbers are also in the 10 times-table. They will be able to explain that numbers ending in '0' are even and all numbers in the 2 times-table table are even, as are *some* numbers in the 5 times-table.

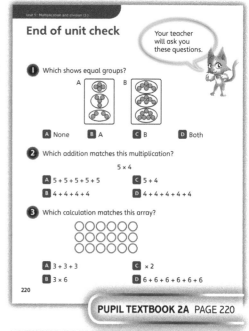

PUPIL TEXTBOOK 2A PAGE 220

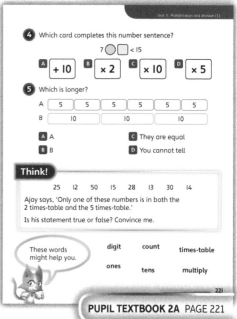

PUPIL TEXTBOOK 2A PAGE 221

Q	A	WRONG ANSWERS AND MISCONCEPTIONS	STRENGTHENING UNDERSTANDING
1	A	Children may think Diagram B contains equal groups as they look similar, whereas the groups in Diagram A look uneven.	When faced with multiple choice questions on matching number sentences, children should make or draw each of the options to help eliminate incorrect options. This will help you to assess what the child understands or misunderstands about the question. For example, if children draw question 2 A (5 + 5 + 5 + 5 + 5) as an array, they should be able to spot that there are five rows and five columns, meaning that this repeated addition sentence cannot represent 5 × 4.
2	D	Hopefully children do not choose C, as that is an additive relationship. Children need to carefully count each 4 and 5 in each sentence to match them to the original sentence.	
3	B	Although the repeated addition sentences could be correct, both A and D have repeated the number as the number of groups. Only B represents the number of rows and columns.	
4	B	Children may automatically think that A will give the smallest answer because multiplication 'makes things much bigger'. By looking at B, C and D they should know that × 2 will give the smaller amount as the others multiply by a higher number.	
5	C	If children want to choose D, they do not see that two 5s represent one 10 and that they are proportional. 3 times a bigger number will always give a bigger answer and a longer representation as a bar model.	

My journal

WAYS OF WORKING Independent thinking

ANSWERS AND COMMENTARY

First, children can write out their 2 times-table and 5 times-table. If they are struggling, they could do jumps on a number line in different colours or circle numbers on a 100 square in different colours. If children quickly remember these times-table facts, can they explain the pattern of digits in each of the times-tables?

Now ask children to look back at the list of numbers given. Can any be eliminated right away? Why would 13 be in neither times-table? Children should identify that this is not just because it is odd but because it does not end in a 5, which is the only odd number that the 5 times-table can end in.

When children come across a number that fits into one of the times-tables, such as 25 or 14, ask children to explain why it is not in both, using the representations they used to write down the times-table. When only 50 and 30 are left, can children articulate that they are both even and both end in 0 and therefore can be in both times-tables? Prompt them to use Sparks's key words in their explanation.

Power check

WAYS OF WORKING Independent thinking

ASK

- *Do you understand what × means?*
- *Do you feel confident doing multiplications?*
- *Can you remember any times-table facts?*

Power play

WAYS OF WORKING Pair work

IN FOCUS Children practise what they have learned about groups and multiplying the number of items in a group by the number of groups. There are an odd number of counters to start and children need to continually take different groups until their partner only has one counter left. The wording '1 group of 3 counters or 2 groups of 3 counters' has been used instead of saying '3 or 6 counters' so that children continue to think in terms of groups of numbers.

ANSWERS AND COMMENTARY There will always be one counter left at the end of the game as 31 is a multiple of 3 + 1 and a multiple of 2 + 1. However, children can start to predict and calculate how many groups they can take away to ensure that their partner always has one counter left. This requires knowledge of multiples of numbers and thinking of 3 and 2 as groups rather than as total amounts. Encourage children who are unsure how to make generalisations or find a pattern to practise using the times-tables in their head and grouping together different numbers.

PUPIL PRACTICE BOOK 2A PAGE 161

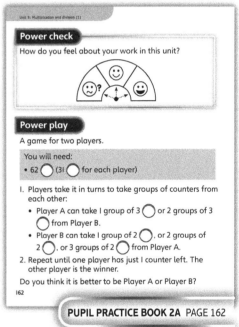

PUPIL PRACTICE BOOK 2A PAGE 162

After the unit ⏸

- How did children respond to questions asking them to explain? Did they rely on physical resources to show things or were they able to articulate their thinking?
- Have you seen an improvement in children's recall of times-table facts outside lessons?

Strengthen and **Deepen** activities for this unit can be found in the *Power Maths* online subscription.

Published by Pearson Education Limited, 80 Strand, London, WC2R 0RL.

www.pearsonschools.co.uk

Text © Pearson Education Limited 2017
Edited by Pearson, Little Grey Cells Publishing Services and Haremi Ltd
Designed and typeset by Kamae Design
Original illustrations © Pearson Education Limited 2017
Illustrated by Laura Arias, Fran and David Brylewski, Nigel Dobbyn, Adam Linley, Nadene Naude and Dusan Pavlic at Beehive
Illustration; and Kamae.
Cover design by Pearson Education Ltd
Back cover illustration © Will Overton at Advocate Art and Nadene Naude at Beehive Illustration.

Series Editor: Tony Staneff
Consultant: Professor Jian Liu

The rights of Tony Staneff, Natasha Dolling, Jonathan East, Julia Hayes, Neil Jarrett and Timothy Weal to be identified as
authors of this work have been asserted by them in accordance with the Copyright, Designs and Patents Act 1988.

First published 2017

20 19
10 9 8 7 6 5 4

British Library Cataloguing in Publication Data
A catalogue record for this book is available from the British Library

ISBN 978 0 435 18982 2

Printed in the UK by Ashford Colour Press

www.activelearnprimary.co.uk

Note from the publisher
Pearson has robust editorial processes, including answer and fact checks, to ensure the accuracy of the content in this
publication, and every effort is made to ensure this publication is free of errors. We are, however, only human, and
occasionally errors do occur. Pearson is not liable for any misunderstandings that arise as a result of errors in this publication,
but it is our priority to ensure that the content is accurate. If you spot an error, please do contact us at
resourcescorrections@pearson.com so we can make sure it is corrected.